VERBUM

Word and Idea in Aquinas

BERNARD J. LONERGAN, S.J.

VERBUM

Word and Idea in Aquinas

Edited by David B. Burrell, C.S.C.

UNIVERSITY OF NOTRE DAME PRESS
NOTRE DAME

The chapters of this book appeared originally as articles in *Theological Studies:* chapter I: VII (1946), 349-92; chapter II: VIII (1947), 35-79; chapter III: VIII (1947), 404-44; chapter IV: X (1949), 3-40; chapter V: X (1949), 359-93.

Copyright © 1967

UNIVERSITY OF NOTRE DAME PRESS

LIBRARY OF CONGRESS CATALOG CARD NUMBER: 67-12126

PRINTED IN THE UNITED STATES OF AMERICA

FOREWORD

This is not the place to celebrate the intellectual prowess and achievements of Bernard J.F. Lonergan. Frederick Crowe, S.J., has engineered this tribute in a special issue of *Continuum* (Autumn, 1964) separately published under the title *Spirit as Inquiry*. Ours is the more modest opportunity of making available Father Lonergan's painstaking investigations into Aquinas' use of the philosophical legacy handed on to him. Here we can observe a reverence for a philosophical tradition as well as acquire a set of tools that will prove liberating and resourceful. In Father Lonergan's hands we can watch these tools turn historical research into authentic philosophical inquiry.

It has been remarked by more than one reviewer that the "*Verbum* articles," as they have come to be called, were an invaluable if not essential interpretative key to Father Lonergan's later and larger work, *Insight*. This has proven to be the case particularly for those trained in philosophy of a more traditional cast. These articles can provide them with a master plan for bridging between old and new. For others not so steeped in a philosophical tradition, research of this cast and quality may help them to appreciate the true worth of an historical perspective when it is properly employed.

There are many accidental factors that have kept Father Lonergan's work from enjoying the attention it most certainly deserves— though one suspects that they also may have contributed to its penetrating character. He has never been in the academic limelight, having spent nearly all of his teaching years with Jesuit scholastics or clerical students seeking advanced ecclesiastical degrees. To this relative academic isolation one must add his insistence on probing matters philosophical while professing to be a theologian. Although the membranes separating these disciplines remain somewhat permeable, professional associations can be exclusive and jealous of recognizing the achievements of an "interloper." Finally, at a time when theologians are concerned with disseminating their results in a relevant manner, Father Lonergan is busy preparing the groundwork for the theologies that can do justice to the impetus of Vatican II. While others keep the field in the limelight, he works to clear away its methodological bases. This relative unconcern for the moment betrays in fact a deep conviction about the role of intelligence in the world. The quality and incisiveness of that intelligence awaits the reader.

I would like first off to thank Father Lonergan himself for his gracious assistance in making this work possible and the warm gratitude with which he met the proposal. John Courtney Murray, S.J., as editor of *Theological Studies*, has generously given permission for the reprinting, and Frederick Crowe, S.J., provided the substance of the indices. My immediate assistants—James Schultz, C.S.C., Francis Faulkner, O.M.I., David Bedan, Joseph DiGiovanna, and Brian Moore—deserve our common gratitude for their painstaking check on notes and references. Finally, the University of Notre Dame Press has shown a care no less warm than it proved thorough and professional.

DAVID B. BURRELL, C.S.C.

INTRODUCTION

In working out his concept of *verbum* Aquinas was engaged not merely in fitting an original Augustinian creation into an Aristotelian framework but also in attempting, however remotely and implicitly, to fuse together what to us may seem so disparate : a phenomenology of the subject with a psychology of the soul.

The Aristotelian framework was impressive. First, it was a general theory of being, a metaphysics. Secondly, it was a general theory of movement, a physics in that now antiquated sense. Thirdly, it was a general theory of life, a biology. Fourthly, it was a general theory of sensitivity and intelligence, a psychology.

Since in this framework the prior components are comprehensive, the latter are not pure but cumulative. Because movements exist, physical statements are not just physical; they are determinations added to metaphysical statements. Because living things move, biological statements are not just biological; they are determinations added to metaphysical and physical statements. Because sentient and intelligent beings are alive, psychological statements are not purely psychological; they presuppose and employ and determine what already has been settled in metaphysics, physics, and biology.

The use of such a framework gave Aristotelian thought its majestic coherence and comprehensiveness. The interlockinig of each part with all the others precluded the possibility of merely patchwork revisions. As Professor Butterfield has observed, to correct Aristotle effectively, one must go beyond him; and to go beyond him is to set up a system equal in comprehensiveness and more successful in inner coherence and in conformity with fact.[1] Still such attempts have been made and, indeed, in two quite different manners. There have been open repudiations of Aristotle, as in modern science and in much modern philosophy. There also has been the more delicate procedure of sublation that developed and transformed Aristotelian positions to the point where the

---

[1] The point is made repeatedly by Herbert Butterfield, *The Origins of Modern Science, 1300-1800*, New York 1960.

incorporation of further and profounder doctrines became possible. Such was the method of Aquinas, and our immediate concern is to find in Aristotle the point of insertion for Augustinian thought.

It is not difficult to discern. I distinguished above four components in the Aristotelian framework. I must hasten to add that, in a sense, the distinction between the third and fourth, between biology and psychology, is not as clear, as sharp, as fully developed, as may be desired. For Aristotle's *De anima* is at once biological and psychological. It does not confuse plants, animals, and men. At the same time it fails to bring out effectively the essential difference between an investigation of plant life and an investigation of the human mind; much less does it work out the methodological implications of that essential difference.

The *De anima* is about soul. If the Platonic *nauta in navi* is suggestive of the subject, the Aristotelian soul is not. It is an inner principle, constituent of life. It is defined as the first act of an organic body.[2] It is found in all organic bodies, in plants no less than in animals and men. Moreover, a single method is worked out for determining the differences of souls and so for investigating each species of the genus. Souls are differentiated by their potencies; potencies are known by their acts; acts are specified by their objects.[3] But what is meant by an object? That is the decisive question. For the meaning given the term "object" will settle the specification given acts; the specification of acts will settle the distinction between potencies; and the distinction between potencies will settle the essential differences between the souls of plants, animals, and men.

A modern reader is apt to take it for granted that by an object Aristotle must mean the intentional term of a conscious act. But quite evidently Aquinas was of a different opinion. In his *Commentary* he defines objects in terms, not of intentionality, but of causality: an object is either the efficient or the final cause of the occurrence of an act in a potency.[4] Nor is it easy to disagree with Aquinas. He goes beyond what is explicit in the text.

---

[2] *De anima* II, 1 412b 4 ff.

[3] *Ibid.* II, 4, 415a 14-20.

[4] In II de An., lect. 6   §305.

But as the book of definitions in the *Metaphysics*[5] reveals, Aristotle used his word for object, τὸ ἀντιπείνενον, in a great variety of meanings. In the immediate context in the *De anima* he illustrates objects not only by the sensible and the intelligible, which are the intentional terms of conscious acts, but also by nutriment, which in the case of plants has not an intention but only a causal relation to acts.

It is at this point that there comes to light the problem to which I have already alluded. No one will complain that Aristotle did not employ introspective techniques in his study of plant life. But one could well complain if a method, suitable for the study of plants, were alone employed in the study of human sensitivity and human intelligence. If the objects of vegetative activity are causal, it remains that the objects of sensitive and intellectual activity are also intentional. If vegetative acts are not accessible to introspection, sensitive and intellectual acts are among the immediate data of consciousness; they can be reached not only by deduction from their objects but also in themselves as given in consciousness. Finally, when conscious acts are studied by introspection, one discovers not only the acts and their intentional terms but also the intending subject, and there arises the problem of the relation of subject to soul, of the Augustinian *mens* or *animus* to the Aristotelian *anima*.

If in Scholastic circles such a *Problematik* is contemporary and indeed, for many, still novel, it is plain that neither Aristotle nor Aquinas handled the matter in a triumphantly definitive fashion. This is not to say, of course, that they anticipated positivists and behaviorists by systematically avoiding any use of introspection or any appeal to the data of consciousness. As we shall see, Aquinas explicitly appealed to inner experience and, I submit, Aristotle's account of intelligence, of insight into phantasm, and of the fact that intellect knows itself, not by a *species* of itself, but by a *species* of its object, has too uncanny an accuracy to be possible without the greatest introspective skill. But if Aristotle and Aquinas used introspection and did so brilliantly, it remains that they did not thematize their use, did not elevate it into a reflectively elaborated technique, did not work out a proper method

---

[5] *Met. Δ,* 10.

for psychology, and thereby lay the groundwork for the contemporary distinctions between nature and spirit and between the natural and the human sciences.

It is time to turn to Augustine: a convert from nature to spirit; a person that, by God's grace, made himself what he was; a subject that may be studied but, most of all, must be encountered in the outpouring of his self-revelation and self-communication. The context of his thought on *verbum* was trinitarian, and its underlying preoccupation was anti-Arian. It followed that the prologue to the Fourth Gospel had to be freed from any Arian implication. To achieve this end Augustine did not employ our contemporary techniques of linguistic and literary history. He did not attempt a fresh translation of the Greek word "λόγος," but retained the traditional *verbum*. Church tradition, perhaps, precluded any appeal to the Stoic distinction between *verbum prolatum* and *verbum insitum*.[6] In any case he cut between these Stoic terms to discover a third *verbum* that was neither the *verbum prolatum* of human speech nor the *verbum insitum* of man's native rationality but an intermediate *verbum intus prolatum*. Naturally enough, as Augustine's discovery was part and parcel of his own mind's knowledge of itself, so he begged his readers to look within themselves and there to discover the speech of spirit within spirit, an inner *verbum* prior to any use of language, yet distinct both from the mind itself and from its memory or its present apprehension of objects.

Though I cannot attempt here to do justice to the wealth of Augustine's thought or to the variety of its expression,[7] at least it will serve to illustrate my meaning if, however arbitrarily, I select and briefly comment on a single passage.

> Haec igitur omnia et, quae per se ipsum, et quae per sensus sui corporis, et quae testimoniis aliorum percepta scit animus humanus, thesauro memoriae condita tenet, et quibus gignitur

---

[6] I would like in this connection to draw attention to a forthcoming work in the series, *Analecta Gregoriana* : S. Biolo, *La coscienza nel "De Trinitate" di S. Agostino.*

[7] On the distinction, G. Kittel, TWNT IV, 84, *12* ff. (Kleinknecht) ; M. Schmaus, *Die psychologische Trinitätslehre des hl. Augustinus*, Münster 1927, p. 33 n. *11.* On the tradition, cf. St. Ambrose, *De fide ad Gratianum*, IV, vii, 72, ML 16, 631 ; also DS 140 can. 8.

verbum verum, quando quod scimus loquimur, sed verbum
ante omnem sonum, ante omnem cogitationem soni. Tunc
enim est verbum simillimum rei notae, de qua gignitur, et
imago eius, quoniam de visione scientiae visio cogitationis
exoritur, quod est verbum linguae nullius, verbum verum de re
vera, nihil de suo habens, sed totum de illa scientia de qua
nascitur. Nec interest quando id didicerit, qui quod scit loquitur; aliquando enim statim ut discit,hoc dicit; dum tamen
verbum sit verum, id est, de notis rebus exortum.[8]

In this passage, then, the Augustinian *verbum* is a nonlinguistic
utterance of truth. It differs from expression in any language, for
it is *linguae nullius*. It is not primitive but derived: *gignitur,
exoritur, nascitur.* Its dependence is total: *nihil de suo habens,
sed totum de illa scientia de qua nascitur.* This total dependence
is, not blind or automatic, but conscious and cognitive: *quod
scimus loquimur; de visione scientiae visio cogitationis exoritur;
qui quod scit loquitur.* Finally, this total dependence as conscious
and known is the essential point. It makes no difference whether
the *verbum* has its ground in memory or in recently acquired knowledge. What counts is its truth, its correspondence with things as
known: *verbum simillimum rei notae; imago eius; verbum verum
de re vera, nihil de suo habens, sed totem de illa scientia de qua
nascitur; dum tamen verbum sit verum, id est, de notis rebus exortum.*

Such, at least in one passage, is what Augustine had to say
about *verbum.* Many more passages might be cited and they would
reveal him saying different things or the same things in a different manner. But sooner or later it would be necessary to advance from the simpler question of what he said to the more difficult question of what he meant. Since I am writing not a study
of Augustine but an introduction to a study of Aquinas, I must
leap at once to the more difficult question, though not to answer
it in detail, but only to indicate the source from which the answer
must proceed.

A blind man may listen to a disquisition on color, but he is
bound to find it obscure. A person who is deaf may read a book
on music, but he will have a hard time deciding whether the author
is talking sense or nonsense. In similar fashion it is only by introspection that one can discover what an introspective psychologist

---

[8] *De trinitate* XV, xii, 22 ; ML 42, 1075.

is talking about. If what Augustine had to say about *verbum*
was true, then it corresponded exactly to what Augustine knew
went on in his own mind. If what Augustine had to say about
verbum was universally true, then it corresponds exactly to what
Augustine knew goes on in any human mind. If one supposes
Augustine to be right and, at the same time, entertains an admiration
for Newman, one is going to ask whether the Augustinian couplet
of *memoria* and *verbum* is parallel to Newman's couplet of illative
sense and unconditional assent. But if one desires to get beyond
words and suppositions to meanings and facts, then one has to
explore one's own mind and find out for oneself what there is to
be meant; and until one does so, one is in the unhappy position
of the blind man hearing about colors and the deaf man reading
about counterpoint.

About such matters Augustine was explicit. *Unde enim mens
aliquam mentem novit, si se non novit? Neque enim ut oculus corporis videt alios oculos et se non videt. . . . Mens ergo ipsa sicut
corporearum rerum notitias per sensus corporis colligit, sic incor-
porearum per semetipsam. Ergo et semetipsam per se ipsam novit. . . .*[9] Moreover, for Augustine, the mind's self-knowledge was
basic; it was the rock of certitude on which shattered Academic
doubt; it provided the ground from which one could argue to the
validity both of the senses of one's own body and, with the me-
diation of testimony, of the senses of the bodies of others. So
the passage we have quoted and explained begins with this threefold enumeration: *quae per se ipsum et quae per sensus sui corporis,
et quae testimoniis aliorum percepta scit animus humanus.* The
enumeration merely summarizes what had been set forth at greater
length in the immediately preceding paragraph;[10] and that paragraph, of course, only resumes a theme that is recurrent from Augustine's earliest writings on.

Clearly enough, it was neither *per sensus sui corporis* nor by
alienorum corporum sensus that Augustine knew of a *verbum* that
was neither Latin nor Greek, neither sound nor even the thought
of sound. The Augustinian affirmation of *verbum* was itself a
verbum. For it to be true, on Augustine's own showing, it had to

---

[9] *De trinitate* IX, iii, 3 ; ML 42, 962 f.
[10] *Ibid.* XV, xii, 21 ; 1073-75.

be totally dependent on what Augustine's mind knew through itself about itself. On the existence and nature of such knowledge
Augustine had a great deal to say, and there is no need for us to
attempt to repeat it here. Though it cannot be claimed that
Augustine elevated introspection into a scientific technique, it
cannot be doubted that he purported to report in his literary
language what his own mind knew immediately about itself.

So we come to Aquinas. Because he conceived theology as in
some sense a science, he needed Aristotle who, more than anyone,
had worked out and applied the implications of the Greek ideal of
science. Because his theology was essentially the expression of
a traditional faith, he needed Augustine, the Father of the West,
whose trinitarian thought was the high-water mark in Christian
attempts to reach an understanding of faith. Because Aquinas
himself was a genius, he experienced no great difficulty either
in adapting Aristotle to his purpose or in reaching a refinement
in his account of rational process—the *emanatio intelligibilis*—
that made explicit what Augustine could only suggest. Because,
finally, Aquinas was a man of his time, he had to leave to a later
age the task of acknowledging the discontinuity of natural and
of human science and of working out its methodological implications.
For performance must precede reflection on performance, and
method is the fruit of that reflection. Aquinas had to be content
to perform.

The present study is divided into five chapters, and the division
is dictated by the quite different systematic contexts in which
Thomist statements about *verbum* are involved. Already I have
noted the cumulative character of Aristotelian categories, in which
psychological statements presuppose biological, biological presuppose physical, and physical presuppose metaphysical. In a somewhat similar fashion Thomist statements about *verbum* will be
theological in their primary intent; they will involve technical
terms drawn from physics and metaphysics; their meaning will
turn on metaphysical explanations of gnosiological possibility;
and embedded in this structural complexity there will be a core
of psychological fact. To reach even an approximation to what
Aquinas meant, it is necessary to explore separately the several
hermeneutical circles that in cumulative fashion are relevant
to an interpretation.

The first two chapters are concerned with the core of psychological fact. Aquinas identified *verbum* with the immanent terminal object of intellectual operation; he distinguished two intellectual operations, a first in answer to the question *quid sit*, and a second in answer to the question *an sit*. So we have a first chapter on *verbum* as definition, and a second on *verbum* as *compositio vel divisio*.

Throughout the first two chapters the reader will be troubled by the recurrence of technical terms of a metaphysical or physical origin. Quite apart from any intrinsic difficulty they may offer, the determination of their meaning is enormously complicated, *first*, by Aristotle's efforts to adapt the Greek language to his own technical purposes, *secondly*, by the imperfect coincidence of the earlier Latin equivalents, mediated by Arabic culture, and the later fruits of direct translation from the Greek, and *thirdly*, for those who approach Aquinas through manuals and commentaries quite innocent of the methods of literary and historical research, by such interpreters' proclivity to smooth out linguistic oddities by giving free rein to their talent for speculative invention. The third chapter is an effort to cut through this jungle.

Our fourth chapter deals with matters intermediate between metaphysics and psychology. Such is the doctrine of abstraction from matter. Such also are the relations between immateriality and knowledge.

Finally, St. Thomas's thought on *verbum* occurs, for the most part, in a trinitarian context. If Thomist philosophers, quite comprehensibly, are reluctant to venture into this field, it remains that a historian must do so. St. Thomas was a theologian. His thought on *verbum* was, in the main, a statement for his technically minded age of the psychological analogy of the trinitarian processions. Its simplicity, its profundity, and its brilliance have long been obscured by interpreters unaware of the relevant psychological facts and unequal to the task of handling merely linguistic problems.[11] So it is that our final chapter deals with the trinitarian

---

[11] This may appear harsh, but I find no other explanation for the startling discrepancies that exist. In his account of intellectual procession no less eminent a theologian than L. Billot could write : Et simile omnino est in imaginatione (*De Deo Uno et Trino*, Roma 1910, p. 335). But St. Thomas

meaning of *imago Dei*, and as there the many levels of our study come together, so there also, I hope, the reader will find some compensation for the heavy labor of ploughing through the preceding pages.

In closing I should, perhaps, note that the present introduction is an afterthought written over fifteen years after the original text was completed and published in *Theological Studies*. May I take this occasion to thank Rev. John Courtney Murray, then as now editor of that review, for allowing this edition.

explicitly restricted the trinitarian analogy to the minds of rational creatures. *Sum. theol.* I, q.93, a. 6c. : . . . nec in ipsa rationali creatura invenitur Dei imago nisi secundum mentem. Cf. *In I Sent.*, d. 3, q. 3, a. 1 ; *De Ver.*, q. 10, aa. 1 § 7 ; *De Pot.*, q. 9, a. 9 *ad fin.* ; *C. Gent.*, IV, 11.

CONTENTS

I

VERBUM: DEFINITION AND UNDERSTANDING

THE GENERAL NOTION OF AN INNER WORD

Etymology and biblical English both favor writing "inner word" or simply "word" as equivalent to the Thomist synonyms, *verbum interius, verbum cordis, verbum mentis,* and, most common of all, simply *verbum.* The only complication arises in connection with the division of words into simple and compound. It is odd, indeed, to speak of a compound word and mean a sentence or judgment; but such speech will be rare; and the disadvantage of its oddity is outweighed, I think, by the convenience of having an English term for the main matter of the discussion.

The first element in the general notion of an inner word is had from a contrast with outer words—spoken, written, imagined, or meant. Spoken words are sounds with a meaning: as sounds, they are produced in the respiratory tract; as possessing a meaning, they are due to imagination according to Aristotle, or, as Aquinas seems to have preferred, to soul; it is meaning that differentiates spoken words from other sounds, such as coughing, which also are produced in the respiratory tract.[1] Written words are simply signs of spoken words;[2] the issue was uncomplicated by Chinese ideograms. A similar simplicity is the refreshing characteristic of the account of *imaginatio vocis;*[3] a term that seems to embrace the whole mnemic mass and sensitive mechanism of motor, auditory, and visual images connected with language. Finally, the outer word that is some external thing or action meant by a word is dismissed as a mere figure of speech.[4]

---

[1] *In II de An.,* lect. 18, § 477.

[2] *In I Periherm.,* lect. 2, § 17: " ... nomina et verba quae scribuntur, signa sunt eorum nominum et verborum quae sunt in voce."

[3] *In I Sent.,* d. 27, q. 2, a. 1 sol. *Sum. Theol.,* I, q. 34, a. 1 c.

[4] *Sum. Theol.,* I, q. 34, a. 1 c.: "Dicitur autem figurative quarto modo verbum, id quod verbo significatur vel efficitur; sicut consuevimus dicere, hoc est verbum quod dixi tibi, vel quod mandavit rex, demonstrato aliquo facto quod verbo significatum est vel simpliciter enuntiantis, vel etiam imperantis."

There is a twofold relation between inner and outer words: the inner word is an efficient cause of the outer; and the inner word is what is meant immediately by the outer. The aspect of efficient causality seems to be the only one noticed in the *Commentary on the Sentences*: the inner word is compared to the major premise of a syllogism; the imagined word to the minor premise; and the spoken word to the conclusion.[5] Later works do not deny this aspect[6] but I think I may say that subsequently the whole emphasis shifted to the second of the two relations mentioned above. Repeatedly one reads that the inner word is what can be meant (*significabile*) or what is meant (*significatum*) by outer words and, inversely, that the outer word is what can mean (*significativum*) or what does mean (*significans*) the inner word.[7] There is no doubt about this matter, though, frankly, it is just the opposite of what one would expect. One is apt to think of the inner word, not as what is meant by the outer, but as what means the outer; the outer word has meaning in virtue of the inner; therefore, the inner is meaning essentially while the outer has meaning by participation. That is all very true, and Saint Thomas knew it.[8] But commonly he asked what outer words meant and answered that, in the first instance, they meant inner words. The proof was quite simple. We discourse on "man" and on the "triangle." What are we talking about? Certainly, we are not talking about real things directly, else we should all be Platonists. Directly, we are talking about objects of thought, inner words, and only indirectly, only in so far as our inner words have an objective reference, are we talking of real things.[9] The same point might be made in another fashion. Logical positivists to the contrary, false propositions are not meaningless; they mean something; what they mean is an inner word,

5 *In I Sent.*, d. 27, q. 2, a. 1 sol.
6 Efficient causality is mentioned in *In Ioan.*, cap. 1, lect. 1.
7 "*De Ver.*, q. 4, a. 2, c.: " ... sive sit conceptio significabilis per vocem incomplexam ... sive per vocem complexam. ..." *C. Gent.*, IV, 11 (ed. Leon., XV, 32b 30ff.): " ... est quaedam similitudo concepta ... quae voces exteriores significant; unde et ipsa intentio verbum interius nominatur, quod est exteriori verbo significatum." Cf. *De Pot.*, q. 8, a. 1 c; q. 9, a. 5 c; *Sum. Theol.*, I, q. 27, a. 1 c; q. 34, a. 1 c; q. 85, a. 2 ad 3 m; *Quodl.* V, a. 9 c; *In Ioan.*, cap. 1, lect. 1.
8 See *De Ver.*, q. 9, a. 1 ad 7 m.
9 *In I Periherm.*, lect. 2.

and only because that inner word is false, does the false proposition lack objective reference.[10]

Such is the first element in the general notion of an inner word. It is connected with the well-known anti-Platonist thesis on abstraction that the mode of knowing need not be identical with the mode of reality, that knowledge may be abstract and universal though all realities are particular and concrete. It also is connected with the familiar Aristotelian statement that "bonum et malum sunt in rebus, sed verum et falsum sunt in mente."[11] Because outer words may be abstract, and true or false, because real things are neither abstract nor true nor false, the immediate reference of their meaning is to an inner word.

The second element to be considered is the nature of the correspondence between inner and outer words. Grammarians divide the latter into eight, or sometimes ten, parts of speech; of these the Aristotelian *Perihermeneias* bothered to notice only nouns and verbs, and included both under the same rubric of the element of meaning.[12] Aquinas, in his commentary, denied a point-to-point correspondence between inner and outer words, arguing that inner words correspond to realities, while outer words are the products of convention and custom, and so vary with different peoples.[13] However, since the inner word is in the intellect, and since apprehension of the singular involves the use of a sensitive potency,[14] it should seem that the correspondence of realities to inner words is,

---

[10] *Ibid.*, lect. 3, § 31: " ... haec vox 'homo est asinus' est vere vox et vere signum; sed quia est signum falsi, ideo dicitur falsa."

[11] *In VI Met.*, lect. 4, § 1230 f.; cf. V lect. 9, § 895 f.; *In I Sent.*, d. 19, q. 5, a. 1 *sol*; *De Ver.*, q. 1, a. 2c; *Sum. Theol.*, I, q. 16, a. 1 c.

[12] The Aristotelian division is of conventionally significant sounds: if the parts have meaning, not merely *per accidens* as "heat" in "cheat," there is a λόγος, which is subdivided into indicative, optative, imperative, etc.; if the parts have no meaning, the division is into names and verbs. Cf. *Periherm.*, I, 2-4.

[13] *In I Periherm.*, lect. 2, § 21: "Ostendit passiones animae naturaliter esse sicut res per hoc quod sunt eaedem apud omnes.... Melius dicendum est quod intentio Aristotelis non est asserere identitatem conceptionis animae per comparationem ad vocem, ut scilicet unius vocis sit una conceptio, quia voces sunt diversae apud diversos: sed intendit asserere identitatem conceptionum animae per comparationes ad res...." Cf. Arist., *Periherm.*, I, 1; 16a 5-8.

[14] Cf. e.g., *Sum. Theol.*, I, q. 86, a. 1, ob. 1a, c. & ad 2m.

at best, like the correspondence between a function and its derivative; as the derivative, so the inner word is outside all particular cases and refers to all from some higher view-point.

A third element in fixing the nature of the inner word is connected intimately with the preceding. What is the division of inner words? On this question, four major works of Aquinas and a large number of his commentators are silent.[15] On the other hand, silence is no argument against positive statement. Four other works of recognized standing divide inner words into the two classes of definitions and judgments, and three of these recall the parallel of the Aristotelian twofold operation of the mind.[16] Moreover, the *De Veritate* argues that there is a *processio operati* in the intellect, though not in the will, on the ground that "bonum et malum sunt in rebus, sed verum et falsum sunt in mente."[17] This clearly supposes that the judgment is an inner word, for only in the judgments is there truth or falsity. On the other hand, while Aquinas does refer frequently to the inner word as a *conceptio, conceptum, conceptus*,[18] one must not give this term its current exclusive connotation; Aquinas employed it to denote judgments.[19] Finally, as stated above, the correspondence of inner words is mainly, not to outer words, but to reality; but reality divides into essence and existence; and of the two Aristotelian operations of the mind "prima operatio respicit quidditatem rei; secunda respicit esse ipsius."[20] It seems beyond doubt that an account of the Thomist inner word has to be an account of judgments no less than of the formation of definitions.

---

[15] The four works are the *Sentences*, the *Contra Gentiles* (which, however, mentions definition but not judgment [I, 53; IV, 11]), the *Summa* (but see I, q. 85, a. 2 ad 3m), and the *Compendium Theologiae*. With regard to the commentators, it is simplest to note that Ferrariensis acknowledges the twofold inner word (*In C. Gent.*, I, 53, § IV *ad fin.* [ed. Leon., XIII, 152]).

[16] *De Ver.*, q. 4, a. 2 c.; q. 3, a. 2 c; ; *De Pot.*, q. 8, a. 1 c.; q. 9, a. 5 c.; *Quodl.* V, a. 9 c.; *In Ioan.*, cap. 1, lect. 1.

[17] *De Ver.*, q. 4, a. 2 ad 7m.

[18] *Sum. Theol.*, I, q. 27, a. 1; q. 34, a. 1; *et passim.*

[19] Cf., e.g., *De Ver.*, q. 11, a. 1, c. " . . . primae conceptiones intellectus, quae statim lumine intellectus agentis cognoscuntur ... sive sint complexa, ut dignitates, sive incomplexa, sicut ratio entis."

[20] *In I Sent.*, d. 19, q. 5, a. 1 ad 7m. *In Boet. de Trin.*, q. 5, a. 3 c. *init.* (ed. Mand., III, 110).

A fourth element in the general notion of an inner word is that it supplies the object of thought. What is abstract, what is true or false, is not, as such, either a real thing or a mere copy of a real thing. It is a product of the mind. It is not merely a product but also a known product; and as known, it is an object. The illuminating parallel is from technical invention. What the inventor comes to know is not some already existing reality; it is simply the idea of what will be a reality if financial backing and a demand on the market are forthcoming; and in itself, apart from practical economic considerations, the invention known by the inventor is merely an idea. Such ideas are the products and fruits of a thinking out, an *excogitare*: certain general principles are known; the inventor's task is to work out practicable applications, to proceed from the properties of uranium to the atomic bomb. A similar process of thought is involved in the plans of every architect, the prescription of every doctor, the reflective pause of every craftsman and mechanic before he sets to work. In invention, creative imagination is needed; in the practical arts, imagination moves in the worn grooves of custom and routine; but in both cases there is the same general form of intellectual process, for in both certain general principles are known, in both a determinate end is envisaged, in both the principles are applied to the attainment of the end, and in both this application leads to a plan of operations that, as such, is, not knowing what is, but only knowing the idea of what one may do. Aquinas was aware of this. Aristotle in his *Metaphysics* had analysed such thinking things out and had arrived at the conclusion that the end, which is first in intention, is last in execution, whereas what is first in execution is last to be arrived at in the order of thought.[21] But Aquinas was troubled with a problem that had not concerned Aristotle, namely, how to reconcile the simplicity of God with the infinity of ideas known by God. To solve this problem, he generalized the Aristotelian theorem on the practical arts. It is not merely the prescription of the doctor, the plan of the architect, the idea of the inventor that, in the first instance, is a product and object of thought. The same holds for every definition and every judgment. As such, the definition is abstract; as such, the judgment is true or false; but no real thing

---

[21] *In VII Met.*, lect. 6, § 1405-10.

is abstract; and no real thing is true or false in the relevant sense
of truth or falsity.

The foregoing, I believe, is a key element in the Thomist concept
of inner word. Its principal expression is to be found, not in trinitarian passages, but in the discussions of the plurality of divine
ideas. It would be premature to attempt a detailed study of this
matter at once, for it pertains properly to an account of the Thomist
position on natural human knowledge of a divine word. On the
other hand, the reader is urged to review at once the Thomist texts
on the issue. The brilliant treatment is in the *De Veritate* (q. 3, a.
2 c.). Detailed treatment is in the *Contra Gentiles* (lib. I, cc. 46-54)
with the central issue in chapter 53. In the *Summa*, I should say
that Aquinas handled the matter automatically, as one does a
question that has ceased to be real problem.[22] In the *Sentences*,
on the other hand, though the essential elements of the solution
are present,[23] I fail to detect the mastery and effectiveness of the
later discussions; on this the reader may check by looking up the
objections of Scotus,[24] and asking himself whether *In I Sententia-
rum* (d. 36, q. 2, a. 2 sol.) really meets them.

Though the principal account of the definition and judgment as
both product and object of thought is to be found in the discussion
of the divine ideas, parallel affirmations are to be had in passages
dealing explicitly with the inner word. The most downright affirmation is the insistence of the *De Potentia*[25] that the inner word
is "primo et per se intellectum." But this view is already present
in the *De Veritate*. [26] On the other hand, the *Contra Gentiles*,

---

[22] *Sum. Theol.*, I, q. 14, aa. 5 & 6; q. 15, aa. 1-3; cf. q. 27, a. 1 ad 3m, which
connects the plurality of ideas with the divine procession of the Word.

[23] Cf. *In I Sent.*, d. 26, q. 2, a. 3 ad 2m; d. 35, q. 1, a. 2.

[24] *In I Sent.* (*Op. Ox*), d. 35, q. unic., n. 7 (ed. Vivès, X, 544). Scotus argues
that the divine ideas cannot be accounted for by adding notional relations to
the divine essence; for the object precedes the knowing, and relations that
precede knowing are not notional but real. The argument does not touch Aquinas' real position, which is that the object as known is not prior and that the
relations pertain only to the object as known.

[25] *De Pot.*, q. 9, a. 5 c.

[26] *De Ver.*, q. 4, a. 1 c.: The inner world is "id quod intellectum est," "ipsum
interius intellectum," "id quod actu consideratur per intellectum"; cf. *ibid.*,
a. 2 c.: it is "id ad quod operatio nostri intellectus terminatur, quod est ipsum
intellectum, quod dicitur conceptio intellectus."

though holding the same position, distinguishes between "res intellecta" and "intentio intellecta": the "intentio" is the inner word
whereas the "res" is the external thing, and the difference between
understanding the former and the latter is the difference between
logic or psychology and, on the other hand, metaphysics.[27] As the
term "intentio" refers to the inner word, so also and more frequently
does the term "ratio": white and black are outside the mind, but
the "ratio albi" is only in the mind.[28] To close the circle, one has
only to recall that the divine ideas, as principles of production, are
exemplars, but as principles of speculative knowledge, properly
are named "ratio."[29]

A fifth element in the general notion of an inner word is that
in it and through it intellect comes to knowledge of things. As this
threatens to engulf us in the epistemological bog, a brief orientation now may save endless confusion later. A useful preliminary
is to note that animals know, not mere phenomena, but things:
dogs know their masters, bones, other dogs, and not merely the
appearances of these things. Now this sensitive integration of sensible data also exists in the human animal and even in the human
philosopher. Take it as knowledge of reality, and there results
the secular contrast between the solid sense of reality and the
bloodless categories of the mind. Accept the sense of reality as
criterion of reality, and you are a materialist, sensist, positivist,
pragmatist, sentimentalist, and so on, as you please. Accept reason
as a criterion but retain the sense of reality as what gives meaning
to the term "real," and you are an idealist; for, like the sense of
reality, the reality defined by it is non-rational. In so far as I
grasp it, the Thomist position is the clear-headed third position:
reason is the criterion and, as well, it is reason—not the sense of
reality—that gives meaning to the term "real." The real is, what
is; and "what is," is known in the rational act, judgment.

The first act of intellect is knowledge of the *quod quid est*, τὸ τί
ἐστιν, the "what is it?" By definition, this knowledge involves

---

[27] *C. Gent.*, IV, 11 (ed. Leon., XV, 32b 33ff).

[28] *In VI Met.*, lect. 4, § 1230. The frequently repeated "ratio quam nomen
significat est definitio rei" stems from *In IV Met.*, lect. 16, § 733. The initial
statement on "ratio" is to be found *In I Sent.*, d. 2, q. 1, a. 3 c. *init.*

[29] *Sum. Theol.*, I, q. 15, a. 3 c.

neither truth nor falsity,[30] for the reason that the question of truth
or falsity is not as yet raised, because as yet one knows, not the
thing, but only the idea of the thing, because as yet one is in a
purely logical order.[31] Hence, "scientia est de aliquo dupliciter.
Uno modo primo et principaliter, et sic scientia est de universalibus
super quas fundatur. Alio modo est de aliquibus secundario, et
quasi per reflexionem quamdam, et sic est de rebus illis quarum
sunt illae rationes.... Ratione enim universali utitur sciens et ut
re scita et ut medio sciendi."[32] As long as one is dealing with ideas
as ideas, there is properly no question of truth or falsity and no
use of the inner word as a medium of knowledge. On the other
hand, the second operation of intellect—by the very nature of its
reflective character,[33] by the very fact that it raises the question
of truth, which is conformity between mind and thing,[34]—introduces
the duality of idea and thing and makes the former the medium
in and through which one apprehends the latter. Thus, our knowledge of God's existence is just our knowledge of the truth of the
judgment, *Deus est.*[35] And, while this knowledge differs from other
knowledge in most respects, it does not differ in the respect now
in question. For just as the inner word is a medium between the
meaning of outer words and the realities meant,[36] so also the inner

---

[30] *In III de An.*, lect. 11, § 746. Parallels are common: *In I Sent.*, d. 19, q. 5,
a. 1 ad 7m; *De Ver.*, q. 1, a. 3; *Sum. Theol.*, I, q. 16, a. 2; *In VI Met.*, lect. 4, §
1231-36.

[31] *In I Sent.*, d. 19, q. 5, a. 1 ad 7m. " ... quidditatis esse est quoddam esse
rationis."

[32] *In Boet. de Trin.*, q. 5, a. 2 ad 4m (ed. Mand., III, 107). This is not contrary
to *Sum Theol.*, I, q. 85, a. 2, which treats of the informing *species* and not of the
consequent *verbum*, except by contrast in the *ad 3m.* Cf. q. 15, a. 2 c.: "ideam
operati esse in mente operantis sicut quod intelligitur; non autem sicut species
qua intelligitur, quae est forma faciens intellectum in actu."

[33] On judicial reflection in general, cf. *In VI Met.*, lect. 4, § 1236; *Sum.
Theol.*, I, q. 16, a. 2 c. Such reflection is pushed to the level of the critical problem in *De Ver.*, q. 1, a. 9 c.

[34] *De Ver.*, q. 1, a. 1; *Sum. Theol.*, I, q. 16, a. 1; cf. *In I Sent.*, d. 19, q. 5, a. 1
sol.

[35] *Sum. Theol.*, I, q. 3, a. 4 ad 2m.

[36] *De Pot.*, q. 9, a. 5 c.: " ... vox exterior significat conceptum intellectus quo
mediante significat rem; ut cum dico 'homo' vel 'homo est animal.'" *De Pot.*,
q. 8, a. 1 c.: " ... vox enim exterior non significat ipsum intellectum [the faculty]

word is a medium between the intellect and the things that are understood.[37]

A sixth element in the general notion of an inner word is its necessity for an act termed *intelligere* which, I believe, is to be taken as meaning "understanding."[38] *Quoad se*, this necessity is universal, holding true in the case of God, of angels, and of men.[39] However, so far as our natural knowledge of God goes, we cannot affirm that His understanding involves the procession of an inner word.[40] Why that is so, is to be explained, I believe, only by an exact grasp of the psychology of the inner word.

A seventh element in the general notion is that the inner word of the human mind emerges at the end of a process of thoughtful inquiry,[41] that, until it emerges, we do not yet understand but are thinking in order to understand,[42] that it emerges simultaneously

---

neque speciem intelligibilem neque actum intellectus sed intellectus conceptionem qua mediante refertur ad rem."

[37] *De Ver.*, q. 3, a. 2c.: " ... quidditas ... compositio vel divisio ... quoddam operatum ipsius; per quod tamen intellectus venit in cognitionem rei exterioris"; *De Ver.*, q. 4, a. 2 ad 3m: " ... conceptio intellectus est media inter intellectum et rem intellectam, quia ea mediante pertingit ad rem"; *De Pot.*, q. 8, a. 1, c.: " ... conceptio intellectus ordinatur ad rem intellectam sicut ad finem; propter hoc enim intellectus conceptionem rei in se format ut rem intellectam cognoscat"; *C. Gent.*, I, 53: " ... ex hoc quod intentio intellecta sit similis alicui rei, sequitur quod intellectus, formando huiusmodi intentionem, rem illam intelligat"; *Quodl. V*, a. 9, ad 1m: " ... intellectus ... format verbum ad hoc quod intelligat rem"; *In Ioan.*, cap. 1, lect. 1: " ... in ipso expresso et formato videt naturam rei intellectae."

[38] *De Ver.*, q. 4, a. 2 ad 5m; *De Pot.*, q. 8, a. 1; q. 9, a. 5; *Sum. Theol.*, I, 27, a. 1 c.

[39] *In Ioan.*, cap. 1, lect. 1.

[40] *De Pot.*, q. 8, a. 1 ad 12m; *De Ver.*, q. 4, a. 2 ad 5m; cf. *Sum. Theol.*, I, q. 32, a. 1 ad 2m.

[41] *In Ioan.*, cap. 1, lect. 1: " ... cum volo concipere rationem lapidis, oportet quod ad ipsam ratiocinando perveniam: et sic est in omnibus aliis quae a nobis intelliguntur: nisi forte in primis principiis, quae cum sint simpliciter nota, absque discursu rationis statim sciuntur. Quamdiu ergo sic ratiocinando intellectus iactatur hac atque illac, necdum formatio perfecta est, nisi quando ipsam rationem rei perfecte conceperit: et tunc primo habet rationem rei perfectae, et tunc primo habet rationem verbi. Et inde est quod in anima nostra est cogitatio, per quam significatur ipse discursus inquisitionis, et verbum, quod est iam formatum secundum perfectam contemplationem veritatis."

[42] *De Pot.*, q. 9, a. 9 c.: "Ipsum enim intelligere non perficitur nisi aliquid in

with the act of understanding,[43] that it is distinct from understanding,[44] that it is a product and effect of the act of understanding,[45] that it is an expression of the cognitional content of the act
of understanding,[46] that the more perfect the one act of understanding, the more numerous the inner words it embraces in a
single view.[47] The problem here is twofold: (1) Does *intelligere*
mean understanding? (2) What is understanding both in itself and

mente concipiatur, quod dicitur verbum; non enim dicimur intelligere, sed cogitare ad intelligendum, antequam conceptio aliqua in mente nostra stabiliatur."
There is a variant—"cognoscere potius aliquid intelligendo"—to be found in
the compilation of texts, mostly from Aquinas, under the title, *De Intellectu
et Intelligibili, Opusc.* LXIII, (ed. Mand., V, 377). For the distinction between
intelligere proprie and *intelligere communiter*, see *De Ver.*, q. 1, a. 12 c. Cf. *In
III Sent.*, d. 35, q. 2, a. 2 sol. 1; *Sum. Theol.*, II-II, q. 8, a. 1 c.

[43] *C. Gent.*, IV, 14 (ed. Leon., XV, 56a 5 ff.): "Similiter etiam verbum quod in
mente nostra concipitur, non exit de potentia in actum nisi quatenus intellectus noster procedit de potentia in actum. Nec tamen verbum oritur ex intellectu
nostro nisi prout existit in actu: simul autem cum in actu existit, est in eo verbum conceptum ... intellectus in actu numquam est sine verbo." One may
recite a definition by rote without understanding; but unless one really understands, one cannot define; and as soon as one understands, one has defined.

[44] *De Pot.*, q. 8, a. 1 c. and q. 9, a. 5 c., are the most insistent texts on this
point.

[45] *De Ver.*, q. 4, a. 2 c.: " ... ipsa enim conceptio est effectus actus intelligendi."
Cf. q. 3, a. 2; q. 4, a. 2, ad 7m; *Sum. Theol.*, I, q. 34, a. 1 ad 3m: " ... intellectus
hominis verbo, quod concipit intelligendo lapidem, lapidem dicit."

[46] *De Ver.*, q. 4, a. 2 c: " ... aliquid expressum a notitia mentis." Cf. *Sum.
Theol.*, I, q. 34, a. 1 c.: "Ipse autem conceptus cordis de ratione sua habet quod
ab alio procedat, scilicet a notitia concipientis."

[47] *Sum. Theol.*, I, q. 85, a. 4; q. 55, a. 3; q. 58, aa. 2-4; q. 12, aa. 8 & 10. Parallels to these texts abound; see also the series on the plurality of divine ideas
(note 22 *supra*). Briefly, there are two points. The first (*In I Eth.*, lect. 11,
ad fin.) is that "Principium enim videtur esse plus quam dimidium totius. Quia
scilicet omnia alia quae restant continentur in principiis. Et hoc est quod subdit,
quod per unum principium bene intellectum et consideratum, multa fiunt mani-
festa eorum quae qaeruntur in scientia." The second is that a process of reasoning ends, not in the multiplicity of the process, but in a synthetic view of
the whole (*Sum. Theol.*, I, q. 14, a. 7 c.): " ... procedentes enim a principiis ad
conclusiones non simul utrumque considerant.... Unde manifestum est quod,
quando cognoscitur primum, adhuc ignoratur secundum. Et sic secundum non
cognoscitur in primo sed ex primo. Terminus vero discursus est, quando secundum videtur in primo, resolutis effectibus in causas; et tunc cessat discursus."
Numerous texts on this matter have been collected by J. Peghaire (*Intellectus
et Ratio*, Institut médiéval d'Ottawa, VI: Ottawa and Paris, 1936, pp. 247 ff.).

its expression? The contention of this paper will be that Aquinas was speaking of understanding and that an interpretation in terms of general metaphysics misses the point; to follow Aquinas here, one must practice introspective rational psychology; without that, one no more can know the created image of the Blessed Trinity, as Aquinas conceived it, than a blind man can know colors.

DEFINITION

In the foregoing section we approached the Thomist concept of inner word in the omnivorous fashion of the fact collector. Under seven headings we listed most of the matter relevant to the inquiry, and in the references we supplied the reader with indications of the sources of fuller and more accurate information.[48] From the cata-

---

[48] It is to be observed that Aquinas discussed the inner word, not directly in his general treatments of intellect, but in trinitarian passages and in discussions of the plurality of divine ideas. I should say that the theological issues forced a development of the basic Aristotelian materials. Further, it is in the *De Veritate* and in the discussion of the plurality of divine ideas (q. 3, a. 2) that the distinction between the twofold form or species is first enunciated effectively even though the general idea is not new (cf. *In I Sent.*, d. 26, q. 2, a. 3 ad 2m; d. 35, q. 1, a. 2 sol.). Finally, though the idea of an inner word is basically the same in the *Sentences* and in later works, still, since the grip is not so firm, statements occur which hardly can be reconciled with the later position. The position is basically the same: a distinction is drawn between the act of understanding ("simplex intuitus intellectus in cognitione intelligibilis") and the ordering of this intelligible to its manifestation; the inner word is some emanation from the intellect as making known (*In I Sent.*, d. 27, q. 2, a. 1; *In II Sent.*, d. 11, q. 2, a. 3); it adds something like thought to the simple intuition of intellect (*In I Sent.*, d. 27, q. 2, a. 1 ad 3m); it follows upon the intuition of intellect (*ibid.*, q. 2, a. 3); it is the "species concepta in qua est similitudo eius quod dicitur" and "quaedam similitudo in intellectu ipsius rei intellectae" (*ibid.*); it follows upon some intellectual light—at least that of the agent intellect and of first principles; consequently, a conclusion is an inner word but not the principles themselves (d. 34, q. 2, a. unic. ad 2m). But I do not think that later Aquinas would have said that the "species concepta interius" is not an inner word unless it is ordained to some manifestation (*In II Sent.*, d. 11, q. 2, a. 3 sol.), that it is not the divine essence as intellect or as understood, but as medium of understanding (*In I Sent.*, d. 27, q. 2, a. 1 ad 4m), that it may be the operation of understanding as such (*ibid.*, a. 2 sol. 1). See G. Chênevert, "Le Verbum dans le Commentaire sur les Sentences de saint Thomas d'Aquin," *Sciences ecclésiastiques*, 13 (1961), 191-223; 359-390.

logue there emerged our thesis, that we must begin by grasping
the nature of the act of understanding, that thence we shall come
to a grasp of the nature of inner words, their relation to language,
and their role in our knowledge of reality. Now, understanding is
of two kinds: there is the direct understanding, parent of the definition, in which the mind clicks, one gets the idea, one feels like
shouting "Eureka" with Archimedes; there is also a reflective
understanding, parent of judgment, in which one sees that one
cannot but judge something to be so. Our first concern will be
the former; our second chapter will deal with the latter; the third
chapter will turn to the metaphysical analysis of intellect; the
fourth to issues that are at once metaphysical and psychological;
the fifth to Thomist trinitarian theory. Such in outline is the plan.

In his zeal to prick complacent bubbles of unconscious ignorance,
Socrates made it a practice to ask people just what things are.
What is virtue? What is moderation? courage? justice? What
is science? On Plato's showing, Socrates had the formula for the
sixty-four-dollar question, but it was Aristotle who made capital
of it. For Aristotle, it would seem, realized that the real catch was
in the form of the question. It may be difficult to define this or
that virtue; but what makes things hopeless is the difficulty of
saying what one wishes to find out when one asks, even of the
most familiar things, "What is it?" Accordingly, one finds the
second book of the *Posterior Analytics* opening with an attempt to
fix the meaning of this type of question. Any question, we are
told—and so any answer and any item of knowledge—can be listed
under one of four headings. Either one asks (*a*) whether there is an
X, or (*b*) what is an X, or (*c*) whether X is Y, or (*d*) why X is Y. The
superficial eye will pair off the first two questions together and
the last two; but the significant parallel is between the first and
the third, and between the second and the fourth. In modern language the first and third are empirical questions: they ask about
matters of fact; they can be answered by an appeal to observation
or experiment. But the fourth question is not empirical; it asks for
a cause or reason; and, at least in some cases, the second question
is identical with the fourth and hence it too is not empirical, but
likewise asks for a cause or reason. Thus, "Why does light refract?"
and "What is refraction?" are, not two questions, but one and
the same. Again, to take Aristotle's stock example, "What is an

eclipse of the moon?" and "Why is the moon thus darkened?" are, not two questions, but one and the same. Say that the earth intervenes between the sun and the moon, blocking off the light received by the latter from the former, and at once you know why the moon is thus darkened, and what an eclipse is. The second and fourth questions, then, ask about causes; but a cause supplies the middle term in the scientific syllogism; and if the cause exists, its consequent necessarily exists. Hence, all four questions are questions about the middle terms of scientific syllogisms. The first and third ask whether there is a relevant middle term; the second and fourth ask what the relevant middle term is.[49]

But this answer only raises a further question. Granted that we know what is meant by "What is X?" when that question can be recast into an equivalent "Why V is X?" yet one may ask, quite legitimately, whether there always is a V. It is simple enough to substitute "Why does light refract?" for "What is refraction?" But tell me, please, what I am to substitute for "What is a man?" or "What is a house?" A good question needs a roundabout answer, and Aristotle considered that question good enough for the answer to be attempted, not in the *Posterior Analytics*, but only in the *Metaphysics*.

Let us go back to Socrates. In the *Meno* he proved a reminiscence of the ideas by summoning a slave and questioning him about a diagram. Aristotle was impressed, more by the questions than by the alleged reminiscence, but most of all by the diagram. At least he made grasp of the intelligible a matter of insight into the sensible or the imagined.[50] In the *Posterior Analytics* he remarked that, if a man were on the moon during its eclipse, he would not have to ask the first question—whether there is an eclipse—for the fact would be obvious; moreover, he would not even have to

[49] *Post Anal.*, II, 2, 89b 36 ff. (*In II Post. Anal.*, lect. 1); any of the four causes may be a middle term (II, 11, 94b 20ff.; lect 9). Aquinas (lect. 1, § 408) remarked of the four questions: "ad quae quattuor reduci potest quidquid est quaeribile vel scibile," and added that the four questions assigned in the *Topics* are only subdivisions of the two empirical questions here considered. He employed the four questions in proving a natural desire for the beatific vision in the angels (*C. Gent.*, III, 50).
[50] *De An.* III, 8, 432a 3-10; cf. 431a 14, b 2 (III, lect. 13, § 791; lect. 12, §§ 772, 777).

ask the second question—what is eclipse—for that too would be
obvious; he would see the earth cutting in between the sun and
himself, and so at once would grasp the cause and the universal.[51]
Grasping the cause is, not an ocular vision, but an insight into the
sensible data. Grasping the universal is the production of the
inner word that expresses that insight. And, Aquinas explains,
if one reached the universal from such brief acquaintance, that
would be a matter of conjecturing that eclipses of the moon always
occurred in that fashion.[52] A similar point comes up in the *Metaphysics*, in the passage that is the source of Aquinas' repeated
"unumquodque cognoscitur secundum quod est actu." Aristotle
made this point from the instance of geometrical problems; they
are difficult when the construction is merely in potency; but draw
in the construction, and one solves the problem almost by inspection. Stare at a triangle as long as you please, and you will not
be any nearer seeing that its three angles must equal two right angles. But through the vertex draw a line parallel to the base, and
the equality of alternate angles ends the matter at once.[53] The act
of understanding leaps forth when the sensible data are in a suitable
constellation.

We may now revert to our main problem—how to transform
questions of the second type into questions of the fourth type in
such ultimate and simple cases as, What is a man? What is a house?
The clue lies in the fact of insight into sensible data. For an insight,
an act of understanding, is a matter of knowing a cause.[54] Presumably, in ultimate and simple cases, the insight is the knowledge
of a cause that stands between the sensible data and the concept
whose definition is sought. Though Aristotle's predecessors knew

---

[51] *Post Anal.*, II, 2, 90a 24 ff. (II, lect. 1, § 416).

[52] *In II Post. Anal.*, lect. 1, § 417.

[53] *Met.*, Θ, 9, 1051a 22 ff. (IX, lect. 10, § 1888 ff).

[54] The Aristotelian analysis of understanding (ἐπίστασθαι) (*Post. Anal.*,
I, 2, 71b 9 ff. [I, lect. 4]) is first its identification with knowing a cause and secondly its expression in scientific syllogism. The *Posterior Analytics* simply
ring the changes on that analysis; the rest of the logical works serve to narrow
attention down to it as to the essential; the non-logical works apply it. Hence,
I should say that to miss the point here is the most effective way of missing
everything.

little of such a cause—for the cause in question is the formal cause[55]
—Aristotle himself made it a key factor in his system; and it was
to the formal cause that he appealed when, in the *Metaphysics*,
he attempted to settle the meaning of such questions as, What is a
man? What is a house?[56] The meaning is, Why is this sort of
body a man? Why are stones and bricks arranged in a certain
way, a house? What is it that causes the matter, sensibly perceived,
to be a thing? To Scholastics the answers are self-evident. That
which makes this type of body to be a man, is a human soul. That
which makes these stones and bricks to be house, is an artificial
form. That which makes matter, in general, to be a thing, is the
causa essendi, the formal cause.[57] The Aristotelian formulation
of understanding is the scientific syllogism (*syllogismus faciens
scire*) in which the middle term is the real cause of the presence
of the predicate in the subject. But the genesis of the terms involved
in scientific syllogisms follows the same model: sense provides the
subject, insight into sensible data the middle, and conceptualization the predicate, which is the term whose genesis was sought.

There remains a final note. The core of meaning in questions of
the second type has been determined by transposing them into
questions of the fourth type. What is a man? is equivalent to,
Why is V a man? —where V stands for the sensible data of a man
and the answer is the formal cause, the soul. Now, this does not
imply that one is to answer the question, What is a man? by the
proposition, A man is his soul. That answer is patently false. The
formal cause is only part of the whole, and part can never be predicated of the whole. The fallacy that leads to this false conclusion
is that, while we have transposed, What is X? into, Why V is X?,
we have yet to transpose the formal cause which answers, Why
V is X? back to the answer of, What is X? That transposition
is from formal cause to essence or quiddity. Neglect of this second
transposition by Aristotle has led to considerable obscurity: for
among the meanings of "substance" Aristotle will write the *causa
essendi*, the τὸ τί ἦν εἶναι, the form.[58] Very accurately Aquinas

---

[55] *Met.*, A, 7, 988a 18ff. (I, lect. 11, esp. § 175); A, 10, 993a 11 ff. (I, lect. 17, esp. § 272).
[56] *Met.*, Z, 17, 1041a 9 ff. (VII, lect. 17, § 1649 ff.).
[57] *Ibid.*, 1041b 4 ff. (§ 1666-68).
[58] E.g., *Met.*, Δ, 8, 1017b 10 ff.

hit upon the root of the confusion: "Essentia enim et forma in hoc conveniunt quod secundum utrumque dicitur esse illud quo aliquid est. Sed forma refertur ad materiam, quam facit esse in actu; quidditas autem refertur ad suppositum, quod significatur ut habens talem essentiam."[59] Questions of the second type ask about the *suppositum*, e. g., What is a man? Transposed to the fourth type, they ask about the matter, e. g., Why is this type of body a man? Common to both questions is inquiry into the *quo aliquid est*, which, relative to the matter, is the form, but relative to the *suppositum*, is the essence, i. e., the form plus the common matter.[60]

"QUOD QUID EST"

Quod quid est is a medieval attempt to find three Latin words corresponding to the Greek τὸ τί ἐστιν; similarly, *quod quid erat esse* is a literal translation of τὸ τί ἦν εἶναι; finally, *quidditas* is of medieval coinage and differs from the preceding as abstract from concrete. It will be convenient to refer to these five as Q_1, T_1, Q_2, T_2, and Q_3 respectively. For our present intention is to write a note on the usage of these terms, and in that our purpose is to confirm the interpretation of Aristotle set forth in the preceding section. The argument here invoked is, then, just a challenge: such and such are the pieces of this jig-saw puzzle; put them together in some other fashion if you can.

T_1 and T_2 are twists of the Greek language which Aristotle turned to technical account. Though they have distinct spheres of influence, still their connotations are closely related and their denotations overlap. That both terms exist, is to be accounted for, I would suggest, by the fact that T_1—the question of the second type—has its meaning defined by transposition to a question of the fourth type, while the answer to this fourth-type question

---

[59] *In V Met.*, lect. 10, § 904.

[60] There is a parallel ambiguity with regard to *species* (*In VII Met.*, lect. 9, § 1473): "Sciendum tamen est, quod nulla materia, nec communis, nec individuata, secundum se, se habet ad speciem prout sumitur pro forma. Sed secundum quod species sumitur pro universali, sicut hominem dicimus esse speciem, sic materia communis per se pertinet ad speciem, non autem materia individualis in qua natura speciei accipitur."

is properly T_2. Thus, the principal meaning of T_1 is essence, and the principal meaning of T_2 is form; of this difference Aristotle was aware, but his emphasis was not on the difference but on the radical equivalence. His argument was against the Platonists, who failed to grasp both insight into phantasm and the idea of formal cause, who consequently wished to derive essences—T_1—not from insight into the form of sensible objects, but from a noëtic heaven. Such a controversial interest would suffice to direct attention away from sharp and perfect differentiation, which, in any case, is more the work of the text-book writing pedant than of the original genius.[61]

T_2 ranges in meaning from the concrete and individual form of a particular thing to the abstract core of identical meaning in a scientific term. To begin from the latter, we learn in the *Topics* that the ἴδιον is convertible with its subject but does not reveal the T_2 of the subject,[62] while the ὅρος is both convertible with the subject and reveals the T_2 of the subject, so that its criterion is an identity of meaning with the meaning of the subject term.[63] At the same time we are warned that if one has the ὁρισμός, then one will have identity of meaning; but the converse does not hold.[64] Now this negative criterion of T_2 is employed in the *Metaphysics;* consideration of the candidacy of T_2 for the role of substance opens with some logical exercises to the effect that "being you" is not "being a musician," and "being a surface" is not "being white."[65]

But T_2 is also a frequent name for the formal cause of a particular thing: if particulars are discrete from their formal causes, they could neither be nor be known.[66] Is this merely a blind leap from the remotely abstract to the concrete? Hardly, for the proof in the *Physics* that there are just four causes turns upon a consideration of material cause, efficient cause, final cause, and, no doubt

---

[61] J. H. Newman put the point, not without a touch of exaggeration, when he wrote (*Grammar of Assent*, London 1870, p. 374): "It is the second-rate men, though most useful in their place, who prove, reconcile, finish, and explain."

[62] *Topics*, I, 5 (102a 18); I, 8 (103b 9f); V, 3 (131b 37—132a 9); V, 4 (133a 1, 6, 9).

[63] *Ibid.*, I, 4 (101b 19, 21); I, 5 (101b 39).

[64] *Ibid.*, I, 5 (102a 14 ff). On definition and its relation to scientific syllogism, cf. *Post. Anal.*, II, 8-10 (II, lect. 7 & 8).

[65] *Met.*, Z, 4, 1029b 13 ff. (VII, lect. 3, § 1308 ff.).

[66] *Met.*, Z, 6 (VII, lect. 5).

what is meant is the formal cause, but the only thing mentioned is T_1; the cause from which the geometer argues is the definition.[67] A similar tendency is to be observed in other treatments of the four causes, though in the other treatments the formal cause is named not T_1 but T_2.[68]

The naturalness of such transitions appears more clearly in Aristotle's environment and problems than in an abstract discussion held over twenty centuries later. Let us turn to these antecedents. Aristotle rebuked Democritus for advancing the statement that the μορφή was revealed by shape and color; the shape and color of a fresh corpse are the shape and color of a man; but a fresh corpse is not a man.[69] On the other hand, Empedocles was applauded more than once for his discernment in affirming that the substance and nature of a bone is, not some one of its elements, or all of them, but the proportion of their combination.[70] The proportion is named λόγος and T_2, and Aristotle's objection was that Empedocles should have held not just bones, but all nature to be such. Aristotle himself, after explaining the meaning of T_1 in the *Metaphysics*, went on to remark that a syllable is not just its component vowels and consonants, that flesh is not just fire and earth; there is a further factor, which is not an element, but a principle and cause—a *causa essendi*—which in natural things is the nature.[71] Thus, a sense is an accidental form, for a sense is to its sense organ, as soul is to body;[72] but though a form, a sense is also named the λόγος, or

[67] *Phys.*, II, 7, 198a 14ff.; cf. II, lect. 10, *ad fin.*, where Aquinas summarized the argument in terms of ontological form.

[68] *Phys.*, II, 3, 194b 16 ff. (II, lect. 5); *Post Anal.*, II, 11, 94a 20 ff. (II, lect. 9) ; *Met.*, A, 3, 983a 26 ff. (I, lect. 4, § 70); Δ, 2, 1013a 27, b 23, b 33 (V, lect.2, §§ 764, 779; lect. 3, § 786).

[69] *De Part. Anim.*, I, 1, 640b 31 ff. Cf. *ibid.*, 641a 18ff ; and *De An.*, II, 1, 412b 20 ff. (II, lect. 2, § 239).

[70] *De Part. Anim.*, I, 1, 640a 20 ff.; *Met.*, A, 10, 993a 17 (I, lect. 17, § 272); cf. *Phys.*, II, 2, 194a 20 (II, lect. 4).

[71] *Met.*, Z, 17, 1041b 11 ff. (VII, lect. 17, § 1672-80).

[72] *De An.*, II, 1, 412b 17ff. (II, lect. 2, § 239). If the whole soul is in each of the parts, it might seem to follow from this Aristotelian position that each of the parts of an animal was equally an animal. Hence, when he wrote *In I Sent.* d. 8, q. 5, a. 3, c., Aquinas seems to have considered the Aristotelian position silly, but had found a saving distinction by the time he wrote *Sum. Theol.*, I, q. 76, a. 8 ob. 3a et ad 3m. (In the Ottawa edition, "anima" instead of "animal" [last word in objection] seems a mere misprint).

proportion, of the organ;[73] and this is considered to account for the fact that violent light, sound, heat, and so on, injure not merely the sense organ but the sense as well, or again for the fact that, though plants are alive and may freeze, yet they do not feel cold because their matter is not in the right proportion.[74] But the crowning sample is the Aristotelian triumph, the definition of soul: soul is the substance as form of a natural body potentially alive;[75] it is the first entelechy of a natural body potentially alive,[76] or of a natural and organic body;[77] it is the substance according to reason[78] and that is the T_2 of a body of such a kind,[79] for if an eye were an animal, its soul would be sight.[80] But one must not be content with an empirical definition.[81] Just as "squaring the rectangle" may be defined empirically as finding a square equal in area to a given rectangle, or causally as finding the mean proportional between the unequal sides of the rectangle—where the former definition follows logically from the latter (for if $A : C : : C : B$, then $AB = C^2$);[82] so too the soul may be defined empirically as the first act of a natural and organic body, but causally as the ultimate principle of our living, feeling, and thinking—where the former definition follows logically from the latter (for the ultimate principle of our living is the first act of our matter).[83] Hence, the soul is not matter or subject, but λόγος τις ἂν εἴη καὶ εἶδος[84] again, the soul is an entelechy and the λόγος of what potentially has such a nature.[85]

---

[73] De An., II, 12, 424a 27 (II, lect. 24, § 555); III, 2, 426b 7 (III, lect. 2, § 592). The significant word is, of course, not the translation, "proportion," but the Greek, λόγος.

[74] De An., II, 12, 424a 28ff. (II, lect. 24, § 556 f.).

[75] De An., II, 1, 412a 20.

[76] Ibid., a 27.

[77] Ibid., b 5.

[78] Ibid., b 9 οὐσία γὰρ ἡ κατὰ τὸν λόγον.

[79] Ibid., b 9-11; cf. Met., Z, 10, 1035b 14 (VII, lect. 10, § 1484).

[80] Ibid., b 18.

[81] De An., II, 2, 413a 12.

[82] Loc. cit.; cf. Post. Anal., II, 8-10 (II, lect. 7 & 8).

[83] De An., 414a 4 ff. (II, lect. 4, § 271-75). It is not Aristotle but Aquinas that dots the I's and crosses the T's on the twofold definition of soul as an application of the pure theory of the Posterior Analytics.

[84] De An., 414a 14.

[85] Ibid., 27.

Now, I think the main point is merely missed by anyone who sees in such passages no more than confused leaping back and forth between ontological and logical considerations. Why was Aquinas able to affirm that intellect penetrates to the inwardness of things? Only because Aristotle had made his point, against the old naturalists and with some help from number-loving Pythagoreans and defining Platonists,[86] that what is known by intellect is a partial constituent of the realities first known by sense. For the materalist, the real is what he knows before he understands or thinks: it is the sensitively integrated object that is reality for a dog; it is the sure and firm-set earth on which I tread, which is so reassuring to the sense of reality; and on that showing, intellect does not penetrate to the inwardness of things but is a merely subjective, if highly useful, principle of activity. To the Pythagoreans the discovery of harmonic ratios revealed that numbers and their proportions, though primarily ideas, nonetheless have a role in making things what they are; and for Aristotle the ratio of two to one was the form of the diaposon.[87] Socratic interest in definition reinforced this tendency,[88] but the Platonist sought the reality known by thought, not in this world, but in another. Aristotle's basic thesis was the objective reality of what is known by understanding: it was a common sense position inasmuch as common sense always assumes that to be so; but it was not a common sense position inasmuch as common sense would be able to enunciate it or even to know with any degree of accuracy just what it means and implies. Aristotle is the representative of unconscious common sense; but conscious common sense found voice in the eminent Catholic doctor and professor of philosophy whom I heard ask, "Will some one please tell me what is all this fuss about *ens*?" When, then, Aristotle calls the soul a λόγος, he is stating his highly original position, not indeed with the full accuracy which his thought alone made possible, but in a generic fashion which suited his immediate purpose; and it is that generic issue that remains the capital issue, for the denial of soul today is really the denial of the

[86] *Met.*, A, 8, 989b 29ff. (I, lect. 13, § 202 f.); A, 7, 988a 34 ff. (I, lect. 11, § 175 ff.).
[87] *Phys.*, II, 3, 194b 27 f. (II, lect. 5); *Met.*, Δ, 2, 1013b 33 (V, lect. 3, § 786).
[88] *Met.*, M, 4, 1078b 9-34.

intelligible, the denial that understanding, knowing a cause, is knowing anything real.

Aquinas employed *quod quid est, quod quid erat esse,* and *quidditas*—Q_1, Q_2, and Q_3. But Q_2 occurs only rarely outside the Aristotelian commentaries[89] and even there the whole tendency is to identify it with Q_1. A discussion will begin with Q_2 as its topic, and a few lines later the discussion will be about Q_1;[90] and however disconcerting this may be, at least it accounts for the emergence of such intermediate forms as *quod quid est esse* and *quid est esse.*[91]. I have attempted to put together a representative, if not exhaustive, account of Thomist usage by listing the references to T_2 in Ross's index to the *Metaphysics* and checking the corresponding passages in the Thomist commentary. In some instances of T_2 Aquinas employed, not so much either Q_1 or Q_2 or Q_3 but *forma* or *causa formalis.*[92] In other instances of T_2 Aquinas employed Q_2 where the meaning of the latter is form, formal cause, formal principle, though this may be obscured or may be made doubtful by a later switch from form to essence. Thus, we are told that Q_2 was not employed by Aristotle in his *Categories,* that it means "neque genus neque species neque individuum sed horum omnium formale principium."[93] More or less in this sense, Q_2 is generated only *per accidens*;[94] it is soul;[95] it is the artist's idea;[96] it is what pertains to form;[97]

---

[89] *De Ente et Essentia,* c. I (ed. Roland-Gosselin, Kain, 1926, p. 3 *ad fin.*): "Et quia id per quod res constituitur in proprio genere vel specie est hoc quod significatur per diffinitionem indicantem quid est res, inde est quod nomen essentie a philosophis in nomen quiditatis mutatur; et hoc est quod Philosophus frequenter nominat quod quid erat esse, id est hoc per quod aliquid habet esse quid."

[90] E.g., *In VII Met.,* lect. 3, § 1308 ff.; lect. 5, § 1363, 1366, 1378.

[91] *In IV Met.,* lect. 7 § 627; V, lect. 7, § 864.

[92] *In I Met.,* lect. 4, § 70; lect. 11, § 175; lect. 17, § 272.

[93] *In VII Met.,* lect. 2, § 1275. Note that the question is the nature of substance; cf. § 1270, where the same term is taken as "quidditas, vel essentia, sive natura rei."

[94] *Ibid.,* lect. 7, § 1421; but cf. § 1422, and lect. 15, § 1608.

[95] *Ibid.,* lect. 10, § 1487; but cf. § 1491.

[96] *Ibid.,* lect. 6, § 1404; but recall that the artist's idea is an inner word that has been thought out and not strictly a form.

[97] *Ibid.,* lect. 13, § 1567.

it is proper to a single subject;[98] it is a principle and cause.[99] At the opposite pole, Q_2 is more or less the same as Q_1, and certainly it is not form, for it is predicable of the whole.[100] In a passage in which Aristotle argued from the properties of T_1 to those of T_2, Aquinas maintained a distinction between Q_1 and Q_2, though it does not seem that Q_2 here means form.[101] Finally, there is the identification of Q_2 with substance. This occasions no difficulty with regard to separate substances which are pure forms;[102] but *Metaphysics* Z deals with material substances,[103] and a measure of ambiguity is introduced into the whole Book by the fact that the centre of interest is not the composite, nor the matter, but substance as form[104] which shortly is referred to as T_2.[105] To some extent this accounts for Thomist corrections of Aristotle's speech, so that the commentary states "substantia, idest forma";[106] however, the ambiguity is perhaps really more fundamental, for such corrections are not confined to Z.[107] It is to be noted that substance and Q_2 are not subjective universals but objective entities: "quod quid erat esse est substantia, et ratio significativa eius est definitio";[108] "substantia rei quae est quod quid erat esse est principium et causa."[109] Finally, with reference to the answer to the question, What is a man? there is a veritable cascade of terms: *substantia, forma, species, causa materiae, principum et causa, quod quid erat esse,* and *quidditas* all occur within the space of two short paragraphs.[110].

[98] *Ibid.*, § 1577.

[99] *Ibid.*, lect. 17, § 1648, 1668, 1678.

[100] *In IV Met.*, lect. 7, § 625; V, lect. 19, § 1048; VII, lect. 3, § 1309; VII, lect. 5, § 1378; VII, lect. 7, § 1422; VII, lect. 10, § 1493.

[101] *In VII Met.*, lect. 4, § 1331 ff., 1339 ff., 1352 ff.

[102] *In VIII Met.*, lect. 3, § 1709.

[103] *In VII Met.*, lect. 1, § 1269.

[104] *Met.*, Z, 3, 1029a 26 ff.

[105] *Ibid.*, 4, 1029b 12.

[106] *In VII Met.*, lect. 10, § 1484, 1487.

[107] *In IX Met.*, lect. 5, § 1828.

[108] *In VIII Met.*, lect. 1, § 1685.

[109] *In VII Met.*, lect. 17, § 1649.

[110] *In VII Met.*, lect. 17, § 1667 f.: "Et similiter cum quaerimus quid est homo, idem est ac si quaereretur propter quid hoc, scilicet Socrates, est homo? quia scilicet inest ei quidditas hominis. Aut etiam idem est ac si quaereretur propter quid corpus sic se habens, ut puta organicum, est homo? Haec enim est materia hominis, sicut lapides et lateres domus. Quare manifestum est quod in talibus

Thus, I think, Thomist usage may be summarized as follows. *Quod quid est* (Q$_1$) is or corresponds to the essential definition as inner word. *Quod quid erat esse* (Q$_2$) is also the essential definition as inner word, but with special reference to the ground of essential definition, namely, the formal cause, so that at times it almost is, or simply is, the formal cause;[111] and precisely because of this uncertainty and ambiguity, the term appears so rarely outside the Aristotelian commentaries. *Quidditas* (Q$_3$) strictly is an abstract term with Q$_1$ as the corresponding concrete term: thus Q$_3$ is to form, as humanity is to the human soul;[112] unlike form, it includes common matter;[113] but this is only the proper meaning of Q$_3$, for at times it is indistinguishable from Q$_1$, a fact to be explained, at least in part, because it can be manipulated grammatically while Q$_1$ was practically indeclinable.[114].

To a superficial thinker, whose grasp of philosophic thought begins and ends with an exact use of language, the foregoing will appear as a horrid blemish. But the fact is that the original genius, precisely because he is original, finds all current usage inept for his purposes and succeeds remarkably if there is any possibility of grasping his meaning from his words; the possibility of exact expression of a philosophic position only arises long after the philo-

---

quaestionibus quaeritur 'causa materiae' idest propter quid materia pertingat ad naturam eius quod definitur. Hoc autem quaesitum quod est causa materiae 'est species' scilicet forma qua aliquid est. Hoc autem 'est substantia' idest ipsa substantia quae est quod quid erat esse. Et sic relinquitur quod propositum erat ostendere, scilicet quod substantia sit principium et causa."

[111] *In V Met.*, lect. 2, § 764: "Et, quia unumquodque consequitur naturam vel generis vel speciei per formam suam, natura autem generis vel speciei est id quod significat definitio, dicens quid est res, ideo forma est ratio ipsius 'quod quid erat esse,' idest definitio per quam scitur quid est res. Quamvis enim in definitione ponantur aliquae partes materiales, tamen id quod est principale, in definitione, oportet quod sit ex parte formae. Et ideo haec est ratio quare forma et causa, quia perficit rationem quidditatis rei." Cf. *In I Met.*, lect. 4, § 70, where however 'quod quid erat esse' occurs presumably in the text but not in the commentary.

[112] *In V Met.*, lect. 10, § 902.

[113] *In VII Met.*, lect. 9, § 1473. See also lect. 2, § 1270; lect. 10, § 1491; lect. 15, § 1606.

[114] E.g., *De Ver.*, q. 1, a. 12, c., where the argument moves from 'essentia' to 'quidditas,' and then on to 'quod quid est' without any apparent difference of meaning.

sopher's death when his influence has moulded the culture which is the background and vehicle of such expression. This is all the more true in matters that are at the very center of philosophic synthesis, and the *quod quid est* is at the very center of Aristotelian and Thomist thought. For *quod quid est* is the first and immediate middle term of scientific syllogistic demonstration; simultaneously, it is the goal and term of all positive inquiry, which begins from wonder about data[115] and proceeds to the search for causes—material, efficient, final, but principally formal; for the formal cause makes matter a thing and, combined with common matter, is the essence of the thing. The *quod quid est* is the key idea not only in all logic and methodology, but also in all metaphysics. *Simpliciter* it is substance; for substance alone is a *quid* without qualification; accidents, too, are instances of *quid*, but only after a fashion, for their intelligibility is not merely what they are, but also includes an added relation to their subject; and this difference in their intelligibility and essence involves a generically different *modus essendi*.[116] There follows the logico-ontological parallel: as methodology moves to discovery of the *quid*, so motion and generation move towards its reality; as demonstration establishes properties from the *quid*, so real essences are the real grounds of real properties. Nor is there only parallel, but also inter-action: the real is the cause of knowledge;[117] inversely, the idea of the technician or artist is the cause of the technical or artistic product;[118] and for Aquinas the latter is the prior consideration, for God is artisan of the universe. Even in this brief and rough delineation, one can perceive the magnificent sweep of genius. Now the issues we have been agitating in this section lie behind this synthesis: The essential definition proceeds from an act of understanding; the real thing is what it is because form has actuated matter. The Aristotelian

---

[115] *In I Met.*, lect. 1, § 2-4; lect. 3, § 54 f., § 66 f.

[116] *In VII Met.*, lect. 4. A less dialectical instance than the snub-nose may make the matter clearer: the intelligibility of circularity is its necessary consequence from equality of radii; but unless one adds the subject, "plane," that intelligibility will not define the circle nor circularity. Substance is a *quid* on its own; but ontological accident is not.

[117] *In IX Met.*, lect. 11, § 1897 ff.

[118] *In VII Met.*, lect. 8, § 1450 ff. See the whole argument, *Met.*, Z, 7-9 (lect. 6-8).

term, T_2, was a logical effort to isolate understanding and form, and one has only to consider the difficulties of such isolation to grasp why Aquinas dropped this Aristotelian effort as abortive and proceeded on lines of his own. Because the act of understanding —the *intelligere proprie*—is prior to, and cause of, conceptualization, because expression is only through conceptualization, any attempt to fix the act of understanding, except by way of introspective description, involves its own partial failure; for any such attempt is an expression, and expression is no longer understanding and already concept. Again, in a sense, the act of understanding as an insight into phantasm is knowledge of form: but the form so known does not correspond to the philosophic concept of form; insight is to phantasm as form is to matter; but in that proportion, form is related to prime matter, but insight is related to sensible qualities; strictly, then, it is not true that insight is grasp of form; rather, insight is the grasp of the object in an inward aspect such that the mind, pivoting on the insight, is able to conceive, not without labor, the philosophic concepts of form and matter.

INSIGHT INTO PHANTASM

Insight into phantasm is the first part of the process that moves from sense through understanding to essential definition. Though Aquinas derived the doctrine from Aristotle,[119] he also affirmed it as a matter of experience: "Quilibet in se ipso experiri potest, quod quando aliquis conatur aliquid intelligere, format sibi aliqua phantasmata per modum exemplorum, in quibus quasi inspiciat quod intelligere studet."[120] However, to many profound minds, so brief a description seems to have been insufficient. Scotus flatly denied the fact of insight into phantasm.[121] Kant, whose critique was not of the pure reason but of the human mind as conceived by Scotus,[122] repeatedly affirmed that our intellects are purely discursive,

[119] Cf. *supra*, note 50.

[120] *Sum. Theol.*, I, q. 84, a. 7 c.

[121] *In I Sent.* (*Op. Ox.*) d. 3, q. 6, n. 10 (ed. Vivès, IX, 250 ff.).

[122] Scotus (*Metaphys.*, II, q. 1, n. 2 [VII, 96]) posits concepts first, then the apprehension of nexus between concepts. His *species intelligibilis* is what is meant immediately by external words (*In Periherm.*, I, q. 2, n. 3; I, 541); it is proved to exist because knowing presupposes its object and indeed its object

that all intuition is sensible. Though the point is elementary, still it is so important that I beg to be permitted to dwell on a plain matter of fact.

The Platonists posited not only sensible objects and eternal forms but also pure mathematical objects; their reason for adding the third category was the fact that mathematical objects are like the forms by their necessity and immobility, but unlike the forms and like sensible objects inasmuch as they are many of the same kind.[123] One and one are two. But I plus myself am not two but

as present (*In I Sent.* [*Op. Ox.*], d. 3, q. 6, nn. 5-14 [IX, 236-53]); its production by agent intellect and phantasm is the first act of intellect, with knowing it as second act or inner word (*ibid.*, q. 8, n. 3 [IX, 401]); it is not necessarily an accident inhering in the intellect but necessarily only a sufficiently present agent cooperating with intellect in producing the act of knowing; ordinarily it is the subordinate, but may be the principal, agent (*ibid.*, q. 7, nn. 21 f. [IX, 362 f.]); sensitive knowledge is merely an occasion for scientific knowledge (*ibid.*, q. 4, nn. 7 ff. [IX, 173 ff.]) ; as our inner word proceeds from the species, so the divine word proceeds from the divine essence (*ibid.*, d. 2, q. 7, n. 15 [VIII, 543]). The Scotist rejection of insight into phantasm necessarily reduced the act of understanding to seeing a nexus between concepts; hence, while for Aquinas, understanding precedes conceptualization which is rational, for Scotus, understanding is preceded by conceptualization which is a matter of metaphysical mechanics. It is the latter position that gave Kant the analytic judgments which he criticized; and it is the real insufficiency of that position which led Kant to assert his synthetic apriori judgments; on the other hand, the Aristotelian and the Thomist positions both consider the Kantian assumption of purely discursive intellect to be false and, indeed, to be false, not as a point of theory, but as a matter of fact. While M. Gilson (*Arch. d'hist. doct. et litt. du M.-A.*, I [1926], 6-128; II [1927], 89-149; IV [1929], 5-149), has done splendid work on Scotist origins, there is needed an explanation of Scotist influence. Cajetan (*In I Sum. Theol.*, q. 12, a. 2, § XIV; ed. Leon., IV 118) confessed that at one time he held, taught, and may even have published a Scotist view of the beatific vision and this view he names the common run of opinion (*ibid.*). Though Cajetan (*ibid.*, q. 79, a. 2, § XIII; ed. Leon. V, 262) did not believe Scotus to have grasped Aristotle on intellect, P. Hoenen (*Gregorianum*, XIV [1933], 153-84; XIX [1938], 498-514; XX [1939], 19-54, 321-50) seems to have demonstrated conclusively that Cajetan has been overcome by Scotus on knowledge of principles; see also E. Longpré's remark (*La philosophie du B. Duns Scot*, [Paris, 1924] p. 215). Innocently enough, R. P. Minges ("Duns Scotus," *Cath. Encyclopedia*, V, 197) summed up the extent of Scotist influence : "The psychology of Scotus is in its essentials the same as that of St. Thomas." Really !

[123] *Met.*, A, 6, 987b 14 ff. (I, lect. 10, § 157). For the distinction of different Platonist positions; cf. M, 1, 1076a 17 ff.

one. For one and one to be two, the second "one" cannot be identical with the first; but neither can it differ in meaning, in idea, in essence, from the first; else it would not be "one" that was added to "one," but something else. When the geometer argues about two triangles similar in all respects, he deals with two triangles, and not with some one triangle; but if they are similar in all respects, then they do not differ in idea, in essence, in nature, or in any accidental characteristic; there is mere material multiplication. In Aristotelian and in Thomist psychology, the second "one" or the second "triangle" is accounted for, not by a second concept, but by the reflection of intellect back to phantasm where the many instances of the one idea are represented.[124]

Phantasm is involved not only in the employment of abstract concepts but also in their genesis. Euclid's first problem was to construct an equilateral triangle on a given base, AB. His procedure was to draw two circles in the given plane, one with center at A and radius AB, the other with center at B and radius BA. The point of intersection, C, was then joined to A and to B, and that ABC was an equilateral triangle was proved from the equality of the radii, AB and AC, BA and BC, and the axiom that things equal to the same are equal to each other. What Euclid failed to demonstrate was that the two circles would intersect; nor can it be demonstrated from abstract concepts; for there are not two abstract circles, and even if there were, they would be outside space, and so could not intersect. That the circles in question must intersect is known by insight into phantasm; draw or imagine the construction, and you will see this necessity; but you will see the two circles by a sensitive faculty, the necessity by an insight into the sensible presentation. Such insight is involved frequently enough in Euclidean proofs, but it is also involved in grasping primary definitions. A plane curve that possesses neither bumps nor dents, of perfectly uniform curvature, cannot be had if not all radii are equal but must be had if all radii are equal; one sees the curve, the radii, their equality, the presence or absence of bumps or dents by one's eyes or imagination; one cannot know them in any other way, ·for there is only one abstract radius, and it does not move; but the impossibility or necessity of perfectly

---

[124] *In III de An.*, lect. 8, § 713. *Sum. Theol.*, I, q. 86, a. 1; q. 84, a. 7; *et passim.*

uniform curvature is known by intellect alone in the act of insight into phantasm.

Aristotle grasped such facts. Intelligible objects, he maintained, do not exist apart from concrete extension but are in sensible forms and mathematical diagrams; accordingly, a person without sense perception would never learn anything or understand anything; further, speculative thought keeps an eye on phantasm for, in its case, phantasms play the role taken by sensible objects in sense perception.[125] Aquinas repeats Aristotle in such a variety of ways that one can be certain that he grasped the issue himself and was not merely appealing to an authority. Phantasm is to intellect as object to potency, as sensible objects to sense, as color to vision.[126] Phantasm is the object of intellect.[127] It is also the mover of intellect, but it is not the object because it is the mover, and so is the object perhaps only in some mechanical or metaphysical, but non-psychological, sense; it is the mover because it is the object.[128] Human intellect in this life needs phantasms as objects[129]—indeed, as proper objects.[130] Since knowledge requires an object, and since phantasm is the object of intellect, a phantasm is always necessary for intellectual activity, no matter how perfect the *species intelligibilis*.[131] "Potentiae sensitivae sunt necessariae animae ad intelligendum, non per accidens tamquam excitantes ut Plato posuit; neque disponentes tantum sicut posuit Avicenna; sed ut repraesentantes animae intellectivae proprium obiectum, ut dicit Philosophus in III de Anima."[132] In a word, one cannot

---

[125] Cf. *supra*, note 50. On insight into phantasm and modern scientific theory see, *James Clerk Maxwell: A Commemoration Volume*, essays by J. J. Thomson, *et al.*, (Cambridge, 1931), pp. 31, 98, 104, 106.

[126] *In II Sent.*, d. 17, q. 2, a. 1 sol; d. 20, q. 2, a. 2 ad 2m; IV, d. 49, q. 2, a. 6 ad 3m; *In Boet. de Trin.*, q. 6, a. 2 c. [ed. Mand., III, 132]; *De Ver.*, q. 2, a. 6 c.; etc.

[127] *In II Sent.*, d. 24, q. 2, a. 2 ad 1m; III, d. 14, q. 1, a. 3 sol. 2. There is even the early and somewhat incautious statement *In I Sent.*, d. 3, q. 4, a. 3 sol.: " ... oportet quod in definitione huius actus qui est intelligere, cadat phantasma, quod est obiectum eius, ut in III de An., text. 38, dicitur, quod per actum imaginationis repraesentatur intellectui." Cf. *De Ver.*, q. 10, a 2 ad 7m.

[128] *In II Sent.*, d. 17, q. 2, a. 1 sol.

[129] *De An.*, a. 15 ad 3m.

[130] *De Ver.*, q. 18, a. 8 ad 4m.

[131] *De Ver.*, q. 10, a. 2 ad 7m (1a ser.).

[132] *De An.*, a. 15 c., *ad fin.*

understand without understanding something; and the something understood, the something whose intelligibility is actuated, is in the phantasm. To understand circularity is to grasp by intellect a necessary nexus between imagined equal radii and imagined uniform curvature. The terms to be connected are sensibly perceived; their relation, connection, unification, is what insight knows in the sensitive presentation.

Because the necessity of phantasm is the necessity of an object, that necessity regards not merely the genesis but also the use of scientific grasp.[133] It makes no difference how spiritual the object, how far removed from sense; phantasm remains necessary; "etiam Deus cognoscitur a nobis per phantasma sui effectus, inquantum cognoscimus Deum per negationem vel per causalitatem vel per excellentiam."[134] Habitual possession of scientific knowledge is useless without conversion to phantasm "in quo resplendet species intelligibilis sicut exemplar in exemplato vel imagine."[135] The difference between invention or learning and use of science is that, in the first instance, phantasm has to produce the act of insight whereas, in subsequent instances, informed intellect guides the production of an appropriate phantasm;[136] in other words, in the first instance, we are at the mercy of fortune, the sub-conscious, or a teacher's skill, for the emergence of an appropriate phantasm; we are in a ferment of trying to grasp we know not what; but once we have understood, then we can operate on our own, marshalling images to a habitually known end.

The act of intellect with respect to phantasm is an insight: "cum phantasmata comparentur ad intellectum ut obiecta in quibus inspicit omne quod inspicit, vel secundum perfectam repraesentationem vel secundum negationem."[137] Though theoretical science proceeds from principles known of themselves, yet these principles

---

[133] *Boet. de Trin.*, q. 6, a. 2 ad 5m [ed. Mand. III, 154]; *De Ver.*, q. 10, a. 2 ad 7m; *Sum. Theol.*, I, q. 84, a. 7; q. 85, a. 1 ad 5m.

[134] *De Malo*, q. 16, a. 8 ad 3m; cf. *Sum. Theol.*, I, q. 84, a. 7 ad 3m.

[135] *C. Gent.*, II, 73 [ed. Leon., XIII, 462b 11].

[136] *Ibid.*; *De Ver.*, q. 19, a. 1 c.; *In III Sent.*, d. 14, a. 3, sol. 3; sol. 5 ad 3m; contrast *Sum. Theol.*, III, q. 12, a. 2 c., which modifies the position on Christ's human knowledge. See also *In III de An.*, lect. 8, § 700 ff.; *De Malo*, q. 16, a. 8.

[137] *In Boet. de Trin.*, q. 6, a. 2 ad 5m; cf. *C. Gent.*, II, 73.

are obtained from sense as explained in the second book of the
Posterior Analytics.[138] There the account is of a process from many
sensations to a memory, from many memories to an element of
experience, and from many elements of experience to grasp of a
universal.[139] Aquinas noted the parallel in the beginning of the
Metaphysics: The man of experience knows that such and such
medicine cured such and such patients in such and such circumstances; but the technician knows that such a kind of medicine
cures such a kind of disease.[140] Like the senses,[141] the man of
experience merely knows *quia*;[142] but the technician knows causes
—*propter quid*—and so is able to teach and to solve objections.[143]
In other words, the technician knows the abstract universal, which
is an inner word consequent to insight. But the man of experience
merely knows the *universale in particulari*, and that knowledge is
not intellectual knowledge but exists in a sensitive potency variously named the *ratio particularis, cogitativa, intellectus passivus*.
It carries on comparisons of particulars in virtue of the influence
of intellect,[144] and it knows Socrates and Callias, not merely as
Socrates and Callias, but also as *hi homines*,[145] and without this
sensitive apprehension of the universal in the particular it would
be impossible for intellect to reach the abstract universal.[146]

---

[138] *In IV Sent.*, d. 49, q. 2, a. 7 ad 12m; cf. *De An.*, a. 15 ad 20m.

[139] *In II Post. Anal.*, lect. 20.

[140] *In I Met.*, lect. 1, § 19.

[141] *Ibid.*, § 30.

[142] *Ibid.*, §§ 23, 24, 29.

[143] *Ibid.*

[144] *Sum. Theol.*, I, q. 78, a. 4 c., ob. 5a & ad 5m.

[145] *In II Post. Anal.*, lect. 20; cf. *In II de An.*, lect. 13, § 396 ff.

[146] While Scotus posited a knowledge of the singular in intellect (see C. S. R.
Harris, *The Philosophy of Duns Scotus*, [Oxford, 1927], II, 20 ff.), Aquinas, at
least when commenting Aristotle, could affirm the necessity of some knowledge of the universal in sense (*In II Post. Anal.*, lect. 20): "Manifestum est enim
quod singulare sentitur proprie et per se, sed tamen sensus est quodammodo
et ipsius universalis. Cognoscit enim Calliam, non solum inquantum est Callias,
sed etiam inquantum est hic homo; et similiter Socratem inquantum est hic
homo. Et inde est quod tali acceptione sensus praeexistente, anima intellectiva
potest considerare hominem in utroque. Si autem ita esset, quod sensus appre-
henderet solum id quod est particularitatis, et nullo modo cum hoc apprehen-
deret universale in particulare, non esset possibile quod ex apprehensione sensus
causaretur in nobis cognitio universalis." This position is impossible if one

This dependence of human intellect on sense for its object and for the preparatory elaboration of its object implies that human intellect is essentially intellect-in-process or reason. We do have occasional flashes of insight; but angelic, and, still more, divine, knowledge is exclusively that sort of thing, a continuous blaze of the light of understanding. We shout our rare "Eurekas" with Archimedes, but for the most part we have to reason: "Nam cum volo concipere rationem lapidis, oportet quod ad ipsam ratiocinando perveniam: et sic est in omnibus aliis quae a nobis intelliguntur; nisi forte in primis principiis, quae cum sint simpliciter nota, absque discursu rationis sciuntur."[147] This necessity of reasoning arises from the dependence of our intellects on sense: "Ex hoc ipso quod intellectus noster accipit a phantasmatibus, sequitur in ipso quod scientiam habet collativam, inquantum ex multis sensibilibus fit una memoria, et ex multis memoriis fit unum experimentum, et ex multis experimentis fit unum universale principium, ex quo alia concludit; et sic acquirit scientiam, ut dicitur in I Metaphys. in prooem. et in fine Posteriorum."[148] Hence the theory of innate

---

defines intellect as that which alone knows the universal; it is inevitable, if by intellect one means the faculty which is subject of acts of intelligence, understanding, etc. Naturally enough, crypto-Scotism would prefer to consider the passage just cited as representing the mind of Aristotle but not that of Aquinas. I would not contend that everything to be found in the Aristotelian commentaries is the mind of Aquinas. On the other hand, one must insist on some evidence before one can consider that an opinion is merely Aristotelian. With regard to the present question the following is perhaps significant (*De Ver.*, q. 8, a. 11, c., *ad fin.*): " ... omnis forma, inquantum huiusmodi, universalis est.... Omnis autem actio est a forma; et ideo, quantum est ex virtute agentis, non fit aliqua forma a rebus in nobis nisi quae sit similitudo formae; sed *per accidens contingit* ut sit similitudo etiam materialium dispositionum, inquantum recipit in organo materiali, quia materialiter recipit, et sic retinentur aliquae conditiones materiae. Ex quo contingit quod sensus et imaginatio singularia cognoscunt." For a fuller account of this mechanism, cf. *In II de An.*, lect. 24, §§ 551-554. If sense knowledge of the singular is in some sense *per accidens*, it hardly is impossible apriori that a sensitive potency under the influence of intellect should know the universal in the particular. For a documented study of the *cogitativa*, cf. J. Peghaire, "A Forgotten Sense: The Cogitative, according to St. Thomas Aquinas," *Modern Schoolman*, XX (1943), 123-40; 210-19; on knowledge of universal, pp. 138 ff.

[147] *In Ioan.*, cap. 1, lect. 1; cf. *In III Sent.*, d. 23, q. 1, a. 2.

[148] *In III Sent.*, d. 14, q. 1, a. 3 sol. 3; cf. II, d. 3, q. 1, a. 2 sol; *C. Gent.*, III,

ideas—and, one may add, of Kantian apriori forms—contradicts the experience we all have of working from, and on, a sensible basis towards understanding.[149] The Kantian apriori form of space has been junked by the geometers, and the Kantian apriori form of time has been junked by the physicists, for human understanding develops, and its *posse omnia fieri* knows no limit save that set by its natural object,[150] which is *ens*.

Now, just as human intellect is mainly reason, because it operates from sense as a starting-point, so the quiddity known by the human intellect is different in kind from that known by the angelic.[151] The angel has no senses and so his acts of understanding cannot be insights into sensibly presented data; they must be pure acts, though limited, of understanding. Of this more will be said later, but its main Aristotelian elements can be noted at once. As soon as Aristotle arrived at the meaning of the question, What is a man?, he immediately concluded that the separate substances must be objects of a different type of knowledge and inquiry.[152] The Platonist extrapolation to higher regions was modelled on the universal concept, and Aristotle rightly criticized the anthropomorphism of such a procedure.[153] Aristotle's own extrapolation is not from universal concepts, but from the act of insight: it consists in affirming the quality of understanding while removing the sensible object and limitation; the result is a νόησις νοήσεως[154] in which understander and understood are identical.[155] Thus the pure Aristotelian theory of intellect is to be sought in the Aristotelian account of his separate substances, and from that account O. Hamelin rightly derives the main features of his description of Aristotelian

56; *Sum. Theol.*, II-II, q. 180, a. 6 ad 2m; see J. Peghaire, *Intellectus et Ratio*, pp. 103 ff.

[149] *In IV Sent.*, d. 50, q. 1, a. 1 sol; cf. *ibid.*, d. 49, q. 2, a. 6 ad 3m.

[150] *C. Gent.*, II, 83 [ed. Leon., XIII, 523a 26 ff.].

[151] *De An.*, a. 7 ad 1 m; *Comp. Theol.*, c. 104; *In Boet. de Trin.*, q. 6, a. 4; *C. Gent.*, II, 94, "Praeterea"; III, 41.

[152] *In VII Met.*, lect. 17, §§ 1669 ff.

[153] *Ibid.*, lect. 16, § 1642-46.

[154] *Met.*, Λ, 9, 1074b 34; *In XII Met.*, lect. 11.

[155] *De An.*, III, 4, 430a 3; cf. *Sum. Theol.*, I, q. 87, a. 1 ad 3m; *De Ver.*, q. 8, aa. 6 & 7; *De Subst. Sep.*, c. 3 [ed. Mand., I, 81]; *In IX Met.*, lect. 11, § 1904.

intellect.[156] Similarly, the pure Thomist theory of intellect is to be sought in the Thomist account of angelic knowledge, and from that account J. Peghaire rightly begins his investigation of Thomist notions of intellect and reason.[157]

"EMANATIO INTELLIGIBILIS"

The procession of the inner word, we are told, is an *emanatio intelligibilis*.[158] This brings us to our main point. All causation is intelligible, but there are three differences between natural process and the procession of an inner word. The intelligibility of natural process is passive and potential: it is what can be understood; it is not an understanding; it is a potential object of intellect, but it is not the very stuff of intellect. Again, the intelligibility of natural process is the intelligibility of some specific natural law, say, the law of inverse squares, but never the intelligibility of the very idea of intelligible law. Thirdly, the intelligibility of natural process is imposed from without: natures act intelligibly, not because they are intelligent, for they are not, but because they are concretions of divine ideas and a divine plan. On the other hand, the intelligibility of the procession of an inner word is not passive nor potential; it is active and actual; it is intelligible because it is the activity of intelligence in act; it is intelligible, not as the possible object of understanding is intelligible, but as understanding itself and the activity of understanding is intelligible. Again, its intelligibility defies formulation in any specific law; inner words proceed according to the principles of identity, non-contradiction, excluded middle, and sufficient reason; but these principles are not specific laws but the essential conditions of there being objects to be related by laws and relations to relate them. Thus the procession of an inner word is the pure case of intelligible law: one may say that such procession is a particular case of "omne agens agit sibi simile"; but one has only to recall that this agent may be similar to anything, that it is "potens omnia fieri," to see that really one has here

---

[156] O. Hamelin, *Le Système d'Aristote* [éd. 2e; Paris, 1931], Lecture VIII, p. 108 ff.

[157] J. Peghaire, *Intellectus et Ratio*, pp. 29 ff.

[158] *Sum. Theol.*, I, q. 27, a. 1 c., *ad fin.*: "Secundum emanationem intelligibilem, utpote verbi intelligibilis a dicente."

not a particular case but the resumé of all possible cases. Thirdly, it is native and natural for the procession of inner word to be intelligible, actively intelligible, and the genus of all intelligible process; just as heat is native and natural to fire, so is intelligible procession to intelligence in act; for intelligence in act does not follow laws imposed from without, but rather it is the ground of the intelligibility in act of law, it is constitutive and, as it were, creative of law; and the laws of intelligible procession of an inner word are not any particular laws but the general constituents of any law, precisely because of this naturalness of intelligibility to intelligence, precisely because intelligence is to any conceived law as cause to effect.

Now it is only to restate the basic contention of this and subsequent articles to observe that the human mind is an image, and not a mere vestige, of the Blessed Trinity because its processions are intelligible in a manner that is essentially different from, that transcends, the passive, specific, imposed intelligibility of other natural process. Any effect has a sufficient ground in its cause; but an inner word not merely has a sufficient ground in the act of understanding it expresses; it also has a knowing as sufficient ground, and that ground is operative precisely as a knowing, knowing itself to be sufficient. To introduce a term that will summarize this, we may say that the inner word is rational, not indeed with the derived rationality of discourse, of reasoning from premises to conclusions, but with the basic and essential rationality of rational consciousness, with the rationality that can be discerned in any judgment, with the rationality that now we have to observe in all concepts. For human understanding, though it has its object in the phantasm and knows it in the phantasm, yet is not content with an object in this state. It pivots on itself to produce for itself another object which is the inner word as *ratio, intentio, definitio, quod quid est*. And this pivoting and production is no mere matter of some metaphysical sausage-machine, at one end slicing species off phantasm, and at the other popping out concepts; it is an operation of rational consciousness.

I believe there cannot be any reasonable doubt that the foregoing represents the mind of Aquinas. It is true that he does not employ the term *intelligere* exclusively in the sense of understanding.[159]

---

[159] J. Peghaire (*op. cit.* pp. 18-25), lists a dozen senses of *intellectus* in Aquinas.

It remains that the principal meaning of *intelligere* is understanding. Aquinas knew perfectly well what Aristotle meant by *quod quid est*, by the wonder that is the source of all science and philosophy, by insight into phantasm; he can take these positions, fuse and transform them, and come forth with a natural desire for the beatific vision,[160] a position that is notoriously unintelligible to people who do not grasp just what understanding is. He repeatedly affirmed that the *quod quid est* is the proper object of intellect,[161] and his affirmation carried with it all the implications of the Aristotelian ideal of science. A definition always rests on prior knowledge;[162] to know the quiddity, to define, to conceive the form of the thing, are identified;[163] to know the definition is to know in potency the science that is demonstrated from the definition;[164] definition is comprehension, embracing the whole range of implications of the defined.[165] In the *De Veritate* he considered as distinct potencies

[160] A natural desire for the beatific vision is absent from the earlier writings: there is the silence of *In II Sent.*, d. 33, q. 2; a. 2; IV, d. 49, q. 2, a. 1; *Quodl.*, X, a. 7; *De Ver.* q. 8, a. 1; furthermore, it seems positively excluded by *De Ver.*, q. 14, a. 2, with which compare *Sum. Theol.*, II-II, q. 4, a. 1. Its first appearance would seem the masterly discussion of beatitude in *C. Gent.*, III, 25-63; see esp. cc. 25, 48, 50, 63. It is reaffirmed in *Sum. Theol.*, I, q. 12, a. 1 c; a. 8 ad 4m; q. 62, a. 1 c; I-II, q. 3, a. 8; *Comp. Theol.*, c. 104. The origin of the doctrine is Aristotle (*In I Met.*, lect. 1, § 2-4; lect. 3, § 54 f; § 66 f.). This appears most clearly in *C. Gent.*, III, 50, and *Sum. Theol.*, I-II, q. 3, a. 8 c.

[161] The source is *In III de An.*, lect. 8, § 705-19, with the relevant statement in § 717. Affirmations of this position are endlessly recurrent: cf. *In III Sent.*, d. 23, q. 1, a. 2 c.; *De Ver.*, q. 1, a. 12 c.; q. 15, a. 2 ad 3m; *C. Gent.*, III, 56, "Amplius"; *Sum. Theol.*, I, q. 17, a. 3; q. 85, a. 6; q. 85, a. 8; q. 84, a. 7.

[162] *In Boet. de Trin.*, q. 6, a. 3, c. [ed. Mand. III, 136]. "Oportet enim definitionum cognitionem sicut et demonstrationum ex aliqua praeexistente cognitione initium sumere." Cf. *ibid.*, a. 4 c. [p. 140].

[163] *De Ver.*, q. 2, a. 1 ad 9m: "Tunc intellèctus dicitur scire de aliquo quid est, quando definit ipsum, id est quando concipit aliquam formam de ipsa re quae per omnia ipsi rei respondet."

[164] *De Ver.*, q. 2, a. 7 ad 5m: "qui cognoscit definitionem, cognoscit enuntiabilia in potentia quae per definitionem demonstrantur." Search Euclid for a property of the circle that is not demonstrated through the definition of the circle.

[165] *De Ver.*, q. 20, a. 5 c *ad fin.*: "Tunc enim unaquaeque res comprehenditur, quando eius definitio scitur. Cuiuslibet autem virtutis definitio sumitur ex his ad quae virtus se extendit. Unde si anima Christi sciret omnia ad quae virtus Dei se extendit, comprehenderet omnino virtutem Dei; quod est omnino impossibile."

the *scientificum* and the *ratiocinativum*; by the former we know
the necessary; by the latter we know the contingent; but it is the
former that has as its object the *quod quid est*, that through definitions knows principles, and through principles knows conclusions; in
other words the former is intellect in the sense of understanding.[166]
Later, in the *Pars Prima*, he found his way to include knowledge
of the contingent within the same potency, not indeed by changing
his concept of intellect, but by admitting within its range imperfect instances of its object.[167] Whatever intellect knows, it knows
through the *quod quid est* which is the substance of the object:
just as whatever is known by sight is known through color, so
what is known by intellect is known through the *quod quid est*.
What cannot be known by intellect in that manner cannot be
known at all. However, it is true that in the natural, as opposed
to the mathematical, sciences, intellect begins, not from the definition, but from sensible accidents; still, that does not affect the
principle enunciated above; it occurs *per accidens* inasmuch as our
intellectual knowledge proceeds from sense.[168] To grasp the meaning
of these passages is impossible, I believe, without also grasping
that by *intelligere* Aquinas means understanding, the act which,
if frequent, gains a man a reputation for intelligence and, if rare,
gains him a reputation for stupidity.

In the second place, Aquinas considered the inner word to be
a product of the act of understanding;[169] to be expressed from the

[166] *De Ver.*, q. 15, a. 2 ad 3m.
[167] *Sum. Theol.*, I, q. 79, a. 9 ad 3m.
[168] *C. Gent.*, III, 56: "Amplius, nulla virtus cognoscitiva cognoscit rem aliquam nisi secundum rationem proprii obiecti; non enim visu cognoscimus aliquid
nisi inquantum est coloratum. Proprium autem obiectum intellectus est quod
quid est, idest substantia rei, ut dicitur in III de Anima. Igitur quidquid intellectus de aliqua re cognoscit, cognoscet per cognitionem substantiae illius rei:
unde in qualibet demonstratione per quam innotescunt nobis propria accidentia, principium accipimus quod quid est, ut dicitur in II libro Posteriorum.
Si autem substantiam alicuius rei intellectus cognoscat per accidentia, sicut
dicitur in I de Anima quod accidentia magnam partem conferunt ad cognoscen-
dum quod quid est, hoc est per accidens, inquantum cognitio intellectus oritur
a sensu; et sic per sensibilium accidentium cognitionem oportet ad substantiae
intellectum pervenire; propter quod hoc non habet locum in mathematicis sed
in naturalibus tantum. Quidquid igitur est in re quod non potest cognosci per
cognitionem substantiae eius, oportet esse intellectui ignotum."
[169] *De Ver.*, q. 4, a. 2 c.: "omne autem intellectum in nobis est aliquid realiter

knowledge possessed by the mind;[170] of its very nature to proceed from the knowledge of the person conceiving it.[171] Of themselves, these statements do not give one a realization of *emanatio intelligibilis*. For that, examples and instances are necessary, and so we turn to the Thomist division of concepts. In this field the modern development of scientific methodology has added greatly to the precision of our knowledge; such precision no one will expect of Aquinas; but, on the other hand, no great discernment is required to see that his medieval grasp of the nature of intellect was sufficiently penetrating to enable him to anticipate what modern methodologists are apt to fancy a private preserve of their own.

Apart from certain natural concepts, of which we shall speak later, it cannot even be suggested that Aquinas thought of conception as an automatic process. Conceptualization comes as the term and product of a process of reasoning.[172] As long as the reasoning, the fluctuation of discourse, continues, the inner word is as yet unuttered.[173] But it also is true that as long as the reasoning continues, we do not as yet understand; for until the inner word is uttered, we are not understanding but only thinking in order to understand.[174] Hence understanding and inner word are simulta-

---

progrediens ab altero; vel sicut progrediuntur a principiis conceptiones conclusionem, vel sicut conceptiones quidditatum rerum posteriorum a quidditatibus priorum, vel saltem sicut conceptio actualis ab habituali cognitione; et hoc universaliter verum est de omni quod a nobis intelligitur, sive per essentiam intelligatur sive per similitudinem; ipsa enim conceptio est effectus actus intelligendi." I do not believe that the three alternatives listed equate with the full range of possibilities, for they regard the deductions of an adult mind, which would have been the aspect of the matter Aquinas would have considered most familiar to his contemporaries. I do not believe that the general principle affirmed as without exception is to be restricted to the field illustrated by these examples. As to conception from habitual knowledge, it is true, on the one hand, that habitual possession of principles without explicit advertence to them controls actual thinking (*De Malo*, q. 16, a. 6 ad 4m), but on the other hand, it is not true that there is ever conception without understanding in act as cause of the conception (*C. Gent.*, IV, 14 [ed. Leon., XV, 56a 5 ff.] ; cited *supra*, note 43).

[170] *De Ver.*, q. 4, a, 2 c: " ... aliquid expressum a notitia mentis."

[171] *Sum. Theol.*, I, q. 34, a. 1 c.: "Ipse autem conceptus cordis de ratione sua habet quod ab alio procedat, scilicet a notitia concipientis."

[172] *In Ioan.*, cap. 1, lect. 1; cited *supra* note 41.

[173] *Ibid.*; see also note 43 *supra*.

[174] See note 42.

neous, the former being the ground and cause of the latter.[175] What, it may be asked, can be the reasoning that is prior to the emergence of the term? Must there not be three terms before there can be any reasoning at all? Clearly such a difficulty is possible only if one's notions of rational psychology are limited to the data to be found in an abbreviated and very formal text-book on deductive logic. But if one is willing to take a broad view on reasoning, to conceive syllogism with some of the intellectual suppleness of Aristotle, one will be willing to grant that every question either asks whether there is a middle term, or asks what the middle term is; that when one asks what a stone is, one asks for the middle term between the sensible data and the essential definition of the stone; between those two, there has to occur an act of understanding, and leading up to such understanding there is the discourse or reasoning of scientific method; finally, such discourse differs with the progress of the human mind, for Aquinas, under the misapprehensions of Aristotelian physics, probably thought of stones as things while any modern thinker would pronounce them to be accidental aggregates. Already we have seen that from the fact that human understanding had its object in phantasm, Aquinas deduced that human intellect was mostly reason; one should not be surprised when he goes on to affirm that we have to reason in order to form concepts.

The rational character of conceptualization has, as its corollary, human ignorance and human progress. The first philosophers were babbling babes,[176] yet all our predecessors render us the double service either of hitting off the truth for us or of missing the mark, and so of challenging us to get to the root of the matter ourselves.[177] No one knows truth perfectly, and no one knows none at all; individual contributions are inevitably small but the common sum is great.[178] Ignorance may force us to use accidental in place of essential differences.[179] There are many properties of nature that

---

[175] See note 43.

[176] *In I Met.*, lect. 17, § 272; cf. *Sum. Theol.*, I, q. 44, a. 2.

[177] *In II Met.*, lect. 1, § 287 f.

[178] *Ibid.*, § 275 f.

[179] *In VII Met.*, lect. 12, § 1552; *De Ver.*, q. 10, a. 1 ad 6m; *Sum. Theol.*, I, q. 77, a. 1 ad 7m.

are totally unknown, and even those that fall under our observation do not readily yield their secrets.[180] There is no one who is not caught in some error, or is not at least ignorant of what he wishes to know or obliged to conjecture where he would have certitude.[181] The fact of indefinite human progress precludes the possibility of beatitude being placed in this life.[182] "Intellectus enim humanus se habet in genere rerum intelligibilium ut ens in potentia tantum, sicut et materia prima se habet in genere rerum sensibilium, unde possibilis nominatur."[183]

Besides implying human ignorance and progress, the rational character of conceptualization also implies a psychological account of abstraction. No doubt, a great deal of what Aquinas has to say of abstraction is on the metaphysical level; to that we hope to attend, inasmuch as it enters into our inquiry, in due course. But our immediate concern is to observe that not a little of the Thomist theory of abstraction is psychological. As a preliminary, we may recall that knowing the universal in the particular, knowing what is common to the instances in the instances, is not abstraction at all; it is an operation attributed by Aquinas to the sensitive potency which he names the *cogitativa*. As a second preliminary, we may explain that by a psychological account of abstraction we mean the elimination by the understanding of the intellectually irrelevant because it is understood to be irrelevant. That, we submit, is the very point of the celebrated three degrees of abstraction. What is variously termed *materia in individualis*, *materia designata*, *materia signata*, the *hic et nunc*, cannot be an explanatory factor in any science; it is irrelevant to all scientific explanation; it is irrelevant apriori; time and place as such explain nothing, for the reason for anything, the cause of anything, is never this instance at this place and time, but always a nature which, if found here, can be found elsewhere, if found now, can be found later. Hence natural scientist, mathematician, and

---

[180] *C. Gent.*, I, 3, *ad fin.*

[181] *Ibid.*, III, 48, "Praeterea."

[182] *C. Gent.*, III, 48: "Quamdiu aliquid movetur ad perfectionem, nondum est in ultimo fine. Sed omnes homines cognoscendo veritatem semper se habent ut moti et tendentes ad perfectionem, quia illi qui sequuntur superinveniunt alia ab illis quae a prioribus inventa sunt, sicut dicitur in II Metaphys."

[183] *Sum. Theol.*, I, q. 87, a. 1 c.

metaphysician all abstract from individual matter,[184] "quae est materia dimensionibus substans."[185] Intellect abstracts from the *hic et nunc*.[186] One cannot account for divine or angelic knowledge of the particulars of sense by accumulating any number of universal predicates, for the resultant combination will not be singular but "communicabile multis";[187] it could occur in any number of other possible worlds or, on the ancient hypothesis, in any number of completely similar cycles of one world. The astronomer can predict all the eclipses of coming centuries; but his science as such will not give him knowledge of any particular eclipse as particular "sicut rusticus cognoscit";[188] for in so far as the astronomer knows future eclipses as particular, it is only by relating his calculations to a sensibly given here and now. Properly, intellect does not remember; to know the past as past, like knowing the present, is the work of sense.[189] Why are all these statements made so confidently? Because it is common to all science to consider the *per se* and disregard the *per accidens*.[190] In other words, the "here and now," or the "there and then," as such are irrelevant to understanding, explanation, the assigning of causes; and from them intellect abstracts, inasmuch as, and because, it understands that irrelevance. The datum "round" is understood as necessitated by equal radii in a plane surface; "equal radii in a plane surface" is abstracted as common matter from phantasm and spoken in an inner word; no more is abstracted, because no more is relevant and, proximately, because understanding grasps that no more is relevant. The theorem on abstraction from individual matter is a theorem with respect to all

184 *Ibid.*, q. 85, a. 1 ad 2m.

185 *De Ver.*, q. 10, a. 5 c.

186 *De Ver.*, q. 2, a. 6 ad 1m; *Sum. Theol.*, I, q. 57, a. 2c.

187 *In II Sent.*, d. 3, q. 3, a. 3 sol. The basic discussion is Aristotle's argument that the Platonic ideas, because singular things, do not admit definition. Cf. *In VII Met.*, lect. 15; Aquinas drew the relevant conclusion in § 1626.

188 *De Ver.*, q. 2, a. 5 c.; cf. *De An.*, a. 20 c.

189 *De Ver.*, q. 10, a. 2 c.

190 *In Boet. de Trin.*, q. 5, a. 3 c., *ad fin.*: "Tertia secundum oppositionem universalis a particulari, et haec competit etiam physicae, et est communis omnibus scientiis, quia in omni scientia praetermittitur quod est per accidens, et accipitur quod est per se." The whole of this opusculum, but especially questions 5 and 6, are a monument to Aquinas' devotion to *Met.*, Z, 10-15 (VII, lect. 9-15).

our acts of understanding, to the effect that the "here and now" always pertains to the sensible residue and never enters into the relevant, the essential, that is abstracted.

The second degree of abstraction is similar to the first: as all science prescinds from the "here and now,"[191] so all mathematics prescinds from all sensible qualities—from colors, sounds, tactile experiences, tastes, odors;[192] the color of the geometrical figure, of the arithmetical or algebraic symbol, is never relevant to the mathematical theorem. The difference between a perspective geometry and a science of optics is that the manner in which light actually does move is relevant to the latter but irrelevant to the former;[193] if it is true that light rays bend, then optics has to be corrected, but not perspective geometry; for the physicist that overlooks matters of sensible fact falls into error, but the theorem and the judgment of the geometer are independent of sensible fact and are content with imagination.[194] Nor does the discovery of the more remote and generic types of non-Euclidean geometry invalidate this posi-

[191] It might be thought that, while Euclidean geometry abstracts from "here" and "there" in the sense that they are irrelevant to theorems, non-Euclidean geometry consists in attaching a significance to "here" or "there" as such. Such a view is mistaken. All geometries suppose a manifold of merely empirical differences which as such are not significant; the various geometries differ by the laws which relate the elements of the manifold; and Euclidean geometry has its unique position because it employs, for the most part unconsciously, the simplest laws. One cannot imagine, much less, see, indefinitely large space; one imagines a certain amount and conceives the addition of further amounts according to some sets of laws which may be, but are not necessarily, of the type named Euclidean.

[192] There is left the space-time continuum which is the pure matter of the *sensibilia communia*, namely, magnitude, shape, number, motion, rest. One cannot imagine any of these without also imagining some of the *sensibilia propria*; but while the *sensibilia communia* are essential to both pure and applied mathematics and enter into its object, the *sensibilia propria*, though necessarily present in imagination, are irrelevant to theorems.

[193] This probably was the occasion of the distinction between sensible and intelligible matter. See *Phys.*., II, 2, 193b 23 ff. (2 lect. 3); *In I Met.*, lect. 10, § 157; VI, lect. 1, § 1145; VII, lect 10, § 1494-96; VII, lect. 11, § 1507 f.; VIII, lect. 5, § 1760; *Met.*, M, 3, 1078a 14 ff.; *In Lib. de Caelo*, I, lect. 19, § 4; *In III de An.*, lect. 8, § 707 f., 714; *In Boet. de Trin.*, q. 5, a. 3; *De Ver.*, q. 2, a. 6 ad 1m; *Sum. Theol.*, I, q. 85, a. 1 ad 2m; etc.

[194] *In Boet. de Trin.*, q. 6, a. 2 c.

tion: they still reduce to an imagination, though not to the imagination that we possess; they presuppose an intellect capable of the third degree of abstraction, of transcending its own imagination; but they do not move within the third degree of abstraction, for they deal with a numercial multiplicity, not merely as a category—as does metaphysics—but as an essential factor in their proper object. Finally, the third degree of abstraction prescinds from all matter, individual and common, sensible and intelligible, to treat of "ens, unum, potentia et actus, et alia huiusmodi."[195] It does so, because metaphysical theorems are valid independently of any sensible matter of fact and of any condition of imagination. Conceptualization is the self-expression of an act of understanding; such self-expression is possible only because understanding is self-possessed, conscious of itself and its own conditions as understanding; in so far as the understanding has its conditions all within the intelligible order, the expression abstracts from all that is sensible and imaginable, and so is in the third degree; in so far as the understanding has conditions in the imaginable, but not in the empirical, order of sensible presentations, the abstraction is of the second degree; in so far as the understanding has conditions within the empirical order of sensible presentations, the abstraction is of the first degree; but there is always some abstraction; for the "here and now" of sensible presentation or of imagination is never relevant to any understanding. The Aristotelian and Thomist theory of abstraction is not exclusively metaphysical; basically, it is psychological, that is, derived from the character of acts of understanding. On the other hand, it is in the self-possession of understanding as the ground of possible conceptualization that one may best discern what is meant by saying that the self-expression of understanding is an *emanatio intelligibilis*, a procession from knowledge as knowledge, and because of knowledge as knowledge.

The concept is the definition, provided there is a definition.[196] Perhaps enough has been said to make the point that defining is a fruit of intelligence, the *quid rei* of understanding the thing, and the *quid nominis* of understanding the language. But what about ultimate concepts that defy definition? Are we to say that

195 *Sum. Theol.*, I, q. 85, a. 1 ad 2m.
196 *In I Sent.*, d. 2, q. 1, a. 3 sol.

DEFINITION AND UNDERSTANDING

they too proceed from acts of understanding? Or must not some less psychological, some more purely metaphysical, process be invoked in their case? Let us consider them.

Aristotle explained whence we obtain the ultimate concepts of potency and act. One begins from the sensible and concrete: "Inducendo in singularibus per exempla manifestari potest illud quod volumus dicere."[197] Relevant examples are the comparison of the sleeping and the waking, eyes closed but not blind and eyes that are seeing, the builder and the raw materials, the raw materials and the finished product. In these cases we are asked to notice a proportion and, indeed, different kinds of proportions. As eyes are to sight, so ears are to hearing (*auditus*, the faculty). As sight is to seeing, so hearing (*auditus*) is to hearing (*audire*) or—to adapt the example to the resources of our language—so taste is to tasting. The former is the proportion of matter to form; the latter is the proportion of operative potency to operation.[198] Now, can this be put in different terms? I think so. One begins by imagining the instances. The comparisons of the *cogitativa* prepare one for an act of insight, seeing in the data what itself cannot be a datum; when we express this insight by a concept, we say "possibility." In closed eyes we discern the possibility of actual seeing; in eyes we discern the possibility of sight; what is possible is the act, and its possibility is the potency; both are objective, but the act is objective when it occurs, the potency when the act is possible; and that objectivity of possibility is, for instance, what makes the difference between an invention and a mere bright idea. Ultimate concepts, like derived concepts, proceed from understanding.

I think much less ink would be spilt on the concept of *ens*, were more attention paid to its origin in the act of understanding. Tell any bumpkin a plausible tale and he will remark, "Well now, that may be so." He is not perhaps exercising consciously the virtue of wisdom which has the function of knowing the "ratio entis et non entis."[199] But his understanding has expressed itself as grasp of possible being. Intelligibility is the ground of possibility, and possibility is the possibility of being; equally, unintelligibility

---

[197] *In IX Met.*, lect. 5, § 1826.
[198] *Ibid.*, § 1827-29.
[199] *Sum. Theol.*, I-II, q. 66, a. 5 ad 4m.

is the ground of impossibility, and impossibility means impossibility
of being. To affirm actual being, more than a plausible tale is
wanted; for experience, though it is not as such the source of the
concept of being—else, as Kant held, the real would have to be
confined to the field of possible experience—still it is the condition of
the transition from the affirmation of the possibility to the affirmation of the actuality of being. Hence, the first operation of
intellect regards quiddities, but the second, judgment, regards
esse, the *actus essendi*.[200] Note, however, that being is not reduced
through possibility to intelligibility as to prior concepts; being
is the first concept;[201] what is prior to the first concept is, not a
prior concept, but an act of understanding; and like other concepts,
the concept of being is an effect of the act of understanding.[202]
Hence, when it was stated above that intellect from intelligibility
through possibility reaches being, an attempt was being made to
describe the virtualities of the act of understanding in its self-
possession, to conceptualize reflectively the pre-conceptual act of
intelligence that utters itself in the concept "being." Now it is
impossible to state that Aquinas himself attempted such descriptive
psychology; but though he kept such matters secret, rather amaz-
ingly he hit off the implications of such an analytic description.
From this it follows that the concept of being is natural to intellect;
for intelligibility is natural to intellect, for it is its act; and conceptualization is natural to intellect, for it is its activity; but the
concept of being, on the above showing, is the conceptualization
of intelligibility as such, and so it too is natural to intellect.[203]
Again, it follows that the content of the concept of being is indeterminate;[204] for it is conceived from any act of understanding
whatever; it proceeds from intelligibility in act as such. Again,

---

200 *In I Sent.*, d. 19, q. 5, a. 1 ad 7m; *In Boet. de Trin.*, q. 5, a. 3 c.

201 *In I Sent.*, d. 19, q. 5, a. 1 ad 2m; *In Boet. de Trin.*, q. 1, a. 3 ob. 3a; q.
6, a. 4c; *De Ver.*, q. 1, a. 1; *In I V Met*, lect. 6, § 605; *In I Post. Anal.*, lect. 5;
De Ente et Essentia Prooem.; *Sum. Theol.*, I, q. 5, a. 2 c; I-II, q. 94, a. 2c.

202 See note 169 *supra*.

203 *C. Gent.*, II, 83 [ed. Leon., XIII, 523a 26 ff.]: "Est eius (intellectus) unum
naturale objectum cuius per se et naturaliter cognitionem habet ... non est
aliud quam ens. Naturaliter igitur intellectus noster cognoscit ens et ea quae
sunt per se entis inquantum huiusmodi.... "

204 *Sum. Theol.*, I, q. 13, a. 11 c.

it follows that the concept of being cannot be unknown to intellect;[205] for its sole condition is that intellect be in any act of understanding. Again, it follows that being is the object of intellect: for intellect would not be intellect were it not at least *potens omnia fieri*, in potency to any intelligibility;[206] but what of its nature is *potens omnia fieri* must have being as its object.[207] Finally, it is impossible to recount in a sentence or so the position of Aquinas on analogy; but one may note briefly that, on the above showing, the concept of being cannot but be analogous; being is always conceived in the same way—as the expression of intelligibility or intelligence in act; but the content of one act of intelligibility or intelligence differs from the content of another; it is the identity of the process that necessitates the similarity of the proportion, and it is the diversity of the content that makes the terms of the proportion different. In brief, we may not claim to have investigated the Thomist concept of being; but at least it is not plausible that the concept of being has to be ascribed to some metaphysical mechanism and must lie outside the field of introspective and analytic psychology.

CONCLUSION

The hypothesis on which we have been working is this: The human mind offers an analogy to the trinitarian processions because it is rational in its conceptualizations, in its judgments, in its acts of will. A fragment of the complicated evidence on the thought of Aquinas has been examined. There remain to be considered the psychology of judgment, the metaphysical analysis of insight, of conceptualization, and of judgment, and the metaphysical and psychological elements in the Thomist concept of God as known both naturally and through divine revelation. Until all the evidence on all the points has been passed in review, there can be no conclusions.

I have begun, not from the metaphysical framework, but from the psychological content of Thomist theory of intellect: logic

---

[205] *De Ver.*, q. 11, a. 1 ad 3m.

[206] This underlies the argument of *In III Sent.*, d. 14, q. unica, a. 1 sol. 2 c.; *Sum. Theol.*, I, q. 79, a. 2; *C. Gent.*, II, 98; cf. *In III de An.*, lect. 13, § 790; *De Ver.*, q. 1, a. 9 c.

[207] *Sum. Theol.*, I, q. 79, a. 7 c.; *De Ver.*, q. 1, a. 2 ad 4m.

might favor the opposite procedure but, after attempting it in a variety of ways, I found it unmanageable. Though I do not expect every reader, at this stage, to see how objections—especially from the metaphysical quarter—might be answered, perhaps the following points may be granted. The Thomist concept of inner word is rich and nuanced: it is no mere metaphysical condition of a type of cognition; it aims at being a statement of psychological fact and the precise nature of those facts can be ascertained only by ascertaining what was meant by *intelligere*. Behind the notion of quiddity there lies the speculative activity that began with Socrates, was pushed forward at the Academy, and culminated in Aristotle: the *quod quid est* is central to a logic, a psychology, a metaphysic, and an epistemology; and this unity is intimately connected both with the metaphysical concept of form and the psychological experience of understanding. This conclusion is reinforced by the insistence of Aquinas on insight into phantasm, by the turn he gave to the notion of an inner word, by the psychological nature of his theory of abstraction. No less powerfully is it confirmed by the psychological wealth of his pages on intellect as contrasted with the psychological poverty of the pages of other writers who mean by *intelligere*, not principally the act of understanding, but any cognitional act of an alleged spiritual nature.

II

VERBUM: REFLECTION AND JUDGMENT

The plan of our inquiry has been, first, to determine the intro-spective psychological data involved in the Thomist concept of a *verbum mentis* or inner word; secondly, to review the meta-physical categories and theorems in which these introspective data were expressed by Aquinas; thirdly, to follow the extrapolation from the analysis of the human mind to the account of the divine intellect as known naturally; fourthly, to study the theory of the procession of the divine Word. The first task of introspective psychology fell into two parts corresponding to the two different types of inner word, namely, the definition and the judgment. Both types pro-ceed from an *intelligere*, but a difference of product postulates a difference of ground; in the preceding chapter of this book it was argued that the *intelligere* whence proceeds the definition is a direct act of understanding, an insight into phantasm; in the present article the contention will be that the *intelligere* from which the judgment proceeds is a reflective and critical act of understanding not unlike the act of Newman's illative sense.

It may be helpful to indicate at once the parallel between the two types of procession of inner words. Both definition and judg-ment proceed from acts of understanding, but the former from direct, the latter from reflective understanding. Both acts of understanding have their principal cause in the agent intellect, but the direct act in the agent intellect as spirit of wonder and inquiry, the reflective act in the agent intellect as spirit of critical reflection, as *virtus iudicativa*.[1] Again, both acts of understanding have their instrumental or material causes, but the direct act has this cause in a schematic image or phantasm, while the reflective act reviews not only imagination but also sense experience, and direct acts of understanding, and definitions, to find in all taken together the sufficient ground or evidence for a judgment. Hence, while the direct act of understanding generates in definition the

---

[1] *De Spir. Creat.*, a. 10 ad 8m.

expression of the intelligibility of a phantasm, the reflective act generates in judgment the expression of consciously possessed truth through which reality is both known and known to be known.

COMPOSITION OR DIVISION

Compositio vel divisio is the usual Thomist name for the second type of inner word. Its origin lies in the Aristotelian use of grammar for the specification of philosophic problems. In the *Categories* one is told to distinguish between simple and composite forms of speech: the latter are illustrated by "the man runs," "the man wins"; the former by "man," "runs," "wins."[2] In the *Periherme-neias* there is set forth the concomitance of truth or falsity in the mind and, on the other hand, linguistic synthesis: one means the true or false not by any single word, not even by the copula, but only by a conjunction of words; apparent exceptions arise, not because any single word by itself really means the true or false, but only because one can at times enounce a single word and have others, as the grammarians say, understood.[3] This passage Aquinas discussed at length, drawing an illuminating distinction between the primary and the consequent meanings of the verb "Est." Primarily, "Est simpliciter dictum significat in actu esse"; but consequently and implicitly, "Est" means the true or false. For the primary meaning of "Est" is the actuality of any form or act, substantial or accidental; but consequently, because actuality involves synthesis with the actuated, and implicitly because the actuated subject is understood when actuality is affirmed, there is the connotation of truth or falsity in this and other verbs.[4]

This distinction may be paralleled by the standard Aristotelian and Thomist division of *ens* into *ens* that is equivalent to *verum* and, on the other hand, *ens* that is divided by the ten categories.[5] But from the viewpoint of a genetic analysis of judgment a prior, though related, distinction must claim our immediate attention. As the name, "compositio," suggests, there is to the judgment a purely synthetic element. It is on this ground that we are told that truth

---

[2] *Categories* 2, 1a 17.
[3] *Periherm.*, I, 3; 16b 19-25.
[4] *In I Periherm.*, lect. 5, *ad fin.*
[5] *In V Met.*, lect. 9, §889 ff., §895 ff.; *De Ente et Essentia*, c. 1, *init.; et passim.*

or falsity resides in the conjunction as such and not in the terms that are conjoined. However, besides this element of synthesis, there is to judgment a further element by which synthesis is posited. If one compares the terms of a judgment to matter and the synthesis of the terms to form, then this act of positing synthesis by affirmation or denial may be likened to existence, which actuates the conjunction of matter and form. Without such positing there may be synthesis, as in a question or an hypothesis, but as yet there is no judgment. Again, synthesis, though not posited, may be true or false, but as yet it is not known to be true or false. Finally, as long as synthesis is not posited, the peculiar objective reference of the judgment is lacking; as yet the primary meaning of "Est," the affirmation (or negation) of an "in actu esse," is not involved. In Aristotle, it is true, this distinction between the merely synthetic element in judgment and, on the other hand, the positing of synthesis is not drawn clearly. In Thomist writings, I believe, the use of Aristotelian terminology obscures to some extent a more nuanced analysis. In any case it was only by making this distinction that I was able to organize the materials I had collected, and so the rest of this section will be devoted to the synthetic element in judgment, while following sections will take up successively different aspects of the more important and more difficult element by which synthesis is posited.

With regard to the synthetic element in judgment, certain preliminary distinctions must be drawn: there is the real composition in things themselves; there is the composition of inner words in the mind; there is the composition of outer words in speech and writing. The last of these three is obvious: spoken words are conjoined in a vocal and temporal cadence; written words are joined by using punctuation marks. Roughly parallel to the composition of outer words is the composition of inner words, so that at times, it may be difficult to say which composition is in question, as in the second part of the statement, "esse ... significat compositionem propositionis quam anima adinvenit coniungens praedicatum subiecto."[6] However, there is no doubt about the existence of an inner composition: it arises from the discursive character of our intellects, which form separate concepts to know first the subject

[6] *Sum. Theol.*, I, q. 3, a. 4 ad 2m.

and then the accident, which move from knowledge of the one to knowledge of the other, which attain knowledge of the inherence of accidents in subjects by some sort of combination or union of *species*.[7] Finally, the ground and cause of the composition that occurs in the mind and in speech is a real composition in the thing. Thus, the proposition, "Socrates is a man," has its ground and cause in the composition of a human form with the individual matter of Socrates; the proposition, "Socrates is white," has its ground and cause in the composition of a real accident, whiteness, with a real subject, Socrates.[8]

The one point to be noted here is that truth is not merely the subjective, mental synthesis. It is the correspondence between mental and real synthesis. More accurately, in our knowledge of composite things, truth is the correspondence of mental composition with real composition or of mental division with real division; falsity is the non-correspondence of mental composition to real division or of mental division to real composition.[9] But besides our knowledge of composite substances there are three other cases in which the foregoing account of truth suffers modal variations: in our knowledge of simple substances the *incomplexa* are known *complexe*; inversely, when simple substances know composite objects, the *complexa* are known *incomplexe*;[10] finally, in the self-knowledge of the absolutely simple substance, knowing and known are an identity and so truth can be named a correspondence in that case only by the artifice of a double negation; one cannot say that divine intellect is similar to divine being, for similarity supposes duality; one can say only that divine intellect is not dissimilar to divine being.[11] However, for the present, the significance of these modal variations is merely that they serve to stress the fact that mental synthesis is one thing and that judgment involves another. Judgment includes knowledge of truth;[12]

---

[7] *De Ver.*, q. 2, a. 7 c. *post med.*

[8] *In IX Met.*, lect. 11, §1898.

[9] *Ibid.*, §1896; *In VI Met.*, lect. 4, §1225 ff.

[10] The basic discussion is *In IX Met.*, lect. 11, §1901 ff.; cf. *De Ver.*, q. 2, a. 7; q. 8, aa. 14-15; *Sum. Theol.*, I, q. 14, a. 14; q. 58, aa. 2-4; q. 85, aa. 4-5; II-II, q. 1, a. 2 c; *et loc. par.*

[11] *Sum. Theol.*, I, q. 16, a. 5 ad 2 m.

[12] *Ibid.*, a. 2.

but knowledge of truth is knowledge not merely of mental synthesis but essentially of the correspondence between mental synthesis and real synthesis. The immediate issue is the nature of the origin and genesis of the mental synthesis, of the conjunction simply as conjunction in the mind and so as prior to knowledge of its correspondence to real conjunction.

Mental synthesis is of concepts. As one defined term proceeds from one insight into phantasm, so two defined terms proceed from two insights. Such multiple insights and definitions may be separate, isolated, atomic. But it also happens that one insight combines with another, or that a first develops so as to include a second. Such a process of developing insight is the whole task of catching on to a science; and, perhaps, it was this very point that obscurely was uppermost in Aristotle's mind when he drew his distinction between the two operations of intellect, namely, knowledge of the indivisible and knowledge of the composite. For he appealed to the naive, evolutionary theory of Empedocles that fancied an initial state of nature in which heads existed apart from necks and trunks apart from limbs; later, concord brought such separate members together into the harmonious wholes of the animals that, by a well-known law, alone have survived. In like manner, Aristotle contended, intellect puts together what before were apart. It is one thing to understand that the diagonal stands to the side of a square as root two to unity; it is another to grasp that that proportion is an irrational; it is a third to see that an irrational cannot be a measure. One may understand in isolation both the nature of measurement and the ratio of the diagonal to the side. But if one also understands the nature of irrationals, one has the scientific middle term for grasping that the diagonal of a square is incommensurable with its side; and in this final state one deals with concepts not in isolation but in intelligible unity; one sees, as it were in a single view, the diagonal as an irrational, and the irrational as an incommensurable.[13]

Note the nature of the conjunction: it is not that two concepts merge into one concept; that would be mere confusion; concepts remain eternally and immutably distinct. But while two concepts remain distinct as concepts, they may cease to be two intelligibili-

---

[13] *In III de An.*, lect. 11, §747-49; on irrationals, *In V Met.*, lect. 17, §1020.

ties and merge into one. "Symmetrum et diametrum aliquando separatim et seorsum intellectus intelligit, et tunc sunt duo intelligibilia; quando autem componit, fit unum intelligibile et simul intelligitur ab intellectu."[14] How do two concepts become one intelligibility? Not by a change in the concepts but by a coalescence or a development of insights: where before there were two acts of understanding, expressed singly in two concepts now there is but one act of understanding, expressed in the combination of two concepts. This combination of two, as a combination, forms but a single intelligible, a single though composite object of a single act of understanding.

The psychological fact that insights are not unrelated atoms, that they develop, coalesce, form higher unities, was fully familiar to Aquinas. Repeatedly he spoke of an *intelligere multa per unum*: many acts of understanding cannot be simultaneous in one intellect; but one act of understanding can and does grasp many objects in a single view.[15] Understanding a house is not understanding severally the foundation, the walls, and the roof; it is understanding one whole.[16] The object of judgment is not the several terms but the one proposition.[17] Knowledge of first principles is not exclusively a matter of comparing abstract terms or concepts; no less than the terms, the nexus between them may be directly abstracted from phantasm, so that, just as the concept, so also the principle may be the expression of an insight into phantasm.[18] The synthetic character of understanding is illustrated not only in the concept of a whole, such as a house, and in the grasp of a principle, but also in the learning of a science; for the less intelligent type of mind has to have things explained in painful detail, while the more intelligent catches on from a few indications.[19]

---

[14] *In III de An.*, lect. 11, §749.

[15] *In II Sent.*, d. 3, q. 3, a. 4; *In III Sent.*, d. 14, q. 1, a. 2, sol. 4 c. et 1m; *Quodl.* VII, a. 2; *De Ver.*, q. 8, a. 14; *C. Gent.*, I, 55; *De An.*, a. 18, ad 5m; *Sum. Theol.*, I, q. 85, a. 4.

[16] *In VI Met.*, lect. 4, §1229.

[17] *Ibid.*; *In III Sent.*, d. 14, q. 1, a. 2, sol. 4; *De Ver.*, q. 8, a. 14 c. *ad fin.* *C. Gent.* I, 55 (ed. Leon., XIII, 157a 22 ff.)

[18] See P. Hoenen, "De Origine Primorum Principiorum Scientiae," *Gregorianum*, XIV (1933), 153-84; XIX (1938), 498-514; XX (1939), 19-54; 321-50.

[19] *Sum. Theol.*, I, q. 55, a. 3 c.

Moreover, it is this synthetic character of understanding that is peculiarly evident in the theory of angelic and of divine knowledge. Angels need *species* to know things other than themselves; but the higher angels are higher because they grasp more by fewer *species* than do the lower with more numerous *species*; their acts of understanding are wider in sweep and more profound in penetration.[20] The summit of such sweep and penetration is the divine intellect; for the divine act of understanding is one, yet it embraces in a single view all possibles and the prodigal multiplicity of actual beings.[21] Finally, it is to such a view of all reality that human intellect naturally aspires. The specific drive of our nature is to understand, [22] and indeed to understand everything, neither confusing the trees with the forest nor content to contemplate the forest without seeing all the trees. For the spirit of inquiry within us never calls a halt, never can be satisfied, until our intellects, united to God as body to soul, [23] know *ipsum intelligere* and through that vision, though then knowing aught else is a trifle,[24] contemplate the universe as well. [25]

If to thirst, however obscurely, for this consummation is natural, still to achieve it is supernatural.[26] But besides supernatural, there is also natural achievement, progress in understanding within the natural ambit of our development. Such progress, as progressing, is reason; for reason is to understanding, as motion is to rest. Reason is not one potency, and understanding another potency; on the level of potency the two are identical; they differ only as process to a term differs from achievement in the term.[27] This point merits illustration.

---

[20] *Ibid.*; *In II Sent.*, d. 3, q. 3, a. 2; *De Ver.*, q. 8, a. 10; *C. Gent.*, II, 98.

[21] *C. Gent.*, I, 46 ff.; *In I Sent.*, d. 35-36; *De Ver.*, qq. 2-3; *Sum. Theol.*, I, q. 14, aa. 5-6; q. 15, aa. 1-3.

[22] *De Ver.*, q. 14, a. 1 c.: ". . . intellectus . . . proprium terminum . . . qui est visio alicuius intelligibilis."

[23] *C. Gent.*, III, 51.

[24] *Sum. Theol.*, I, q. 12, a. 8 ad 4m.

[25] *Ibid.*, I-II, q. 3, a. 8.

[26] *C. Gent.*, III, 52; see Henri Rondet, "Nature et surnaturel dans la théologie de s. Thomas d'Aquin," *Rech. sc. rel.*, XXXIII (1946), 56-91.

[27] *In II Sent.*, d. 9, q. 1, a. 8 ad 1 m; *De Ver.*, q. 15, a. 1; *Sum. Theol.*, I, q. 79, a. 8 c.; cf. J. Peghaire, *Intellectus et Ratio selon S. Thomas d'Aquin* (Inst. méd. d'Ottawa, VI; Ottawa and Paris, 1936).

It is objected, frequently enough, that syllogism does not represent the manner in which, as a matter of fact, we learn and think. This difficulty has its ground, partly in the identity of reason and understanding, partly in the type of examples of syllogism commonly found in the text-books. Syllogism may represent either reasoning or understanding. When we understand, we no longer are reasoning or learning; we have reached the term and apprehend the many as one; but the stock examples of syllogism represent acts of understanding, matters that may have puzzled us long ago, but now are taken for granted. It follows that such syllogisms do not illustrate learning or reasoning for current consciousness. But take a syllogism in a field in which your grasp is not too ready; define the terms; demonstrate the premises; and you will find that this reasoning is bringing an understanding to birth and that, with understanding achieved, you no longer reason but apprehend the many in a synthetic unity. For instance, why is the diagonal of a square incommensurable with the side? First, what is a measurement? It is a fourfold proportion in which, where M and N are integers, M:N : : measurable object: standard unit. What is the ratio of the diagonal to the side? It is root two. Now demonstrate that there cannot be two integers, M and N, such that $M/N = \sqrt{2}$. As long as reasoning continues, understanding is not achieved. But with the reasoning process successfully completed, understanding is achieved: *ratio terminatur ad intellectum*.[28]

It is in its relation to the pyschological experience of understanding that reasoning or discourse is characterized by Aquinas. There is a difference between knowing one thing in another, and

---

[28] *Sum. Theol.*, II-II, q. 8, a. 1 ad 2m: "Dicendum quod discursus rationis semper incipit ab intellectu et terminatur ad intellectum; ratiocinamur enim procedendo ex quibusdam intellectis, et tunc rationis discursus perficitur quando ad hoc pervenimus ut intelligamus id quod prius erat ignotum." Note that the phrase "terminatur ad intellectum" is ambiguous; very frequently it refers to a critical return to *intellectus* as *habitus principiorum;* in the text cited it has to mean the arrival at some hitherto unknown object of understanding, which cannot be the object of the naturally known first principles employed in all reasoning. On this issue, see J. Peghaire, *op. cit.*, pp. 261 ff., 269 ff. With regard to the distinction between natural and chro-, nological priority of knowledge of premises over knowledge of conclusions, see *In I Post. Anal.*, lect. 2.

knowing one thing from knowing another; the former involves a single movement of mind; the latter involves a twofold movement, as in syllogism where first one grasps principles and then conclusion.[29] In the *Summa* the analysis is pushed further by the introduction of a distinction between the temporal and the causal elements in discursive knowledge. In discourse there is temporal succession, for we know first one thing and then another; there is also causal connection, for it is because we know the first that we come to know the second. But in God there is no temporal succession, for He knows all at once; and there is no causal connection between different acts of knowing, for His knowing is a single act. Still, though God's knowledge is uncaused, it does not follow that He does not know causes. For all discursive knowledge comes to a term in the intuitive apprehension of a field of implications, inter-relations, dependencies; from knowing a second because we know a first, we move to knowing a second in the first; but in God that final state is eternal, for He knows all things in their cause, which is Himself.[30]

Reasoning was not characterized by Aquinas with a reference to a text on formal logic; it was characterized as the development of understanding, as motion towards understanding. This fact throws a light backward on an issue raised in the preceding article. Conceive reasoning in terms of deductive logic and there can be no reasoning unless one already is in possession of the necessary three terms, subject, middle, and predicate. But conceive reasoning as understanding in development and there is not the slightest difficulty about the Thomist view that we have to reason to grasp even the terms : "nam cum volo concipere rationem lapidis, oportet quod ad ipsam ratiocinando perveniam; et sic est in omnibus aliis, quae a nobis intelliguntur, nisi forte in primis principiis."[31] Just how Aquinas reasoned out his concept of a stone, I cannot say; but in the second book of the *Contra Gentiles* there is the magnificent reasoning out of the concept of the human soul; it runs through no less than forty-five chapters ;[32]   and that long

---

[29] *De Ver.*, q. 8, a. 15.
[30] *Sum. Theol.*, I, q. 14, a. 7 c.
[31] *In Ioan.*, cap. 1, lect. 1.
[32] *C. Gent.*, II, 46-90.

argument provides an excellent example of what exactly Aquinas
meant by knowledge of essence. For him, understanding was a
knowledge penetrating to the inward nature of a thing. Angels
know such essences directly, for they have no senses; but men
reach essences only through the sensible doors that surround
them; they have to reason from effects to causes and from properties to natures. Hence properly human understanding is named
reason, though—it is not to be forgotten—reasoning terminates
in understanding inasmusch as inquiry eventually yields knowledge
of essence.[33]

Reasoning not merely terminates in understanding; equally
it begins from understanding; for unless we understood something,
we never should begin to reason at all. Accordingly, to avoid
an infinite regress, it is necessary to posit a *habitus principorium*,
also termed *intellectus*, which naturally we possess. Such a natural
habit differs both from acquired habit and from infused habit.
The natural habit, though it has a determination from sense,
results strictly from intellectual light alone; the acquired habit
has in sense not only a determination but also a cause.[34] Thus,
the natural habit is more like the infused than the acquired: the
infused virtue of faith is not caused but only receives a determination from the preaching of the gospel.[35] This is very subtle,
introspective psychology. To grasp it one has to compare two
types of first principle. Thus, there is at least a certain self-evi-
dence to the principle of inverse squares; but is it not a self-evi-
dence that can be apprehended without an image of spatial extension. On the other hand, the evidence of the principle of non-
contradiction is of a different type; with regard to it, any sensible
instance is equally relevant and none is more than an illustration;
for this principle does not arise from an insight into sensible
data but from the nature of intelligence as such; and so its field
of application is not limited to the realm of possible human experience, as the principle of inverse squares is limited to the imaginable and as certain geometrical principles to the Euclidean imaginable.

[33] *In III Sent.*, d. 35, q. 2, a. 2, sol. 1; cf. *De Ver.*, q. 1, a. 12 c; *In VI Eth.*
lect. 5; *Sum. Theol.*, II-II, q. 8, a. 1 c.
[34] *In II Sent.*, d. 24, q. 2, a. 3 sol.; *De Ver.*, q. 8, a. 15 c. *fin.*
[35] *In III Sent.*, d. 23, q. 3, a. 2 ad 1m.

Nowhere, to my knowledge, did Aquinas offer to give a complete list of naturally known principles. His stock examples are the principle of non-contradiction and of the whole being greater than the part.[36] But it does not follow that the list of such principles is quite indeterminate. As there are naturally known principles, so also there is an object which we know *per se* and naturally. That object is *ens*; and only principles founded upon our knowledge of *ens* are naturally known.[37] The nature of our natural knowledge of *ens* already has been touched upon in the previous article,[38] and to it we shall have to return later in this article.

If we are correct in urging that intelligibility is the ground of possibility and that possibility is possibility of being, so that the concept of being is known naturally because it proceeds from any intelligibility in act (= any intelligence in act), then it is equally clear that the principle of non-contradiction is known naturally; for as that principle is the natural law of the procession of any concept from intelligence in act, so it is the first principle ruling all conceptualization; and as Aquinas affirmed,[39] it is the first principle governing all judgment.

The other stock example of a naturally known principle is that the whole is greater than the part.[40] However, quantitative wholes and quantitative parts are known, not naturally, but through insight into phantasm; and it seems difficult to show that the discovery of the relation of quantitative whole to quantitative part is not an ordinary coalescence of insights. Still, it does not follow that St. Thomas was mistaken in stating that we naturally know the whole to be greater than the part. For, as every being is one, so every finite being is a whole compounded of parts, an *ens quod* made up of *entia quibus.* Moreover, we know this naturally. Natural form stands to natural matter, as intelligible form stands to sensible matter;[41] and when by a natural spontaneity we ask

---

[36] *In II Met.*, lect. 1, §277; IV, lect. 6, §605; *In II Sent.*, d. 24, q. 2, a. 3 sol.; *et passim.*

[37] *C. Gent.*, II, 83 (ed. Leon., XIII, 523a 26 ff.)

[38] See pages 43f above.

[39] *In IV Met.*, lect. 6, §605.

[40] *In II Met.*, lect. 1, § 277; *In II Sent.*, d. 24, q. 2, a. 3; *Sum. Theol.*, I-II, q. 66, a. 5 ad 4m.

[41] *De Ver.*, q. 10, a. 8 ad 1m (1ae ser.).

quid sit, we reveal our natural knowledge that the material or sensible component is only a part and that the whole includes a formal component as well. Similarly, when by a natural spontaneity we a**s**k *an sit,* we again reveal our natural knowledge that the whole is not just a quiddity but includes an *actus essendi*[42] as well.[43]

This section on the synthetic element involved in judgment may be concluded with a resumé. Insight into phantasm expresses itself in a definition. Such an expression *per se* is neither true nor false. Next, many insights into many phantasms express themselves severally in many definitions; none of these singly is true or false; nor are all together true or false, for as yet they are not together. Thirdly, what brings definitions together is not some change in the definitions; it is a change in the insights whence they proceed. Insights coalesce and develop; they grow into apprehensions of intelligibility on a deeper level and with a wider sweep; and these profounder insisghts are expressed, at times indeed by the invention of such baffling abstractions as classicism or romanticism, education, evolution, or the *philosophia perennis*, but more commonly and more satisfactorily by the combination, as combination, of simple concepts. Fourthly, such synthetic sweep and penetration comes at first blush to the angel, but man has to reason to it; his intellect is discursive. Still it is not pure discourse. Without initial and natural acts of understanding, reasoning would never begin; nor would there be profit or term to reasoning, did it not naturally end in an act of understanding in which the multiple elements of the reasoning process come into focus in a single view. Fifthly, reasoning in its essence is simply the development of insight; it is motion towards understanding. In the concrete such development is a dialectical interplay of sense, memory, imagination, insight, definition, critical reflection, judgment; we bring to bear on the issue all the resources at our command. Still, the more intelligent we are, the more we are capable of knowing *ex pede Herculem;* then the more

[42] *In I V Met.*, lect. 2, § 553: "Sciendum est enim quod hoc nomen *Homo* imponitur a quidditate sive a natura hominis; et hoc nomen *Res* imponitur a quidditate tantum; hoc vero nomen *Ens* imponitur ab actu essendi."

[43] This paragraph has been rewritten. See *Theological Studies*, 8 (1947), 45.

rapid is our progress to the goal of understanding and the less is our appeal to the stylized reasoning of text-books on formal logic. Again, once we understand, we no longer bother to reason; we take in the whole at a glance. With remarkable penetration Aquinas refused to take as reason the formal affair that modern logicians invent machines to perform. He defined reason as development in understanding; and to that, formal reasoning is but an aid.

JUDGMENT

The act of judgment is not merely synthesis but also positing of synthesis. The preceding section argued that the pure synthetic element in judgment arises on the level of direct understanding and consists in the development of insights into higher unities. The present section will study the more elementary aspects of the act of positing the synthesis. This act may be characterized by the fact that in it there emerges knowledge of truth. So far we have considered the mental *compositio* in its basic stage; we now have to consider knowledge of the correspondence between the mental and the real *compositio*.

The issue, then, is not knowledge as true or false but knowledge as known to be true or false. Even sense knowledge may be true or false. Just as good and bad regard the perfection of the thing, so true and false regard the perfection of a knowing. True knowing is similar, false is dissimilar, to the known. But though sense knowledge must be either similar or dissimilar to its object, it neither does nor can include knowledge of its similarity or dissimilarity. Again, a concept must be either similar or dissimilar to its object; but intellectual operation on the level of conceptualization does not include knowledge of such similarity or dissimilarity. It is only in the second type of intellectual operation, only in the production of the second type of inner word, that intellect not merely attains similitude to its object but also reflects upon and judges that similitude.[44]

Such reflection presents a familiar puzzle. To judge that my knowing is similar to the known involves a comparison between

---

[44] *In VI Met.*, lect. 4, §1232-36; *Sum. Theol.*, I, q. 16, a. 2 c.

the knowing and its standard; but either the standard is known or it is not known; if it is known, then really the comparison is between two items of knowledge, and one might better maintain that we know directly without any comparing; on the other hand, if the standard is not known, there cannot be a comparison. This dilemma of futility or impossibility frightens the naive realist, who consequently takes refuge in the flat affirmation that we know, and that is all there is about it. It perhaps will not be out of place to indicate at once that Aquinas met this issue in a different manner.

He admitted the necessity of a standard in judgment: "nomen mentis a mensurando est sumptum";[45] "iudicium autem de unoquoque habetur secundum illud quod est mensura eius."[46] Not only did he admit the necessity of a standard, but also he does not seem to have considered as standard either of the alternatives against which the above dilemma is operative; for his standard was neither the thing-in-itself as thing-in-itself and so as unknown, nor was it some second inner representation of the thing-in-itself coming to the aid of the first in a futile and superfluous effort to be helpful. The Thomist standard lay in the principles of the intellect itself : "nomen mentis dicitur in anima, sicut et nomen intellectus. Solum enim intellectus accipit cognitionem de rebus mensurando eas quasi ad sua principia."[47] Just what is meant by intellect measuring things by its own principles, can appear only in the sequel. Three points are to be considered, though only two of the three in the present section. First, something must be said on the effect of such measuring by a standard, namely, on assent and certitude. Secondly, something must be added with regard to such measurement on the common criteriological level; namely, granted that some judgments are true, how can we tell the true from the false? Or, in other words, even if no judgments really are true, still some are at least subjectively necessary; what then are the grounds and motives of such subjective necessity? Thirdly, there remains the critical issue; granted the subjective necessity of some judgments as knowable and known, how does

---

45 *De Ver.*, q. 10, a. 1 c.
46 *Ibid.*, a. 9 c.
47 *Ibid.*, a. 1 c.

the mind proceed from such immanent coercion to objective truth and, through truth, to knowledge of reality? In the investigation of Thomist thought on these questions we may hope to discover the nature of the procession of the second type of inner word from an *intelligere*.

On assent we may be brief. It is an act of the possible intellect.[48] It is, accordingly, contrasted with consent which is an act of the will. The good is in things, but the true is in the mind; consent is a motion of the will with respect to the thing, but assent is a motion of the intellect with respect to a conception.[49] Again, the object of an assent is either side of a contradiction. We do not assent by defining; again, we do not assent when we doubt or merely opine. We assent to first principles, to demonstrable conclusions, to the affirmations of reliable authority.[50] Assent occurs when we judge a conception of the thing to be true.[51] It must be motivated; thus intellectual light moves us to assent to first principles and first principles in turn move us to assent to demonstrable conclusions.[52] In a word, assent appears to be identical with judgment but to emphasize its subjective and reflective aspects; it is the judgment as a personal act, committing the person, and a responsibility of the person; it is the judgment as based upon an apprehension of evidence, as including an awareness of its own validity, as a truth in the subject rather than as a truth absolutely and as a *medium in quo* reality is apprehended.[53]

Assent or judgment, on the criteriological level, is reached by a *resolutio in principia*. Unfortunately, this expression is ambiguous. At times it is connected with the contrast between the *via compositionis* and the *via resolutionis*, that is, between the different orders in which a science might be studied. Thus one might study chemistry only in the laboratory in a series of ex-

---

[48] *Ibid.*, q. 14, a. 1 c.
[49] *De Malo*, q. 6, a. 1 ad 14m.
[50] *De Ver.*, q. 14, a. 1 c.
[51] *De Malo*, q. 6, a. 1 ad 14m.
[52] *In Boet. de Trin.*, q. 3, a. 1 ad 4m.
[53] See *In III Sent.*, d. 23, q. 2, a. 2, sol. 3; *De Ver.*, q. 14, a. 1; *In Boet. de Trin.*, q. 3, a. 1; *Sum. Theol.*, II-II q. 2, a. 1. On truth as a *medium in quo*, cf. *Sum. Theol.*, I, q. 3, a. 4 ad 2m.

periments that followed the history of the development of the
science; one would begin from common material objects, learn
the arts of qualitative and quantitative analysis, and very gradually
advance to the discovery of the periodic table and the sub-atomic
structures. But one might begin at the other end with pure mathematics, then posit hypotheses regarding electrons and protons
and neutrons, work out possible atomic and then molecular structures, develop a method of analysis, and finally turn for the first
time to real material things. Both of these lines of approach
are mere abstractions, for actual thinking oscillates dialectically
between the two methods. Still, even if they are abstractions,
they merit names, and the former is the *via resolutionis* while
the latter is the *via compositionis*.[54] It is this *via resolutionis* that
is meant by the *resolutio in principia*, when we are told that the
right way to know that the three angles of a triangle are equal
to two right angles is not to take the proposition on faith but to
resolve it as a conclusion to its first principles.[55]

However, there is another meaning to the expression, *resolutio
in principia*, and in this case it coincides with the *via iudicii* as
opposed to the *via inventionis vel inquisitionis*. This is a distinct
contrast, for the *via inventionis* may be the *via compositionis*[56]
and it may be the *via resolutionis*.[57] On the other hand, the *via
iudicii* has to do with the reflective activity of mind assaying
its knowledge. There are truths that naturally are known; they
form the touch-stone of other truth; and judging is a matter of
reducing other issues to the naturally known first principles.[58]

---

54 *In II Met.*, lect. 1, §278.

55 *De Ver.*, q. 12, a. 1 c; q. 15, a. 3 c.

56 *Sum. Theol.*, I, q. 79, a. 8 c.: "Ratiocinatio humana secundum viam inquisitionis vel inventionis, procedit a quibusdam simpliciter intellectis, quae
sunt prima principia."

57 *Ibid.*, a. 9 c.: "Secundum viam inventionis, per res temporales in cognitionem devenimus aeternorum, secundum illud Apostoli, 'invisibilia Dei per
ea quae facta sunt, intellecta, conspiciuntur.'"

58 *Ibid.*, a. 8 c.: "Ratiocinatio humana . . . in via iudicii revolvendo redit
ad prima principia, ad quae inventa examinat." *Ibid.*, a. 12 c.: "Ratiocinatio
hominis, cum sit quidam motus, ab intellectu progreditur aliquorum, scilicet
naturaliter notorum absque investigatione rationis, sicut a quodam principio
immobili; et ad intellectum etiam terminatur, inquantum iudicamus per principia naturaliter nota de his quae ratiocinando inveniuntur." Cf. note 28 *supra*.

Thus, in demonstrations certitude is attained by a resolution to first principles;[59] such a resolution is the efficient cause of the certitude;[60] until the resolution reaches the first principles, doubt is possible, but once it has reached them, doubt is excluded.[61] For in the demonstrative sciences the conclusions are so related to the principles that, were the conclusions false, the principles would have to be false; hence the mind is coerced by its own natural acceptance of the principles to accept the conclusions as well.[62] With regard to the *quod quid est* and with regard to principles known immediately from such knowledge of quiddity, intellect is infallible; but with regard to further deductions intellect may err; still, such error is excluded absolutely, whenever a correct *resolutio in principia* is performed.[63]

This reflective activity of judging has its psychological conditions. People who syllogize in their sleep regularly find on awakening that they have been guilty of some fallacy.[64] Though dreamers may be aware that they are dreaming,[65] still their self-possession is never more than partial.[66] It is because the ligature of the senses in sleep prevents proper judging that moral fault in that state is not imputed.[67] The existence of such a pyschological condition points to the conclusion that judging is an activity involving the whole man. Knowledge of the *quod quid est* takes us outside time and space; but the act of *compositio vel divisio* involves a return to the concrete. In particular, whatever may be hymned about eternal truths, human judgments always involve a specification of time.[68] Indeed, since truth exists only in a mind, and since only the mind of God is eternal, there can be but one eternal truth.[69] In our minds truth ordinarily consists in the application of abstract universals to sensible things, and such an

[59] *In II Sent.*, d. 9, q. 1, a. 8 ad 1m.
[60] *In III Sent.*, d. 23, q. 2, a. 2, sol. 1.
[61] *In II Sent.*, d. 7, q. 1, a. 1 c.
[62] *De Ver.*, q. 22, a. 6 ad 4m; q. 24, a. 1 ad 18m.
[63] *Ibid.*, q. 1, a. 12 c.
[64] *Sum. Theol.*, I, q. 84, a. 8 ad 2m.
[65] *De Ver.*, q. 12, a. 3 ad 2m.
[66] *Sum. Theol.*, I, q. 84, a. 8 ad 2m.
[67] *Ibid.*, "Sed contra."
[68] *In III de An.*, lect. 11, §749-51; *In IX Met.*, lect. 11, § 1899f.
[69] *In I Sent.*, d. 19, q. 5, a. 3; *Sum. Theol.*, I, q. 16, a. 7.

application involves a temporal qualification.[70] Even when thought rises to the third degree of abstraction, our expressions retain a temporal connotation; and this is only natural, for the proper and proportionate object of our intellects is the nature of sensible things, and it is by an extrapolation from sensible natures that we conceive any other.[71]

A free and full control of our senses as well as of our intellects is, then, a necessary condition of judgment.[72] But sense is relevant to judgment in another fashion, for sense is the beginning of our knowledge; what we know by sense determines judgment, though it does so decreasingly as we ascend the degrees of abstraction. Automatically, the natural scientist who neglects sense falls into error; his work is to judge things as they are presented to the senses. On the other hand, the mathematician is not to be criticized because no real plane surface touches no real sphere at just one point; the criterion of mathematical judgment is not sense but imagination. Similarly, metaphysical entities are not to be called into question because they cannot be imagined; for metaphysics transcends not only sense but imagination as well.[73]

Judgment, then, may be described as resulting, remotely and as it were materially, from developing insight which unites distinct intelligibilities into single intelligibilities, but proximately and as it were formally, from a reflective activity of reason. This reflective activity involves the whole man, and so it is conditioned pyschologically by a necessity of being wide awake. Again, human knowledge has a twofold origin—an extrinsic origin in sensitive impressions, and an intrinsic origin in intellectual light in which virtually the whole of science is precontained.[74] Hence the reflective activity whence judgment results is a return from the syntheses effected by developing insight to their sources in sense

[70] *C. Gent.*, II, 96, *ad fin.*, (ed. Leon., X III, 572b 18-38).

[71] *Sum. Theol.*, I, q. 84, a. 7 ad 3m.

[72] Discussion of this issue had its origin in the skeptical problem, How do we know we are not asleep? See *In IV Met.*, lect. 14, §698; lect. 15, §708 f. It was extended by a consideration of the resultant theological problem, How can we trust prophetic judgment performed in ecstatic trance? See *Sum. Theol.*, II-II, q. 173, a. 3 c. et ad 3m; q. 172, a. 1 ad 2 m; *De Ver.*, q. 12, a. 3 ad 2m.

[73] *In Boet. de Trin.*, q. 6, a. 2 c. (ed. Mand., III, 132, f.).

[74] *De Ver.*, q. 10, a. 6 c., *ad fin.*

and in intellectual light. The latter element of the return is mentioned more frequently; it is described as in instance of "ratio terminatur ad intellectum"; and as the context makes clear, the *intellectus* in question is the *habitus principiorum*,[75] the naturally known first principles that peculiarly are an effect of intellectual light.

However, as we have seen, the phrase, "ratio terminatur ad intellectum," has another and distinct meaning. It also refers to the fact that reason is understanding in process, that reasoning ends up as an act of understanding.[76] This definition of reasoning holds no less of reflective than of direct thought; and we may infer that the reflective activity of reason returning from the synthesis of intelligibilities to its origin in sense and in naturally known principles terminates in a reflective act of understanding, in a single synthetic apprehension of all the motives for judgment, whether intellectual or sensitive, in a grasp of their sufficiency as motives and so of the necessity of passing judgment or assenting. For no less than the first type of inner word, the second also proceeds from an *intelligere*.[77] No less than the procession of the first type, the procession of the second is an *emanatio intelligibilis*.[78] Indeed much more palpably in the latter than in the former is there the determination of reasonableness by sufficient reason, for clearly judgment arises only from at least supposed sufficient ground. We assent to first principles because of intellectual light, to conclusions because of their necessary connection with principles; but because of probabilities we no more than opine; for however strong probabilities may be, they are not a sufficient determinant of reason, do not coerce assent, do not yield a perfect judgment.[79]

The general outline of Thomist analysis of human intellect is now, perhaps, discernible. There are two levels of activity, the direct and the reflective. On the direct level there occur two

---

[75] See J. Peghaire, *op. cit.*, pp. 269-72.
[76] *Ibid.*, p. 261 ff. Cf. note 28 *supra*.
[77] *De Ver.*, q. 3, a. 2 c; q. 4, a. 2 c; *De Pot.*, q. 8, a. 1 c; q. 9, a. 5 c; *Quodl.* V, a. 9 c; *In Ioan.*, cap. 1, lect. 1.
[78] See pages 33-45 above.
[79] *In Boet. de Trin.*, q. 3, a. 1 ad 4m (ed. Mand., III, 64).

types of events: there are insights into phantasm which express themselves in definitions; there is the coalescence or development of insights which provide the hypothetical syntheses of simple quiddities. On the reflective level these hypothetical syntheses are known as hypothetical; they become questions which are answered by the *resolutio in principia*. Thus return to sources terminates in a reflective act of understanding, which is a grasp of necessary connection between the sources and the hypothetical synthesis; from this grasp there proceeds its self-expression which is the *compositio vel divisio*, the judgment, the assent.

WISDOM

We have now to penetrate more deeply into our subject. The finer points of Thomist Trinitarian theory cannot be grasped from the analogy of the mere mechanism of human intellect. Again, without a consideration of profounder issues connected with the nature of judgment, it is impossible to assemble and present all the evidence to be found in Thomist writings for the interpretation of his thought that we are offering. Accordingly, an attempt is to be made to integrate with the foregoing what Aquinas has to say of the habit and virtue of wisdom. For wisdom is the virtue of right judgment.[80] Wisdom has to do with knowledge of the real as real,[81] while it is in judgment that we know reality.[82] Indeed, I should say that wisdom, the act of reflec-

---

[80] *Sum. Theol.*, I, q. 1, a. 6 c.: "Sapientis est ordinare et iudicare," Cf. *ibid.*, q. 79, a. 10 ad 3m; II-II, q. 45, a. 1 c; aa. 2 et 5.

[81] *In I V Met.*, lect. 5, §593. Remember that first philosophy is really wisdom (*In I Met.*, lect. 3, §56).

[82] *In I Sent.*, d. 19., q. 5, a. 1 ad 7m. ". . . cum sit duplex operatio intellectus: una quarum dicitur a quibusdam imaginatio intellectus, quam Philosophus (In III de An., lect. 11) nominat intelligentiam indivisibilium, quae consistit in apprehensione quidditatis simplicis, quae alio etiam nomine formatio dicitur; alia est quam dicunt fidem, quae consistit in compositione vel divisione propositionis: prima operatio respicit quidditatem rei; secunda respicit esse ipsius." Cf. *In Boet. de Trin.*, q. 5, a. 3. The *duplex operatio* corresponds to the twofold inner word; on the former, see also *In III Sent.*, d. 23, q. 2, a. 2, sol. 1; *De Ver.*, q. 14, a. 1; *De Spir. Creat.*, a. 9 ad 6m; *In I Periherm.*, lect. 1 et 5; *In I Post. Anal.*, lect. 1; *In I V Met.*, lect. 6, §605; VI, lect. 4, §1232. M. Gaston Rabeau in his erudite and very stimulating work, *Species: Verbum* (Bibl. thomiste, XXII [Paris: Vrin, 1938] p. 159, note 5), would urge that there

tive understanding, and the act of judgment are related as habit, second act, and the act that proceeds from act.

There are, then, three habits of specualtive intellect.[83] Most easily recognized of the three is the habit of science, which has to do with the demonstration of conclusions. However, demonstration does not admit indefinite regress, and so there must be some prior habit that regards first principles. In fact, two such prior habits are affirmed, intellect and wisdom; and these two seem related much as are the two types of act already described, namely, the act of direct understanding and the act of reflective understanding. For the habit of intellect regards the first principles of demonstrations, while the habit of wisdom regards the first principles of reality. The habit of intellect is comparatively simple: grasp of first principles of demonstrations results from knowledge of their component terms; if one knows what a whole is and what a part is, one cannot but see that the whole must be greater than its part; the habit of such seeing is the habit of intellect. On the other hand, the habit of wisdom has a dual role. Principally, it regards the objective order of reality; but in some fashion it also has to do with the transition from the order of thought to the order of reality. Principally, it regards the objective order of reality; for the wise man contemplates the universal scheme of things and sees each in the perspective of its causes right up to the ultimate cause.

must be a *species intelligibilis* of existence prior to its affirmation in judgment. His argument is that to affirm existence of essence one must first have the *species* of existence. It overlooks the fact that existence is the act, the exercise, of essence; that to know essence is to know its order to its act of existence; but, though potential knowledge of existence is contained in the grounds of existential judgment and so is prior to judgment, actual knowledge of the act of existence of any given essence cannot be had prior to the judgment; and there is no existence that is not the act of some essence. To put the point differently, M. Rabeau might argue that without a prior *species* of existence one would not know what one was affirming when one affirmed it; but this is to overlook the essentially reflective character of the act of judgment, which proceeds from a grasp of sufficient grounds for itself. A third line of consideration is following dilemma: Is the *species* of existence one or is it many? If one what happens to the analogy of *ens*? If many, how do the many differ from the content "act of essence" where act is an analogous concept and essence is any or all essences we know?

[83] The following is based mainly on *In VI Eth.*, lect. 5.

While art orders human products, and prudence orders human
conduct, science discovers the order which art prudently exploits;
but there is a highest, architectonic science, a science of sciences—
and that is wisdom.

Still, wisdom is not merely an ontology or natural theology; it
also has some of the characteristics of an epistemology. The habit
of intellect is the habit of knowing the first principles of demonstrations; but knowledge of first principles is just a function of
knowledge of their component terms.   If the simple apprehension
of these terms is a matter of direct understanding, still it is wisdom
that passes judgment on the validity of such apprehensions and
so by validating the component terms validates even first principles
themselves.[84] Again, science depends upon the habit of intellect
for the theorematic web of interconnections linking conclusions
with principles; but wisdom passes judgment upon that connection.
Hence both intellect and science depend upon the judgment of
wisdom.   Intellect depends upon wisdom for the validity of the
component terms of principles; science depends upon wisdom for
the validity of its consequence from intellect;[85] so that wisdom,
besides being in its own right the science of the real as real, also
is "virtus quaedam omnium scientiarum."[86]

It would seem fair to conclude that, with regard to speculative
intellectual habits, Aquinas drew the same distinctions that, in the
preceding section, we were led to draw with regard to speculative
intellectual acts.   Where Aquinas spoke of the habits of intellect,
science, and wisdom, we were led to distinguish between direct
understanding, the development of direct understanding, and reflective understanding.   For the characteristics ascribed by Aquinas to the habits of intellect, science, and wisdom, may be ascribed
also to acts of direct understanding that grasp the intelligibility
of data represented schematically in the imagination, to acts of
developing understanding that spin the logical network of science,
and to acts of reflective understanding in which judgment is passed
upon the validity of direct understanding and of its development,

---

[84] *Ibid.*; *Sum. Theol.*, I-II, q. 66, a. 5 ad 4m.
[85] *Sum. Theol.*, I-II, q. 57, a. 2 ad 2m.
[86] *In VI Eth.*, lect. 5.

and thereby the transition is effected from a mental construction on an imagined basis to knowledge through truth of reality.

Acknowledgement of an epistemological element in the habit of wisdom goes back to its classical exposition in the *Metaphysics* of Aristotle. First philosophy really is wisdom; only the pretensions of the sophists led the wise to name their pursuit not wisdom itself but love of wisdom.[87] The comparison of lower and higher animals, of animals and men, of men of experience with men of science, brings one to the conclusion that wisdom is a matter of knowing causes.[88] Again, the six characteristics which common consent would attribute to the wise man may all be deduced from the assumption that wisdom is a speculative science concerned with ultimate causes and principles.[89] Further, it is the desire to know causes that moves men, as of old, so also today to the search and study of philosophy ;[90] and it is the achievement of knowledge of causes that is meant by science.[91] Hence, the remainder of the first book of the *Metaphysics* is devoted to an examination of the four causes. But for a resumption of the objective view-point so established, one must leap to book six (E). There one finds an account of the real, followed by accounts of substance or essence,[92] of potency and act,[93] of unity and opposition,[94] and of the separate substances.[95] But the intervening books two to five are gnoseological, methodological, almost epistemological. Knowledge of causes has to be true. But truth is peculiar; no one is totally without it, but no one possesses it in full.[96] Again, no one can make any great contribution to it; but many in collaboration, especially in the collaboration that extends over time and operates through the accumulations of a stable culture, can assemble a rather notable achievement.[97] One may say that philosophers are in the position

---

[87] *In I Met.*, lect. 3, §56.
[88] *Ibid.*, lect. 1.
[89] *Ibid.*, lect. 2.
[90] *Ibid.*, lect. 3.
[91] *Ibid.*, lect. 4, §70.
[92] *In VII et VIII Met.*
[93] *In IX Met.*
[94] *In X Met.*
[95] *In XII Met.*
[96] *In II Met.*, lect. 1, §275.
[97] *Ibid.*, §276.

of people walking the streets; to know the façades of houses is easy, but to know their interiors difficult. So, too, there are palpable truths and hidden truths.[98] In particular, knowledge of the separate substances is hard to come by, for in their regard we are just owls in daylight;[99] for the separate substances are pure intelligibilities, but our intellects are built to know intelligibility, not in its pure form, but only as informing sensible matter.

Still, the problem is not desperate; just as there exist dialectical techniques, unknown even at the time of Socrates, by which we can determine the methodology of the study of contraries without previous knowledge of their essences,[100] so, too, may we approach the larger issue of universal reality even though much of it is hidden from us. Thus, truth and reality are parallel: what has a cause of its reality, also has a cause of its truth;[101] again, as the reality that grounds other reality is the more real, so the truth that grounds other truth is the more true;[102] as an infinite regress in the demonstration of truths is untenable, so also is an infinite regress in the grounding of one reality by another.[103] There is, then, something of which the reality is most real and the truth most true, and it is the object of wisdom.[104]

There follow methodological considerations. Different sciences have to be tackled in different manners.[105] The approach to metaphysics lies in collecting and completing the list of metaphysical problems.[106] Such a list leads one to the definition of first philosophy: it is concerned with ultimate reality. But the science dealing with ultimate reality also will deal with any instance of the real as real,[107] so that first philosophy is the science of being, substance and accident, unity, multiplicity, and opposition.[108] Nor

---

[98] *Ibid.*, § 277.
[99] *Ibid.*, §285.
[100] *Met.*, M, 4 (1078b 25 ff.).
[101] *In II Met.*, lect. 2, §298.
[102] *Ibid.*, §292 ff.
[103] *Ibid.*, lect. 3 et 4.
[104] *Ibid.*, lect. 2, §292 ff.
[105] *Ibid.*, lect. 5.
[106] *In III Met.*, lect. 1-15.
[107] *In IV Met.*, lect. 5, §593.
[108] *Ibid.*, lect. 1-4.

is this the whole story. The first philosopher has to treat, not only of the real as real, but also of the first principles of demonstrations.[109] He is not to skimp this task. He must be satisfied with the validity of the principles of non-contradiction and excluded middle.[110] He must envisage the problem of appearance and reality.[111] Above all, he must scrutinize each of the terms entering into the first principles which intellect grasps and on which his science rests,[112] for "cognitio et veritas principiorum indemonstrabilium dependet ex ratione terminorum.... Cognoscere autem rationem entis et non entis, et totius et partis, et aliorum quae consequuntur ad ens, ex quibus sicut ex terminis constituuntur principia indemonstrabilia, pertinet ad sapientiam."[113]

It is to be observed that the Aristotelian concept of wisdom, or first philosophy, while it does contain an epistemological element, still can hardly be said to raise the critical problem. Aristotle was content with a generalization of the criteriological issue. For him it was enough that one cannot but think according to the principle of non-contradiction, and that that impossibility was only part of the more general impossibility that is known through knowing the principle itself.[114] Again, the wise man knows the difference between appearance and reality. He is ready to refute the sophistries that would confound the two, but he is not prepared to discuss how our immanent activities also contain a transcendence. Aristotelian gnoseology is brilliant but it is not complete: knowledge is by identity; the act of the thing as sensible is the act of sensation; the act of the thing as intelligible is the act of understanding; but the act of the thing as real is the *esse naturale* of the thing and, except in divine self-knowledge, that *esse* is not identical with knowing it.

---

[109] *Ibid.*, lect. 5, §595.
[110] *Ibid.*, lect. 5-10, 16, 17.
[111] *Ibid.*, lect. 11-15.
[112] *In V Met.*, lect. 1-22.
[113] *Sum. Theol.*, I-II, q. 66, a. 5 ad 4m.
[114] *In IV Met.*, lect. 6, §606: "Ex hoc enim quod impossibile est esse et non esse, sequitur quod impossibile it contraria simul inesse eidem, ut infra dicetur. Et ex hoc quod contraria non possunt simul inesse, sequitur quod homo non potest habere contrarias opiniones, et per consequens quod non possit opinari contradictoria esse vera, ut ostensum est."

But, while it should be granted that Aristotle was content with criteriology, it remains that he opened a door to further speculation along the same line. Such speculation may appear to modern Schoolmen a very alien thing, a fascinating but perilous distraction born of Cartesian doubt and Kantian criticism. But Aquinas could have had no such prejudice; his predecessors were neither Descartes nor Kant but Aristotle and Augustine. If the very logic of the Aristotelian position makes it clear that our knowledge of forms, whether sensible or intelligible, can be accounted for by identity, still the same logic forces the conclusion that our knowledge of essence and of existence has to be differently grounded. "Sensibile in actu est sensus in actu, et intelligibile in actu est intellectus in actu. Ex hoc enim aliquid sentimus vel intelligimus, quod intellectus noster vel sensus informatur in actu per speciem sensibilis vel intelligibilis. Et secundum hoc tantum sensus vel intellectus aliud est a sensibili vel intelligibili, quia utrumque est in potentia."[114a] But the problem of knowledge, once it is granted that knowledge is by identity, is knowledge of the other. As long as faculty and object are in potency to knowing and being known, there is as yet no knowledge. Inasmuch as faculty and object are in act identically, there is knowledge indeed as perfection but not yet knowledge of the other. Reflection is required, first, to combine sensible data with intellectual insight in the expression of a *quod quid est*, of an essence that prescinds from its being known, and then, on a deeper level, to affirm the existence of that essence. Only by reflection on the identity of act can one arrive at the difference of potency. And since reflection is not an identity, the Aristotelian theory of knowledge by identity is incomplete.[115]

But it is well to grasp just where the strength of the Aristotelian position lies. One might side with Plato and say knowing of its nature is knowing the other. But this brings up insoluble difficulties with regard to knowledge in the absolute being; for even Plato was

---

[114a] *Sum. Theol.*, I, q. 14, a. 2 c.

[115] Hence to the Aristotelian theorem of knowledge by immateriality Aquinas had to add a further theorem of knowledge by intentionality. The difference between the two appears clearly in the case of one immaterial angel knowing another immaterial angel without the former's knowledge being the latter's eality. See *Sum. Theol.*, I, q. 56, a. 2 ad 3m.

forced to admit, in virtue of his assumptions, that absolute being, if it knows, must undergo motion.[116] That difficulty does not exist for the Aristotelian. Maintain that knowing is identity, and it follows that "in his quae sunt sine materia idem est intelligens et intellectum."[117] The unmoved mover may remain unmoved and yet know, because, with knowing an identity, the being and knowing of the absolute coincide.

Aquinas was quite aware of this profound cleavage between Platonist and Aristotelian gnoseology:"Et hoc quidem oportet verum esse secundum sententiam Aristotelis, qui ponit quod intelligere contingit per hoc quod intellectum in actu sit unum cum intellectu in actu.... Secundum autem positionem Platonis, intelligere fit per contactum intellectus ad rem intelligibilem...."[118] Quite clearly, Aquinas opted systematically for the Aristotelian position. It was a problem for him that God should know anything distinct from the divine essence,[119] and that problem he solved by appealing to the analogy of the human inner word.[120] Rational reflection has to bear the weight of the transition from knowledge as a perfection to knowledge as of the other.

The Thomist validation of rational reflection is connected with the Augustinian vision of eternal truth. Augustine had argued that we know truth not by looking without but by looking within ourselves. Still, we all may know the same truths, and you do not know them by looking within me, nor I by looking within you, so that knowledge of truth is not merely a matter of looking each within himself. Our inward glance really is directly upward to what is above us, and it is in a vision of one eternal truth that all can find the same truth. Now the Platonism of this position is palpable, for its ultimate answer is not something that we are but something that we see; it supposes that knowledge essentially is not identity with the known but some spiritual contact or confrontation with the known. Such a view Aquinas could not accept. One knows by what one is. Our knowledge of truth is not to be

[116] Plato, *Sophistes*, 248e.

[117] *De Anima*, III, 4 (430a 3 f.). Cf. *Sum. Theol.*, I, q. 87, a. 1 ad 3m.

[118] *C. Gent.*, II, 98, ad fin. (ed. Leon., XIII, 582b 13, 22).

[119] *In I Sent.*, d. 35, q. 1, a. 2 ad 1m; *De Ver.*, q. 2, a. 3 ad 1m; *C. Gent.*, I, 51, "Adhunc"; *Sum. Theol.* I, q. 14, a. 5 ad 2m.

[120] *De Ver.*, q. 3, a. 2; *C. Gent.*, I, 53; *Sum. Theol.*, I, q. 15, a. 2 c.

accounted for by any vision or contact or confrontation with the other, however lofty and sublime. The ultimate ground of our knowing is indeed God, the eternal Light; but the reason why we know is within us. It is the light of our own intellects; and by it we can know because "ipsum enim lumen intellectuale quod est in nobis, nihil est aliud quam quaedam participata similitudo luminis aeterni."[121]

The act of the thing as sensible is the act of sensation; the act of the thing as intelligible is the act of understanding; but we can proceed from these identities to valid concepts of essence and true affirmations of existence, because such procession is in virtue of our intellectual light, which is a participation of eternal Light. Such is the Thomist ontology of knowledge. But is there also a Thomist epistemology? It is all very well to validate rational reflection by attributing the light of our intellects to the eternal Light that is God. But such a procedure presupposes that already we know validly both ourselves and God. As an ontology of knowing it is satisfactory; as an epistemology, it is null and void. Is one to say that Aquinas was innocent of modern, critical complications? Or is one to say that, since we know by what we are, so also we know that we know by knowing what we are? While we cannot here discuss that issue to the satisfaction of epistemologists, neither can we omit it entirely; for it is the highest point in rational reflection, and it was in rational reflection that Aquinas found the created analogy to the eternal procession of the divine Word.[122]

Now there happens to be a text in which Aquinas did maintain that our knowledge of truth is derived from our knowledge of ourselves. Sense knowledge, because unreflective, is irrelevant to the procession of the Word.[123] For exactly the same reason, namely, because it is not reflective, sense does not include knowledge of truth. On the other hand, intellect does include knowledge of truth because it does reflect upon itself: "secundum hoc cognoscit veritatem intellectus quod supra se ipsum reflectitur."[124] Sense knowledge is true; sense is aware of its own acts of sensation.

[121] *Sum. Theol.*, I, q. 84, a. 5 c.
[122] *C. Gent.*, IV, 11.
[123] *Loc. cit.*
[124] *De Ver.*, q. 1, a. 9 c.

But sense, though true and though conscious, nevertheless is not conscious of its own truth; for sense does not know its own nature, nor the nature of its acts, nor their proportion to their objects. On the other hand, intellectual knowledge is not merely true but also aware of its own truth. It is not merely aware empirically of its acts but also reflects upon their nature; to know the nature of its acts, it has to know the nature of their active principle, which it itself is; and if it knows its own nature, intellect also knows its own proportion to knowledge of reality. Further, this difference between sense and intellect is a difference in reflective capacity, In knowing, we go outside ourselves; in reflecting, we return in upon ourselves. But the inward return of sense is incomplete, stopping short at a merely empirical awareness of the fact of sensation. But the intellectual substance returns in upon itself completely. It is not content with mere empirical awareness; it penetrates to its own essence.[125]

I cannot take this passage as solely an affirmation of the reflective character found in every judgment.[126] Not in every judgment do we reflect to the point of knowing our own essence and from that conclude our capacity to know truth. Rather, in this passage Aquinas subscribed, not obscurely, to the program of critical thought: to know truth we have to know ourselves and the nature of our knowledge, and the method to be employed is reflection. Still, it is one thing to subscribe to the critical program and quite another to execute it; to what extent such execution is to be found in the writings of Aquinas, is the issue next before us. In tackling it, we shall have in view another end as well, namely, a justification of the procedure followed in these articles, a presentation of the evidence for our belief that the Thomist theory of intellect had an empirical and introspective basis.

SELF-KNOWLEDGE OF SOUL

From Aristotle Aquinas derived a method of empirical introspection. In the second book of the *De Anima*, after defining soul in general, there arose the problem of distinguishing different kinds

---

[125] *Loc. cit.*

[126] Cf. *Sum. Theol.*, I, q. 16, a. 2, or *In VI Met.*, lect. 4, §1236.

of soul. But souls differ by difference in their potencies. Since
potency is knowable only inasmuch as it is in act, to know the different potencies it is necessary to know their acts. Again, since
one act is distinguished from another by the difference of their
respective objects, to know different kinds of acts it is necessary
to discriminate between different kinds of objects. Knowledge of
soul, then, begins from a distinction of objects; specifying objects
leads to a discrimination between different kinds of act; different
kinds of act reveal difference of potency; and the different combinations of potencies lead to knowledge of the different essences
that satisfy the generic definition of soul.[127]

Thus the human soul does not know itself by a direct grasp of its
own essence; that is the prerogative of God and of the angels.[128]
Did man know his own soul in such immediate fashion, the roundabout process through objects, acts, and potencies would be superfluous.[129] The fact is that human intellect is *in genere intelligibilium*
just a potency; unless its potency is reduced to act, it neither
understands nor is understood.[130] On the other hand, the acquisition of an understanding of anything, of any habitual scientific
knowledge, makes our intellects habitually capable not only of
understanding the scientific object in question but also of understanding itself.[131] We can know what understanding is by understanding anything and reflecting on the nature of our understanding;
for the *species* of the object understood also is the *species* of the
understanding intellect. It was by scrutinizing both the object
understood and the understanding intellect that Aristotle investigated the nature of possible intellect. And, indeed, we can have
no knowledge of our intellects except by reflecting on our own
acts of understanding.[132] Evidently, the Aristotelian and Thomist
program is not a matter of considering ocular vision and then
conceiving an analogous spiritual vision that is attributed to a
spiritual faculty named intellect. On the contrary, it is a process
of introspection that discovers the act of insight into phantasm

[127] *In II de An.*, lect. 6, §304-308.
[128] *In III de An.*, lect. 9, §726.
[129] *In II de An.*, lect. 6, §308.
[130] *In III de An.*, lect. 9, §725.
[131] *Ibid.*, lect. 8, §704.
[132] *Ibid.*, lect. 9, §724.

and the definition as an expression of the insight, that almost catches intellect in its forward movement towards defining and in its backward reference to sense for the concrete realization of the defined.[133]

If the *Commentary on the De Anima* adds to the Aristotelian text the enrichment due to a fully developed metaphysical system, there is to be found in the independent Thomist writings not a few additional points of introspective psychology. Of these the most fundamental is the distinction between what we should call an empirical awareness of our inner acts and a scientific grasp of their nature. The scientific grasp is in terms of objects, acts, potencies, essence of soul. It is reached only by study; it is a matter of which many are ignorant, on which many have erred; it is universal knowledge; it is knowledge that we attain only discursively, but angels and devils intuitively, so that even the devils know the essence of our souls better than we do ourselves.[134] This scientific knowledge is what philosophers acquire by arguing from the universality of concepts to the immateriality and other properties of the soul;[135] it is the knowledge that Aquinas himself set forth in masterly fashion in the long argument that begins in chapter forty-six of the second book of the *Contra Gentiles* to end only in chapter ninety. On the other hand, empirical knowledge of our own souls is knowledge of the existence of their acts,[136] knowledge of what is proper to the individual,[137] knowledge of the inner movements of the heart which are hidden from the intuitive, but exclusively essential, knowledge of the devils.[138] Of this self-knowledge Aristotle spoke in the *Ethics* when he remarked that one perceives one's own seeing and hearing and moving and understanding.[139] When such knowledge is in act, it is a matter of our

---

[133] *Ibid.*, lect. 8, §713.

[134] *In I Sent.*, d. 3, q. 4, a. 5 sol.; *In III Sent.*, d. 23, q. 1, a. 2 ad 3m; *De Ver.*, q. 10, a. 8 c; *C. Gent.*, II, 75 (ed. Leon., XIII, 475a 45 ff.); *C. Gent.*, III, 46; *Sum. Theol.*, I, q. 87, aa. 1-4; and for the devils' knowledge of us, *De Malo*, q. 16, a. 8 ad 7m.

[135] *De Ver.*, q. 10, a. 8 c.

[136] *In III Sent.*, d. 23, q. 1, a. 2 ad 3m.

[137] *De Ver.*, q. 10, a. 8.

[138] *De Malo*, q. 16, a. 8 ad 7m.

[139] *Ethics*, IX, 9 (1170a 29-34).

knowing ourselves as in act by our acts;[140] for it is not the eye that sees nor the intellect that understands, but the man by means of his eyes sees and by means of his intellect understands.[141] On the other hand, empirical self-knowledge may be considered not as act but as habit. Now, just as we habitually know we possess a habit of science not by a further habit but simply by our ability to produce the acts of the habit, similarly for the habitual possession of empirical self-knowledge we need nothing more than the soul itself, which is present to itself and capable of eliciting conscious acts.[142]

The relation of empirical to scientific self-knowledge is charted clearly enough; the former is the basis of the latter. The appeal to experience in Thomist psychological theory, though without the benefit of a parade of modern methodology, nonetheless is frequent and even not inconspicuous. The standard argument against the Averroists was the affirmation, "hic homo intelligit": deny such a proposition and, since you too are an instance of *hic homo*, you put yourself out of court as one who understands nothing; but admit it and you must also admit that each individual has his own private *intellectus possibilis* by which he understands.[143] Equally in affirming the immanence of an agent intellect in each of us, the appeal to experience is employed: if we had no experience of abstracting intelligibilities and receiving them in act, then it never would occur to us to talk and argue about them.[144] Again, with regard to our knowledge of separate substances, the issue is settled "secundum Aristotelis sententiam quam magis experimur," and "secundum modum cognitionis no-

---

[140] *De Ver.*, q. 10, a. 8.

[141] *De Spir. Creat.*, a. 10 ad 15m; cf. *In I de An.*, lect. 10, §152; *De Ver.*, q. 2, a. 6 ad 3m; *Sum. Theol.*, I, q. 75, a. 2 ad 2m.

[142] *De Ver.*, q. 10, a. 8; cf. *Sum. Theol.*, I, q. 87 a. 1.

[143] *In III de An.*, lect. 7, §690 : "Manifestum est enim quod hic homo intelligit. Si enim hoc negetur, tunc dicens hanc opinionem non intelligit aliquid, et ideo non est audiendus : si autem intelligit, oportet quod aliquo formaliter intelligat. Hic autem est intellectus possibilis, de quo Philosophus dicit : 'Eico autem intellectum quo intelligit et opinatur anima.'" Cf. *In II Sent.*, d. 17, q. 2, a. 1 ; *De Unit. Intellectus*, §71-79 ; *De Anima*, a. 2; *De Spir. Creat.*, a. 2; *Comp. Theol.*, c. 85 ; *Sum. Theol.*, I, q. 76, a. 1 c.

[144] *C. Gent.*, II, 76 (ed. Leon., XIII, 482a 35 ff.); *De Spir. Creat.*, a. 10 c ; *De Anima*, a. 5 c; *Sum. Theol.*, I, q. 79, a. 4 c., *ad fin.*

bis expertum."[145] Finally, the introspective method employed in this and the preceding article may be said to rest upon an explicit statement: "anima humana intelligit se ipsum per suum intelligere, quod est actus proprius eius, perfecte demonstrans virtutem eius et naturam";[146] grasp the nature of your acts of understanding and you have the key to the whole of Thomist psychology. Indeed, you also have what Aquinas considered the key to Aristotelian psychology: "unde et supra Philosophus per ipsum intelligere et per illud quod intelligitur, scrutatus est naturam intellectus possibilis."[147]

But, I think, one can go further than this. For Aquinas the term "intellectual light" is not simply a synonym for the Aristotelian term "agent intellect." He debated with the Avicennists whether agent intellect was immanent or transcendent. But he never thought of debating whether intellectual light is immanent or transcendent. Indeed, when he argued that agent intellect was immanent, he was arguing for an identification of agent intellect with the ground of intellectual light. Hence he could frame his conclusion in this significant fashion: "unde nihil prohibet ipsi lumini animae nostrae attribuere actionem intellectus agentis; et praecipue cum Aristoteles intellectum agentem comparet lumini."[148] Both the nature of agent intellect and, in particular, Aristotle's comparison of agent intellect with light, lead one to identify agent intellect with the immanent cause of what we call the flash of understanding, the light of reason. What is, then, this *lumen animae nostrae?*

First, the mere fact that one is understanding something, does not make it inevitable that one reflexly directs one's attention to the intellectual light involved in the act.[149] Secondly, whenever an object is understood, it is understood only as illustrated by the light of agent intellect and received in possible intellect. Just as corporal light is seen in seeing any color, so also intelligible

---

[145] *Sum. Theol.*, I, q. 88, a. 1 c.

[146] *Ibid.*, a. 2 ad 3m. Note that *intelligere* is the *proprius actus* not only of the human soul but of the separate substances as well (*C. Gent.*, II, 97). Also, that repeatedly God is *ipsum intelligere.*

[147] *In III de An.*, lect. 9, § 724.

[148] *C. Gent.*, II, 77; *ad fin.*

[149] *Quodl.* X, a. 7 ad 2m.

light is seen in apprehending any intelligibility. Again, just as corporal light is seen, not as an object, but in knowing an object, so also intelligible light is seen, not as an object, but "in ratione medii cognoscendi."[150] Thirdly, intellectual light is a medium not in the sense that it is a known object by means of which another object is known; it is a medium in the sense that it makes other objects knowable. Just as the eye need not see light except in so far as colors are illuminated, so a medium in the given sense need not be known in itself but only in other known objects.[151] Fourthly, with these restrictions we may say that the light of agent intellect is known *per se ipsum.* The soul does not know its own essence by its own essence; but in some fashion it does know its own intellectual light by its own intellectual light, not indeed to the extent that that light is an object, but inasmuch as that light is the element making *species* intelligible in act.[152]

There is, then, a manner in which the light of our souls enters within the range of introspective observation. The most conspicuous instance seems to be our grasp of first principles. Scientific conclusions are accepted because they are implied by first principles; but the assent to first principles has to have its motive too, for assent is rational; and that motive is the light that naturally is within us.[153] Again, the light of agent intellect is said to manifest first principles, to make them evident.[154] In that light the whole of science virtually is ours from the very start.[155] Just as conclusions are convincing because principles are convincing, so our intellectual light derives its efficacy from the *prima lux* which is God.[156] Hence the divine and the human teachers may collaborate without any confusion of role. The human teacher teaches inasmuch as he reduces conclusions to principles; but all the certitude we possess, whether of conclusions or of prin-

---

[150] *In I Sent.*, d. 3, q. 4, a. 5 sol.
[151] *In Boet. de Trin.*, q. I, a. 3 ad '1m (ed. Mand., III, 37).
[152] *De Ver.*, q. 10, a. 8 ad 10m (2ᵃᵉ ser.).
[153] *In Boet. de Trin.*, q. 3, a. 1 ad 4 m (ed. Mand., III, 64).
[154] *In III Sent.*, d. 23, q. 2, a. 1 ad 4m; cf. *C. Gent.*, III, 46, "Amplius."
[155] *De Ver.*, q. 10, a. 6 c., *ad fin.*: "In lumine intellectus agentis nobis est quodammodo omnis scientia originaliter indita."
[156] *In Boet. de Trin.*, q. 1, a. 3 ad 1m (ed. Mand., III, 37).

ciples, comes from the intellectual light within us by which God speaks to us.[157]

However, the experienced effects of intellectual light as the evidence of principles, the motive of assent, the immanent ground of certitude, are not the only instances in which intellectual light, in its indirect fashion, enters into the range of consciousness. It is constitutive of our very power of understanding.[158] It is the principle of inquiry and of discourse; man reasons discoursing and inquiring by his intellectual light, which is clouded with temporal continuity because man obtains his knowledge from sense and imagination.[159] As the principle of inquiry, intellectual light is the source of that search for causes which reveals the natural desire of man for the beatific vision.[160] Our knowledge has a twofold source—an extrinsic origin on the level of sense, but an intrinsic origin in the light of our intellects.[161] Sense is only the *materia causae* of our knowledge. [162] The object of understanding is supplied and offered to us, as it were materially, by the imagination; formally, as object of understanding, it is completed by intellectual light.[163] Perhaps, agent intellect is to be given the function of the subconscious effect of ordering the phantasm to bring about the right schematic image that releases the flash of understanding; for agent intellect is to phantasm, as art is to artificial products.[164] When the soul is separated from the

[157] *De Ver.*, q. 11, a. 1 ad 13m.

[158] *I Boet. de Trin.*, q. 1, a. 3 c (ed. Mand., III, 35): " . . . lux naturalis per quam constituitur vis intellectiva, . . . "

[159] *In II Sent.*, d. 3, q. 1, a. 2 sol.

[160] *Sum. Theol.*, I-II, q. 3, a. 8 c.

[161] *De Ver.*, q. 10, a. 6 c. *ad fin.*

[162] *Sum. Theol.*, I, q. 84, a. 6 c. *ad fin.*

[163] *In II Sent.*, d. 20, q. 2, a. 2 ad 2m. One might suggest that sense data as not illuminated by agent intellect are the mere data of the positivist, whereas sense data as illuminated are partial knowledge of hylemorphically conceived reality. For the positivist, any knowledge apart from sense data is merely subjective; for the Aristotelian, intellectual knowledge is as objective as sensitive; and the illumination of phantasm is the assumption that there is an intelligibility to be known.

[164] *De Anima*, a. 5 c. It would seem that this influence of agent intellect on phantasm is mediated by the sensitive potency named the *cogitativa*. See *Sum. Theol.*, I, q. 78, a. 4 ob. 5a et ad 5m.

body, there are neither senses nor imagination; then *species*, bestowed by the separate substances, are received directly in the possible intellect; but the power of understanding is had by the agent intellect.[165]

With regard to the act of understanding itself, at all times a distinction is drawn between possible intellect, habit of science, and the actuation of this habit; but in earlier writings there is a further distinction introduced within the habit of science between an element of light and, on the other hand, *species* as element of determination.[166] Though this distinction does not recur in the same form in later writings, equivalent affirmations are to be found. Both agent intellect and phantasm concur in producing the act of understanding, but in their cooperation each has its respective role. Just as corporal light, it was supposed, did not include in itself the various colors of the spectrum but only reduced to act either the colors themselves or the *diaphanum* through which the colors were perceived, similarly agent intellect did not include the specific determinations of the various natures of material things but only was capable of making any such nature intelligible in act.[167] Hence, while phantasm caused in possible intellect the determination of the act of understanding, agent intellect caused the element of immaterialization, of intelligibility in act.[168]

This distinction seems relevant to the distinction between the twofold inner word, between concept in the narrower modern sense and, on the other hand, judgment. For we read that human intellectual operation is perfected in two manners, by intelligible *species* and by intellectual light; in virtue of the former we have our apprehensions of things; but in virtue of the latter we pass judgment upon our apprehensions.[169] Now we have seen that the inner word, whether definition or judgment, is the self-expression of the self-possessed act of understanding: the definition is the

---

[165] *De Anima*, a. 15 ad 9m.

[166] *In I Sent.*, d. 3, q. 5, a. 1 ad 1m; *In III Sent.*, d. 14, q. 1, a. 1, sol. 2; *ibid.*, sol. 3; *Quodl.* VII, a. 1; *De Ver.*, q. 10, a. 6; q. 18, a. 8 ad 3m.

[167] *In III de An.*, lect. 10, §739; *De Malo*, q. 16, a. 12 ad 1m et ad 2m.

[168] *In III de An.*, lect. 10, §737 ff.; *C. Gent.*, II, 77; *Sum. Theol.*, I, q. 79, a. 4 ad 4m; *De Spir. Creat.*, a. 10 ad 4m; *De An.*, a. 5 c.

[169] *De Malo*, q. 16, a. 12 c.

expression both of and by an insight into phantasm; the judgment is the expression both of and by a reflective act of understanding. On the division enounced above, these two types of expression have their grounds respectively in the two elements of determination and light found in the act of understanding. Inasmuch as the act of understanding grasps its own conditions as the understanding of this sort of thing, it abstracts from the irrelevant and expresses itself in a definition of essence. But inasmuch as the act of understanding grasps its own transcendence-in-immanence, its quality of intellectual light as a participation of the divine and uncreated Light, it expresses itself in judgment, in a positing of truth, in the affirmation or negation of reality.

Now this relation of intellectual light to judgment goes beyond the Aristotelian theory of agent intellect. Aristotle had argued that, since we understand now in potency and now in act, there must be in us both an active and a passive principle of understanding.[170] This active principle is like a habit, but as Aquinas noted, it is not to be confused with the *habitus principiorum*.[171] Unlike Plato, Aristotle did not consider that the essences of material things existed separately, and were of themselves intelligible in act; hence he had to have a cause to effect their immaterialization, to reduce them from potential to actual intelligibility.[172] Like the possible intellect, the agent intellect is separable, impassible, unconfused with matter; but as well it is of its nature ever in act.[173] Though it is a participation of the intellectual light of the separate substances, still it is an immanent and private possession of each of us.[174] In a word, Aquinas had no scruples about fitting the Aristotelian text into a context of contemporary medieval speculation; but even so he did not manage in his *Commentary* to relate agent intellect to judgment.

That relation is affirmed clearly and repeatedly in his independent writings. For it is the light of intellect that replaces the Augustinian vision of eternal truth; and regularly one reads that we know,

---

[170] *In III de An.*, lect. 10, §728.

[171] *Ibid.*, §729; cf. *In II Sent.*, d. 17, q. 2, a. 1 sol.; *De An.*, a. 5 c.

[172] *In III de An.*, lect. 10, §730 f.

[173] *Ibid.*, §732 f. Cf. *In II Sent.*, d. 3, q. 3, a. 4 ad 4m; *In III Sent.*, d. 14, q. 1, a. 1, sol. 2 ad 2m; *De Ver.*, q. 10, a. 8 ad 11m; *Sum. Theol.*, I, q. 54, a. 1 ad 1m.

[174] *In III de An.*, lect. 10, §734-39.

we understand, we judge all things by a created light within us which is a participation, a resultant, a similitude, an impression of the first and eternal light and truth.[175] Nor is the relation of intellectual light to judgment confined to such general affirmations. The range of a cognitional potency is fixed by the light under which it operates: ocular vision extends to all colors; the human soul can know all that falls under the light of agent intellect; the prophet knows by the divine light that manifests anything, corporal or spiritual, human or divine.[176] Knowing truth is a use or act of intellectual light,[177] and so judgment occurs according to the force of that light.[178] Hence the prophet judges according to an infused light, and the essence of prophecy lies in such judgment for a prophet need not be the recipient of a revelation but only pass judgment on data revealed to another; such was the case of Joseph, who judged Pharaoh's dreams;[179] such also perhaps was the case of Solomon, who judged with greater certitude and from a divine instinct what naturally is known about nature and human morals.[180]

In particular, there is a relevance of intellectual light to the critical problem, for it is by intellectual light that we can get beyond mere relativity to immutable truth and that we can discern appearance from reality.[181] As already has been seen, it is by reflection on the nature of intellect and especially on the nature of the active principle of intellectual light that we come to know truth.[182] But it is somewhat hazardous to attempt to specify the exact course of such reflection. Aquinas himself did not offer an account of the pro-

[175] *In IV Sent.*, d. 49, q. 2, a. 7 ad 9m; *Quodl. X*, a. 7 c.; *In Boet. de Trin.*, q. 1, a. 3 ad 1m; *De Ver.*, q. 1, a. 4 ad 5m; q. 10, a. 8 c. *ad fin* ; q. 11, a. 1 c. *ad. fin*; *Sum. Theol.*, I, q. 12, a. 11 ad 3m; q. 16, a. 6 ad 1m; q. 84, a. 5; q. 88, a. 3 ad 1m; *De Spir. Creat.*, a. 10 c. et ad 8m.

[176] *Sum. Theol.*, II-II, q. 171, a. 3 c; cf. I-II, q. 109, a. 1c.

[177] *Ibid.*, I-II, q. 109, a. 1 c. *init.*

[178] *Ibid.*, II-II, q. 173, a. 2 c.

[179] *De Ver.*, q. 12, a. 7 c.

[180] *Ibid.*, a. 12 c.

[181] *Sum. Theol.*, I, q. 84, a. 6 ad 1m: "Requiritur enim lumen intellectus agentis per quod immutabiliter veritatem in rebus mutabilibus cognoscamus, et discernamus ipsas res a similitudinibus rerum."

[182] *De Ver.*, q. 1, a. 9 c.

cedure he would follow; so it is only by piecing together scattered materials that one can arrive at an epistemological position that may be termed Thomistic but hardly Thomist. However, two basic points may be thought to be sufficiently clear. Epistemological reflection will involve a sort of reasoning, but that reasoning is not a deduction, since no premises may be assumed, but rather a development of understanding by which we come to grasp just how it is that our minds are proportionate to knowledge of reality. This point follows from the analysis of judgment already given; it squares with the nature of the problem; it need not be enlarged. The other point has to do with the precise content of the act of reflective and critical understanding. It should seem that this act consists in a grasp of the native infinity of intellect; for on the one hand, Thomist thought does stress that native infinity, and, on the other hand, from such infinity one can grasp the capacity of the mind to know reality.

Thomist thought stresses the native infinity of intellect; for the nature of intellect as active is *potens omnia facere*; as passive, it is *potens omnia fieri*. This is not merely an Aristotelian commonplace which Aquinas endlessly repeated; he also knew how to transpose and apply it in rather startling fashion. Now any finite act of understanding has to be a *pati*, because intellect as intellect is infinite.[183] Because of its infinite range, the object of intellect must be *ens*;[184] this object cannot be unknown;[185] it is known *per se* and naturally.[186] As there are different types of intellect, so there are different modes of knowing *ens*. Since understanding is by identity and *ens* includes all reality, only infinite understanding can be the direct and immediate apprehension of the proper object of intellect, *ens intelligibile*.[187] Man's intellect is potency. But as the hand is the instrument capable of using any instrument, so the human soul is the form capable of receiving any form.[188] While God is *totum ens* without qua-

[183] *In III Sent.*, d. 14, a. 1, sol. 2; *C. Gent.*, II, 98; *Sum. Theol.*, I, q. 79, a. 2 c.
[184] *De Ver.*, q. 1, a. 2 ad 4m; *Sum. Theol.*, I, q. 79, a. 7 c.
[185] *De Ver.*, q. 11, a. 1 ad 3m.
[186] *C. Gent.*, II, 83 (ed. Leon., XIII, 523a 26 ff.).
[187] *Ibid.*, 98.
[188] *In III de An.*, lect. 13, §790.

lification, [189] man is *totum ens* only *quodammodo*.[190] Hence in his
direct acts of understanding man enters into identity with the
intelligibility of only this or that material nature; it is in an act
of reflective understanding in which the nature of understanding
is itself understood as *potens omnia facere et fieri*, that man becomes capable of grasping the analogous concept of *ens*. For
to know being and not-being, whole and part, and the other concepts that flow from the concept of being, pertains not to the
direct habit of intellect nor the derived habit of science but to
the reflective and critical habit of wisdom.[191] For the concept
of *ens* is not just another concept, another *quod quid est*, another
but most general essence; the concept of *ens* is any concept, any
quod quid est, any essence, when considered not as some highest
common factor nor again simply in itself but in its relation to
its own *actus essendi*,[192] which is known in the act of judgment.[193]
Only on condition that human intellect is *potens omnia facere
et fieri* is the concept of all concepts really commensurate with
reality—really the concept of *ens*. On the other hand, if intellect is *potens omnia facere et fieri*, then since we know by what
we are, *per se* and naturally we do know *ens*, further, since we
know we know by knowing what we are, it is by reflection on
the nature of intellect that we know our capacity for truth and
for knowledge of reality.[194] But the native infinity of intellect
as intellect is a datum of rational consciousness. It appears in
that restless spirit of inquiry, that endless search for causes which,

[189] *C. Gent.*, II, 98.

[190] *In III de An.*, lect. 13, §790.

[191] *Sum. Theol.*, I-II, q. 66, a. 5 ad 4m.

[192] *De Ente et Essentia*, cap. 1 (ed. Roland-Gosselin, p. 4). This is the account of *ens* in the principal meaning of the term : not as *ens per accidens*,
nor as *ens* that is equivalent to the truth of a proposition (*est* in the sense of *yes*),
but as *ens* that is divided by the ten categories. In this meaning *ens* is determined
by real essence, and so there is the definition of essence : "Essentia dicitur
secundum quod per eam et in ea ens habet esse." Cf. *In V Met.*, lect. 9, for
the classical account.

[193] *In I Sent.*, d. 19, q. 5, a. 1 ad 7m: "Prima operatio (intellectus) respicit
quidditatem rei; secunda respicit esse ipsius." The *esse* known in the second
operation, judgment, is the real; there is an *esse* pertaining to the quiddity as
such, but (*loc. cit.*) "quidditatis esse est quoddam esse rationis."

[194] Hence *De Ver.*, q. 1, a. 9 c.

Aquinas argued, can rest and end only in a supernatural vision of God.[195] It appears in the absolute exigence of reflective thought which will assent only if the possibility of the contradictory proposition is excluded.[196] Just as Thomist thought is an ontology of knowledge inasmuch as intellectual light is referred to its origin in uncreated Light, so too it is more than an embryonic epistemology inasmuch as intellectual light reflectively grasps its own nature and the commensuration of that nature to the universe of reality. [197]

A comment may be permitted; for in the measure one grasps the character and implication of the act by which intellectual light reflects by intellectual light upon intellectual light to understand itself and pronounce its universal validity, in that measure one grasps one of the two outstanding analogies to the procession of an infinite Word from an infinite Understanding. On the other hand, the foregoing argument, precisely because it clung closely to Thomist texts to avoid all unnecessary appearance of airy speculation, is apt to find little echo in a modern mind. Two remarks may increase the resonance. First, our knowledge of the real is not knowledge of some note or aspect or quality of things. The whole of each thing is real; and by reality we mean nothing less than the universe in the multiplicity of its members, in the totality and individuality of each, in the interrelations of all. To know the real is to know the universe. As our intellects are potential, so our knowledge of the real is a development. The child has to learn to distinguish sharply between fact and fiction; the young man has not yet acquired a sufficiently nuanced grasp of human living for the study of ethics to be profitable; each of us, confronted with something outside the beaten track of our experience, turns to the expert to be taught just what it is. Still, in all this progress we are but discriminating, differentiating, categorizing the details of a scheme that somehow we possessed from the start. To say that any X is real is just to assign it a place in that scheme; to deny the reality of any Y is to deny it a place in the universal scheme.

---

[195] *Sum. Theol.*, I-II, q. 3, a. 8 c.
[196] *In Boet. de Trin.*, q. 3, a. 1 ad 4m.
[197] *De Ver.*, q. 1, a. 9 c.

But how do we grasp the scheme itself? At its root it is just the principle of excluded middle: X either is or else is not. And in its details the scheme is just the actuation of our capacity to conceive any essence and rationally affirm its existence and its relations. Since within that scheme both we ourselves and all our acts of conceiving and of judging are no more than particular and not too important items, the critical problem—and this is our second remark—is not a problem of moving from within outwards, of moving from a subject to an object outside the subject. It is a problem of moving from above downwards, of moving from an infinite potentiality commensurate with the universe towards a rational apprehension that seizes the difference of subject and object in essentially the same way that it seizes any other real distinction. Thus realism is immediate, not because it is naive and unreasoned and blindly affirmed, but because we know the real before we know such a difference within the real as the difference between subject and object. Again, the critical problem has the appearance of insolubility only because the true concept of the real is hidden or obscured, and in its place there comes the false substitute that by the real we mean only another essence, or else that by the real we mean the object of modern existentialist experience—the mere givenness of inner or outer actuality, which truly is no more than the condition for the rational transition from the affirmation of possible to the affirmation of actual contingent being.

THE UNITY OF WISDOM

Wisdom, as first philosophy, deals at once with the real as real and with the first principles of demonstrations.[198] It is, in the very definition of its object, a duality. So far from mitigating that violent contrast of object and subject, the current pedagogical convenience of separate books and courses on metaphysics and on epistemoloy rather tends to make it appear ultimate and irreducible. But being is not just one thing, with knowing quite another. We know by what we are; we know we know by knowing what we are; and since even the knowing in "knowing what we are"

[198] *In IV Met.*, lect. 5, §595.

is by what we are, rational reflection on ourselves is a duplication of ourselves. In us the principle and term of that doubling are not identical. In the procession of the divine Word the principle and the term of the doubling are identical, but the relations of principle to term and of term to principle remain real, opposed, subsistent, eternal, equal personalities—Father and Son in the consubstantiality of intellectual generation.[199] Even in the Godhead the duality of wisdom is not overcome utterly; even there in some sense one may speak of a *sapientia genita*.[200] But though the duality of wisdom never disappears totally, yet it tends towards that limit. Some remarks on the approach towards the limit are our concluding concern.

There is a common element to all our acts of understanding. It is a pure quality, coming to be when we inquire *quid sit* and *an sit*, partially realized when we directly understand some essence and again when we reflectively understand the necessity of affirming its existence. This pure quality is intellectual light. But in its pure form we have no experience of it.   It never is just inquiry but always inquiry about something. It never is pure understanding but always understanding this or understanding that. Even so, we may discern it introspectively, just as externally we discern light in seeing color. But while the external and corporal light that strikes and stimulates our eyes could not be produced, even in fanciful thought, to an infinity, there is to intellectual light an inner nisus towards the infinite. Aristotle opened his *Metaphysics* with the remark that naturally all men desire to know. But Aquinas measured that desire to find in the undying restlessness and absolute exigence of the human mind that intellect as intellect is infinite, that *ipsum esse* is *ipsum intelligere* and uncreated, unlimited Light, that though our intellects because potential cannot attain naturally to the vision of God, still our intellects as intellects have a dynamic orientation, a natural desire, that nothing short of that unknown vision can satisfy utterly.

---

[199] *C. Gent.*, IV, 11.

[200] The difficulty with this expression is that *sapientia* is identical with the divine essence, and the divine essence is neither generating nor generated. See *In I Sent.*, d. 5, q. 1, a. 2 sol. ; d. 32, q. 2, aa. 1 & 2; *De Ver.*, q. 4, a. 2 ad 2m; a. 4 ad 3m; a. 5 c. med.; *C. Gent.*, IV, 12; *In I Cor.*, cap. 1, lect. 3, *ad fin.*; *Sum. Theol.*, I, q. 34, a. 1 ad 2m et ad 4m.

For Augustine our hearts are restless until they rest in God; for Aquinas, not our hearts, but first and most our minds are restless until they rest in seeing Him.

The basic duality of our wisdom is between our immanent intellectual light and the uncreated Light that is the object of its groping and its straining. The same duality is also the basic instance of the opposition and distinction between what is first *quoad nos* and what is first *quoad se* : ontologically the uncreated Light is first; epistemologically our own immanent light is first, for it is known not by some *species* but *per se ipsum* as the actuating element in all intelligible *species*. Known with this qualified immediacy, it justifies itself as the potentially boundless base whence we can posit and through our positing know the universe; and as the principle of our knowledge of reality, it also is the most convincing sample in us of the stuff of which the Author of the universe and of our minds consists. Between these poles, the highest in us and in God the most like us, our wisdom moves to knowledge of itself and of its source. Were our wisdom substantial, it would not be subject to that type of duality. But in fact it is accidental, a perfection that relates us to Perfection. Not only is it accidental, but also it is acquired gradually. Towards it we are moved in a dialectical oscillation, envisaging more clearly now one pole and now another, with each addition to either at once throwing more light on the other and raising further questions with regard to it.

Perhaps in this connection we may note most conveniently a particular aspect of the soul's self-knowledge. The most nuanced account of this is to be found in the *De Veritate*,[201] where three types of self-knowledge are distinguished. There is the empirical self-knowledge, actual or habitual, based upon the soul's presence to itself; there is the scientific and analytic self-knowledge that proceeds from objects to acts, from acts to potencies, from potencies to essence; but besides this pair with which we are already familiar, there is also a third. It lies in the act of judgment which passes from the conception of essence to the affirmation of reality. Still, it is concerned not with this or that soul, but with what any soul ought to be according to the eternal reasons; and so the reality

[201] *De Ver.*, q. 10, a. 8c.

of soul that is envisaged is not sorry achievement but dynamic norm. Now knowledge of the norm, of the ought-to-be, cannot be had from what merely happens to be and, too often, falls far short of the norm. Normative knowledge has to rest upon the eternal reasons. But this resting, Aquinas explained, is not a vision of God but a participation and similitude of Him by which we grasp first principles and judge all things by examining them in the light of principles.[202]

Wisdom through self-knowledge is not limited to the progress from empirical through scientific to normative knowledge. Beyond the wisdom we may attain by the natural light of our intellects, there is a further wisdom attained through the supernatural light of faith, when the humble surrender of our own light to the self-revealing uncreated Light makes the latter the loved law of all our assents. Rooted in this faith, supernatural wisdom has a twofold expansion. In its contact with human reason, it is the science of theology which orders the data of revelation and passes judgment on all other science.[203] But faith, besides involving a contact with reason, also involves a contact with God. On that side wisdom is a gift of the Holy Spirit, making us docile to His movements in which, even perceptibly, one may be "non solum discens sed et patiens divina."[204]

Our account of the introspective data underlying an interpretation of Thomist trinitarian theory would be incomplete if it contained no mention of the possible relevance of mystical experience. Early in the *Sentences*,[205] in discussing the *imago Dei* in the human soul, it is asked whether knowledge and love of God and of self are constantly in act. In the *Summa* this question is answered negatively for the peremptory reason that everyone now and then goes to sleep.[206] But in the early work the answer is affirmative, and it is given in two forms—first in a context of Augustinian terms, secondly in a context of Aristotelian terms. It would seem that the difference between the two is not merely

---

[202] *Ibid.*

[203] *Sum. Theol.*, I, q. 1, a. 6 c. et ad 2m; cf. a. 8 c.

[204] *In III Sent.*, d. 15, q. 2, a. 1, qc. 2; d. 35, q. 2, a. 1; *De Ver.*, q. 26, a. 3 ad 18 m; *De Div. Nom.*, IV, 2; *Sum. Theol.*, II-II, q. 45, a. 2 c.

[205] *In I Sent.*, d. 3, q. 4, a. 5 c.

[206] *Sum. Theol.*, I, q. 93, a. 7 ad 4m.

terminological; for the second account is introduced by the statement : "Alio tamen modo secundum Philisophos intelligitur quod anima semper se intelligit."[207] Not only does this not sound like the preface to a repetition of the same doctrine in different terms, but also the view of the philosophers, which follows, seems to move on a different plane. It is no more than the view, outlined above, of our perception of intellectual light not as an object but as a medium in our acts of understanding. It amounts to saying that the soul is present to itself in rational consciousness. But from that presence to oneself it is not too easy a step to the presence of God to oneself. Philosophic thought can achieve it through the theorem, mentioned in the preceding article,[208] of divine ubiquity. But it takes a rather marvellous grasp of that metaphysical theorem for constant actual knowledge and love of God to result. In fact, it is rather in the preceding, Augustinian statement that such knowledge and love receive attention. The knowledge in question is not a *discernere* which distinguishes one object from another, nor a *cogitare* which relates the parts of one object to the whole, nor any *intelligere* that fixes attention in a determinate fashion; what is affirmed is some simple and continuous intuition in virtue of presence by which the soul knows and loves both itself and God in some indeterminate manner. Now it is true that, apart from prying introspection, self-knowledge within rational consciousness is neither a *discernere*, nor a *cogitare*, nor an *intelligere* with a fixed object. But must one not enter into the domain of religious experience to find this awareness of one's spiritual self prolonged into an awareness of God? That prolongation does not seem to be a datum within the range of ordinary introspection; on the other hand, one can give Aquinas' words a very satisfactory meaning if one reads the descriptions of mystical writers on the habitual felt presence of God.[209]

A similar, if less acute, question arises in the *De Veritate*, where one reads that the presence of God in the mind is the memory of God in the mind.[210] Such a statement has a mystical ring in-

---

[207] *In I Sent.*, d. 3, q. 4, a. 5 c.

[208] *Ibid.*, a. 4 c.

[209] E.g., A. Poulain, *Des grâces d'oraison* (éd. 10ᵉèm, Paris, 1922), chaps. V et VI.

[210] *De Ver.*, q. 10, a. 7 ad 2m.

asmuch as a presence that is a memory seems to be a known presence. However, the same passage concludes with a remark that confines the interpreter within the range of ordinary experience. A necessary condition of understanding is within nature, and we are told that from the divine presence in the soul intellect receives the light necessary for understanding.[211] Further, if one goes back to Aquinas' explicit accounts of the term, *memoria*, one finds that it is habitual knowledge,[212] and even that the mind is present to itself and God present to the mind before any *species* are received from sense, so that the human *imago Dei* has its constitutive *memoria* before any conscious intellectual act is elicited.[213] To the casual reader it may seem that a presence of God which is a memory must be a known presence; but Aquinas' own explanation of his terms does not substantiate that conclusion.

Perhaps the following series of propositions will do justice to the question: To what extent is mystical experience relevant to the Thomist concept of the *imago Dei*? First, the Thomist description of that experience, in its general form, does supply in an extremely simple fashion the required triad of the *imago*. "Taste and see how the Lord is sweet." "Taste" refers to inner experience, to an *experientia consortii divini*; it supplies the *memoria* in act. "See" refers to a consequent judgment, to a *certitudo intellectus;* it supplies the inner word. "How the Lord is sweet" refers to the second effect of the experience, the ineffable act of love, the *securitas affectus*; it gives the third element of the triad.[214] Secondly, while one should admit the possible relevance of mystical experience to an interpretation of the *imago* and even the deep influence of mysticism upon Aquinas and his thought, one is not to leap from possibility to affirmation of fact. Whatever is true, Aquinas certainly was not exclusively a theologian of the mystical. He was deeply interested in nature; his merit lay in embracing all and in drawing all distinctions; and indubitable references to mystical experience in his discussions of the *imago* at best are few and, at least by later Theresan standards, anything but ex-

---

[211] *Loc. cit.*

[212] *Ibid.*, a. 3 c.

[213] *Ibid.*, a. 2 ob. 5a et ad 5m.

[214] *In* Ps. 33, v. 9. Cf. F. D. Joret, *La contemplation mystique d'après s. Thomas d'Aquin* (Bruxelles, 1923), pp. 117, 126.

plicit. Finally, on Aquinas' own testimony, the image of God is found in men universally. It is found in those without the actual use of reason; it is found in sinners; it is found, clear and fair, in those in the state of grace.[215] It should seem that essentially Thomist theory of the trinitarian processions is in its basic analogy not mystical but psychological. Though the created image becomes clearer as the use of reason develops, though it becomes fairer as grace is added to reason, though it becomes manifest as special graces reveal the potentialities of our *consortium divinum*, still these differences strictly are accidental; they have to do with the development of wisdom and of love in man and not with the essence of what develops.

CONCLUSION

The first part of our inquiry into the concept of *verbum* in the writings of St. Thomas has been completed. In this first part the principal aim has been to build a bridge from the mind of the twentieth-century reader to the mind of the thirteenth-century writer. Both possess psychological experience; in both that experience is essentially the same; both can by introspection observe and analyse such experience. At once the assumption of the method employed and the contention derived from the data assembled in these two chapters have been that Aquinas did practice psychological introspection and through that experimental knowledge of his own soul arrived at his highly nuanced, deeply penetrating, firmly outlined theory of the nature of human intellect. Hence the light of intellect, insight into phantasm, acts of defining thought, reflective reasoning and understanding, acts of judgment, are above all psychological facts. The inner word of definition is the expression of an insight into phantasm, and the insight is the goal towards which the wonder of inquiry tends. The inner word of judgment is the expression of a reflective act of understanding, and that reflective act is the goal towards which critical wonder tends. The former answers the question, *quid sit?* The latter answers the question, *an sit?* No doubt, as expressed by Aquinas, these psychological facts are embedded in

---

[215] *Sum. Theol.*, I, q. 93, a. 8 ad 3m.

metaphysical categories and theorems. But without first grasping in some detail the empirical content so embedded, one risks, if not emptying the categories and theorems of all content, at least interpreting them with an impoverished generality that cannot bear the weight of the mighty superstructure of trinitarian theory. Conversely, it will be found, I believe, that our preliminary concern with psychological fact will lend a sureness, otherwise unattainable, to the interpretation of the metaphysical categories; for the Thomist application of metaphysics to the tasks of psychological analysis cannot be studied in some preliminary vacuum. That application exists only in psychological contexts; and it is easier to interpret metaphysics as applied to psychology when one is aware of the psychological facts involved. Without such awareness interpretation has to limp along on more or less remote and certainly non-psychological analogies. Finally, we beg to observe, the point at which conclusions can be drawn has not yet been reached. If the interpretation of the applied metaphysics depends upon the psychology, so too the interpretation of the psychology depends upon the applied metaphysics. There remains, then, a whole series of questions to be considered before we may claim to have satisfied the data on *verbum* found in Thomist writings.

III.

PROCESSION AND RELATED NOTIONS

Just as a modern exact science is generically mathematics and only specifically mechanics or physics or chemistry so also the Thomist analysis of the *verbum* or inner word is generically metaphysics and only specifically psychology. Two chapters have been devoted to the psychological side of the issue before us.[1] Attention must now be turned to the metaphysics, for the matters of fact that have been assembled in preceding articles find their systematic formulation and structural interrelation in terms of potency, habit, operation, action, passion, object, species.

Since in general it will be possible to assume that the reader is familiar with Thomist metaphysics, our concern in these pages will be with matters of detail. On its objective side the problem arises from the insufficient generality of Aristotelian analyses and from the concomitance in Aquinas of different terminologies which, unless distinguished carefully, yield a crop of pseudometaphysical issues. Perhaps the subjective side of the problem will offer greater real difficulty. For in Aquinas psychology and metaphysics as applied to psychology are so intimately related that any distortion of the one can be had only by a compensating distortion of the other. If then I have been correct in affirming a disregarded wealth in Thomist rational psychology,[2] I now must argue for a simplification and clarification of metaphysics as applied to psychology. In the long run, I believe, simplicity and clarity must win out. In the short run there can hardly fail to occur not only the normal human resistance to change, which is a healthy

---

[1] See chapters I and II above.

[2] I find that similar views are advanced by P. Petrus Hoenen, *La théorie du jugement d'après S. Thomas d'Aquin*, Analecta Gregoriana, XXXIX (Rome, 1946), ser. phil. sect. A, n. 3; this work is a brilliant complement to P. Hoenen's articles in *Gregorianum* already cited (p. 26, note 122). As I was indebted to the articles, so my own work is now supported by the book. Enter on the other side of the ledger, Matthew J. O'Connell, "St Thomas and the *Verbum*: An Interpretation," *Modern Schoolman*, XXIV (1947), 224-34.

conservative force, but also the difficulty of assimilating what has
been long overlooked, of grasping its significance, of assessing
exactly its import and implications. However, with such subjective difficulty I cannot deal here, except by the indirect method
of setting forth, as accurately as I can, the historical evidence
on an historical question.

PROCESSION

In the work on the *Sentences* two types of procession are distinguished: the first is local movement, properly the local movement
of an animal; the second, which alone is considered relevant to
the divine processions, is decribed as "eductio principiati a suo
principio,"[3] and equivalently as "exitus causati a causa."[4] In
the *De Veritate* thought is somewhat more refined. The distinction
is drawn between "processio operationis," the emergence of a perfection from (and in) what is perfected, and "processio operati,"
the emergence of one thing from another. Next, it is argued that,
since in God there is no capacity to be perfected, there can be
in God no possibility of a "processio operationis," such as the
procession of the act of understanding from the intellect or the
procession of the act of love from the will. Accordingly, created
analogy to the divine processions has to be sought in instances
of "processio operati," such as the procession of the inner word
in the intellect.[5]

One may find a parallel distinction to the above in the *Contra
Gentiles* where it is remarked that the origin of the divine Word
is not of act from potency but "sicut oritur actus ex actu."[6] On
the other hand, a new approach is to be recognized in the *De Potentia*. Procession, it is said, primarily denotes a local movement
from a starting point, through intermediate positions taken in
their proper order, towards a goal. But this primary meaning
is to be generalized until procession refers to "omne illud in quo
est aliquis ordo unius ex alio vel post aliud." After a variety

---

[3] *In I Sent.*, d. 13, q. 1, a. 1 sol.

[4] *Ibid.*, a. 3 ad 2m; cf. *ibid.*, a. 1, ad 3m.

[5] *De Ver.*, q. 4, a. 2, ad 7m.

[6] *C. Gent.*, IV, 14, §3. N.B. I shall count paragraphs in the Leonine manual
edition.

of examples of this generalized meaning, attention concentrates on the "duplex actio."[7] The *Summa* proceeds more peremptorily to the same conclusion : all procession is according to some action;[8] and as there are actions that go forth into external matter, so also there are actions that remain in the agent.

Is there any notable significance to be attached to the foregoing variations? I do not think so. In all cases the same term is reached, namely, opposed relations of origin. In earlier works they are reached more directly; for Aquinas there does not shrink from using such terms as "causatum" and "operatum." In later works deference is paid to the usage of Latin Fathers and theologians who rarely or never apply the name "cause" to the divine processions,[9] while the required relations of origin are obtained by recalling the Aristotelian doctrine that relations are founded on actions,[10] or by stating that "actio secundum primam nominis impositionem importat originem motus,"[11] where perhaps only excessive subtlety could distinguish between "origo motus" and the Aristotelian definition of efficient cause, "a quo est principium motus."[12] On the other hand, what the *De Veritate* obtains by denying "processio operationis" in God, namely, the absence of real relations between intellect and the act of understanding, between will and the act of willing, the *Summa* attains by a different route. It conveniently overlooks the definition of potency as "principium actionis" to consider only "principium agendi in aliud";[13] and it insists on the identity of divine intellect with what is understood, of divine will with what is willed.[14]

However, it has been advanced that in one respect the position of the *De Veritate* later underwent change, namely, in its negation of a "processio operati" within the will.[15] The passage that

---

[7] *De Pot.*, q. 10, a. 1 c.

[8] *Sum. Theol.*, I, q. 27, a. 1 c.

[9] *De Pot.*, q. 10, a. 1 ad 8m; *Sum.* Theol., I, q. 33, a. 1, ad 1m.

[10] *De Pot.*, q. 8, a. 1 c.; *Sum. Theol.*, I, q. 28, a. 4 c.

[11] *Sum. Theol.*, I, q. 41, a. 1, ad 2m.

[12] *In II Phys.*, lect. 5, §7.

[13] *Sum. Theol.*, I, q. 27, a. 5, ad 1m; cf. *ibid.*, q. 25, a. 1 c.

[14] *Ibid.*, q. 28, a. 4, ad 1m; cf. *De Pot.*, q. 8, a. 1, ad 11m.

[15] See T. L. Penido, "Gloses sur la procession d'amour," *Ephem. Theol. Lovan.*, XIV (1937), 38.

has so exercised Thomistic writers[16] reads as follows: "et ideo voluntas non habet aliquid progrediens a seipsa quod in ea sit nisi per modum operationis; sed intellectus habet in seipso aliquid progrediens ab eo, non solum per modum operationis, sed etiam per modum rei operatae."[17] Now this passage gives rise to difficulty only inasmush as one may assume that there should be a parallel between intellect and will, that as the inner word proceeds from the act of understanding, so within the will some distinct term proceeds from the act of love. This assumption would seem to be quite justified in interpreting the trinitarian writings of Henry of Ghent[18] or of Scotus.[19] But if one is to interpret Aquinas in the context of what he himself wrote, then the assumption in question is extremely doubtful. Not only does the passage in the *De Veritate* explicitly deny such a parallelism of intellect and will, but Thomist trinitarian theory has no exigence for it. On the contrary, it seems a plain matter of fact that for Aquinas the second procession grounding real relations is not the procession of the act of love from the will, nor the procession of something else from the act of love within the will, but the procession in the will of the act of love from the inner word in the intellect.[20]

---

[16] *Ibid.*, 37-48; see also R. Morency, "L'activité affective selon Jean de S. Thomas," *Laval phil. et théol.*, II (1946), 143-74.

[17] *De Ver.*, q. 4, a. 2, ad 7m. The "nisi" is nòt found in the printed editions but cf. I. Chevalier, *Div. Thom. Plac.*, 1938, 63-69; T. L. Penido, *Ephem. Theol. Lovan.*, XV (1938), 339; also *Bull. Thom.*, 1937, 138; *Angelicum*, 1938, 422; B. Lonergan, *De Deo Trino*, Romae, 1964, Vol. II, pp. 109-114.

[18] His views are summarized by Scotus, *In I Sent. (Op. Ox.)*, d. 2, q. 7, n. 13 (ed. Vives, VIII, 535 f.). P. Häring, P.S.M., has examined the microfilm copy of Henry of Ghent at the Medieval Institute, Toronto, and has assured me that Scotus gives a satisfactory account of Henry's views.

[19] See P. Raymond, "Duns Scot," *Dict. Théol. Cath.*, IV, 1882.

[20] A detailed discussion cannot be undertaken here. See *In I Sent.*, d. 11, q. 1, a. 1, ad 4m: ". . . a Verbo procedit Spiritus sanctus sicut a verbo mentali amor"; *ibid.*, d. 27, q. 2, a. 1 c: ". . . quia potest esse duplex intuitus, vel veri simpliciter, vel ulterius secundum quod verum extenditur in bonum et conveniens, et haec est perfecta apprehensio; ideo est duplex verbum: scilicet rei prolatae quae placet, quod spirat amorem, et hoc est verbum perfectum ; et verbum rei quae etiam displicet. . . aut non placet"; cf. *In III de An.*, lect. 4, §634 f. *C. Gent.*, IV, 24, §12: "Nam amor procedit a verbo: eo quod nihil amare possumus nisi verbo cordis illud concipiamus." *Ibid.*, IV, 19, §8: "Quod autem aliquid sit in voluntate ut amatum in amante, ordinem quem-

Advertence to this repeatedly affirmed dependence of love on inner word puts an end, very simply and very clearly, I think, to an exceptional amount of labored interpretation.

Actus Perfecti

Excessive attention to the metaphysical framework with insufficient attention to the psychological content of the Thomist concept of verbum has led to a good deal of obscure profundity on the meaning of Aquinas' *actus perfecti*. It is necessary for us to set forth the evidence on the meaning of the phrase and, in doing so, it will be well to begin from Aristole, first because it is only a translation of Aristotle's ἐνέργεια τοῦ τετελεσμένου,[21] and secondly, because Aquinas, when first he uses it,[22] takes it

dam habet ad conceptionem quod ab intellectu concipitur . . . non enim amaretur aliquid nisi aliquo modo cognosceretur." *De Pot.*, q. 9, a. 9, ad 3m (2ae ser.): "... nihil enim potest amari cuius verbum in intellectu non praeconcipiatur; et sic oportet quod ille qui procedit per modum voluntatis sit ab eo qui procedit per modum intellectus, et per consequens distinguatur ab eo. Cf. *ibid.*, q. 10, a. 2 c; ad 4m; ad 7m; a. 4 c; a. 5 c: "Non enim potest esse nec intelligi quod amor sit alicuius quod non est intellectu praeconceptum: unde quilibet amor est ab aliquo verbo, loquendo de amore in intellectuali natura." *Sum. Theol.*, I, q. 27, a. 3, ad 3m: "... de ratione amoris est quod non procedat nisi a conceptione intellectus"; *ibid.*, q. 36, a. 2c: "Necesse est autem quod amor a verbo procedat: non enim aliquid amamus, nisi secundum quod conceptione mentis apprehendimus. Unde et secundum hoc manifestum est quod Spiritus sanctus procedat a Filio." *Comp. theol.*, cap. 49: "... Similiter etiam id quod amatur est in amante secundum quod amatur actu. Quod autem aliquid actu amatur, procedit et ex virtute amativa amantis, et ex bono amabili actu intellecto. Hoc igitur quod est esse amatum in amante, ex duobus procedit, scilicet ex principio amativo, et ex intelligibili apprehenso, quod est verbum conceptum de amabili." *De Rationibus Fidei ad Cantorem Antiochenum*, cap. 4: "Manifestum est autem, quod nihil amare possumus intelligibili et sancto amore, nisi quod actu per intellectum concipimus. Conceptio autem intellectus est verbum, unde oportet quod amor a verbo oriatur. Verbum autem Dei dicimus esse Filium, ex quo patet Spiritum sanctum esse a Filio...." In the *De Potentia* the procession of love from word is well integrated into general trinitarian theory; this cannot be said of the *Sentences*, as appears from *In I Sent.*, d. 10, q. 1, a. 5 c; d. 12, q. 1, a. 1, ad 2m; ad 3m; a. 3, ad 3m; d. 13, q. 1, a. 2 sol ; a. 3, ad 4m.

[21] *De An.*, III, 7, 431a, 5 ff.

[22] *In I Sent.*, d. 4, q. 1, a. 1, ad 1m. The correct reference in this text probably is not to *Eth.*, V, but to *Eth.*, X.

for granted that the reader knows his Aristotle and so knows what it means. Our account of Aristotle may be divided into three parts: general contrasts between operation (ἐνέργεια) and movement (κίνησις); the analysis of movement in the *Physics*; and the recurring embarrassment in the *De Anima* occasioned by the specialization of terms in the *Physics*.

In the *Ethics* there is considered a Platonist argument to the effect that pleasure is not the good because pleasure is a movement and so incomplete, while the good must be complete and perfect. It is met with the observation that all movements have velocities, that pleasure has no velocity, and so pleasure cannot be a movement nor be incomplete.[23] On a later page the incompleteness of movement and the completeness of operation are described at greater length. A movement becomes in time; one part succeeds another; and a whole is to be had only in the whole of the time. On the other hand, an operation such as seeing or pleasure, does not become in time but rather endures through time; at once it is all that it is to be; at each instant it is completely itself. In a movement one may assign instants in which what now is, is not what later will be. In an operation there is no assignable instant in which what is occuring stands in need of something further that later will make it specifically complete.[24]

A similar general contrast occurs in the *Metaphysics*. There is a difference between action (πρᾶξις) distinct from its end and action coincident with its end. One cannot at once be walking a given distance and have walked it, be being cured and have been cured, be learning something and have learned it. But at once one is seeing and has seen, one is understanding and has understood, one is alive and has been alive, one is happy and has been happy. In the former instances there is a difference between action and end, and we have either what is not properly action or, at best, incomplete action—such are movements. In the latter instances action and end are coincident—such are operations.[25]

---

[23] *Eth.*, X, 3, 1173a, 29 ff; lect. 3 "non bene."

[24] *Ibid.*, 4, 1174a, 14—b 9; lect. 5.

[25] *Met.*, Θ, 6, 1048b, 18-34; on the authenticity of the passage, cf. Ross, *Metaphysics*, II, 253. Apparently Aquinas did not know it and does not comment on it; but the ideas were familiar to him.

The characteristics of movement, described in the *Ethics* and the *Metaphysics*, are submitted to analysis in the *Physics*. The nature of movement is difficult to grasp because it is a reality that, as reality, is incomplete and so involves the indeterminate.[26] Still, movement may be defined as the act of what is in potency inasmuch as it is in potency, or as the act of the movable just as movable.[27] Again, one may say that what is about to be moved is in potency to two acts: one of these is complete and so admits categorial specification; but this act is the term of another which is incomplete and so does not admit categorial specification; movement is the latter, incomplete act.[28] Since this definition does not presuppose the concept of time, it is employed in defining time.[29] Next it is shown that the incomplete act, movement, can occur in only three categories, namely, place, sensible quality, and physical size.[30] It is insisted that movement can be had only in a corporeal, quantitative, indefinitely divisible subject.[31] From the indefinite divisibility of distance and time it is concluded that in a local movement not only is there a *moveri* prior to every assignable *motum esse* but also there is an assignable *motum esse* prior to every assignable *moveri*;[32] thus analysis pushes to the limit the descriptive contrast betweeen the specific completeness of operation and the specific incompleteness, the categorial indeterminacy, of movement.[33] But just how the demonstrable paradox of local movement was to be extended to alteration, growth, generation, and illumination, was for the commentators an obscure and disputed point.[34]

[26] *Phys.*, III, 2, 201b, 24 ff.
[27] *Ibid.*, 1, 201a, 10 ff.
[28] *In III Phys.*, lect. 2, §5; cf. §3.
[29] *In IV Phys.*, lect. 16-22.
[30] *In V Phys.*, lect. 2-4; cf. VIII, lect. 4-6.
[31] *In VI Phys.*, lect. 5 & 12.
[32] *Ibid.*, lect. 8, §5.

[33] That movement does not square with the categories of thought, is accepted by Aristotle as well as by Bergson ; because Bergson conceives the real as the empirically experienced, he concludes that the categories of thought fall short of the reality of movement; because Aristotle conceives the real as being, convertible with the true, he concludes that the reality of movement falls short of the reality corresponding to the categories of thought.

[34] *In VI Phys.*, lect. 5, §§11-16; lect. 8, §15.

As the *Physics* analyzes movement, so one might expect the *De Anima* to analyze operation. But if that expectation is verified substantially,[35] there is a far more conspicuous embarrassment caused by the specialization of terms in the *Physics*. For in the *De Anima*, despite the alleged wealth of the Greek language, Aristotle needed such words as κίνησις, ἀλλοίωσις, πάθησις, in a fresh set of meanings; but instead of working out the new meanings systematically, he was content, in general, to trust his reader's intelligence and, occasionally, to add an incidental warning or outburst. Three examples of this may be noted. First, there is the remark that, because movement (κίνησις) is an act (ἐνέργεια)) even though it is an incomplete one, we may take it that undergoing change (πάσχειν) and being moved (κινεῖσθαι) and operating (ἐνεργεῖν) are all the same thing.[36] Again, there is the explanation that the phrase, undergoing change (πάσχειν), is not univocal: when the scientist's science becomes actual thought, the becoming is not an alteration or, if it is, then it is alteration of a distinct genus.[37] In similar vein the third book of the *De Anima* contains the statement to which Aquinas regularly referred[38] when contrasting *actus perfecti* and *actus imperfecti*: the movement of a sense is movement of a distinct species; for movement has been defined as the operation or act (ἐνέργεια) of the incomplete, but operation simply so called is of the completed.[39]

The substance of what Aquinas meant by *actus perfecti* and *actus imperfecti* is contained in the foregoing account of Aristotle. He referred to this contrast variously as a difference between *operatio* and *motus*,[40] or as a twofold *operatio*,[41] or finally as a

[35] Movement supposes matter : *In II Met.*, lect. 4, §328; VIII, lect. 1, §1686; XII, lect. 2, §2436. Sensation is without matter: *De An.*, II, 12, 424a, 18; III, 8, 432a, 10. Movement is incomplete and of the incompleted, sensation is of the completed: *De An.*, *II*, 5, 417a, 16; III, 7, 431a, 6.

[36] *De An.*, II, 5, 417a, 14 ff; lect. 10, §356.

[37] *Ibid.*, 417b, 2-7 (cf. 14); lect. 11, §369 ff.

[38] *In I Sent.*, d. 37, q. 4, a 1, ad 1m; *In IV Sent.*, d. 17, q. 1, a. 5, sol 3, ad 1m; *De Pot.*, q. 10, a. 1 c; *C. Gent.*, II, 82, §17; *De Div. Nomin.*, IV, lect. 7; *In VII Phys.*, lect. 1, §7; *Sum. Theol.*, II-II, q. 179, a. 1, ad 3m; q. 180, a. 6 c.

[39] *De An.*, III, 7, 431a, 5 ff; lect. 12, §766.

[40] *In I Sent.*, d. 4, q. 1, a. 1, ad 1m; d. 37, q. 4, a. 1, ad 1m; II, d. 11, q. 2,

twofold *motus*.[42] *Actus imperfecti* was explained by noting that what is moved is in potency, that what is in potency is imperfect, and so that movement is the act of the imperfect.[43] Both early and late works testify to a full awareness that movement is intrinsically temporal and specifically incomplete.[44] In contrast the *actus perfecti* is defined as "actus existentis in actu,"[45] and even as "actus existentis in actu secundum quod huiusmodi";[46] it is specifically complete, an "operatio consequens formam,"[47] the "operatio sensus iam facti in actu per suam speciem,"[48] without need or anticipation of any ulterior complement to be itself,[49] and intrinsically outside time.[50]

What, I may be asked, does this all amount to? In current terminology, then, it is a brilliant and penetrating negation of essentialism. There are elements in reality that correspond to what we know by defining; they are called essences; but they are not the whole of reality. There are also elements of reality that are less than essences, that are, as it were, essences-on-the-way; they are movements, acts that actualize incompletely, acts intrinsically in anticipation of completion and so intrinsically in time. But there also are elements of reality that are over and above essence; sight is an essence, but seeing is more than that

---

a. 1 sol; d. 15, q. 3, a. 2 sol; IJI, d. 31, q. 2, a. 1, sol. 2; *De Ver.*, q. 8, a. 15, ad 3m; *In III de An.*, lect. 12, §766.

[41] *De Ver.*, q. 8, a. 14, ad 12m.

---

[42] *In IV Sent.*, d. 17, q. 1, a. 5, sol. 3, ad 1m; *De Div. Nom.*, IV, lect. 7; *Sum. Theol.*, I-II, q. 31, a. 2, ad 1m; III, q. 21, a. 1, ad 3m; cf. I, q. 18, a. 1 c; q. 53, a. 1, ad 2m; q. 58, a. 1, ad 1m.

[43] *In I Sent.*, d. 4, q. 1, a. 1, ad 1m; *In III de An.*, lect. 12, §766.

[44] *In X Eth.*, lect. 5 "videtur enim"; *In IV Sent.*, d. 17, q. 1, a. 5, sol 3, ad 1m; d. 49, q. 3, a. 1, sol 3; *De Ver.*, q. 8, a. 14, 12m; *Sum. Theol.*, I-II, q. 31, a. 2, ad 1m.

[45] *Sum. Theol.*, I, q. 18, a. 3, ad 1m; I-II, q. 31, a. 2, ad 1m; III, q. 21, a. 1, ad 3m.

[46] *In IV Sent.*, d. 49, q. 3, a. 1, sol. 1, ob. 2a; cf. "actus perfecti inquantum huiusmodi" (*ibid.*, III, d. 31, q. 2, a. 1, sol. 2).

[47] *In III Sent.*, d. 31, q. 2, a. 1, sol. 2.

[48] *In III de An.*, lect. 12, §766.

[49] Cf. footnote 44 with exception of I-II, q. 31, a. 2, ad 1m.

[50] Cf. footnote 44.

essence; still seeing is not a further essence, for seeing and sight have the same definition, which they share as act and potency; this more-than-essence is act, act of what already is completely in possession of essence, act that does not need or anticipate something further to become what it is to be, act that intrinsically stands outside time.

Such is the substance of what Aquinas meant by *actus perfecti* and *actus imperfecti*. But there are also accidental variations; for, so far was Aquinas from the stereotyped terminology that sometimes is attributed to him, that he could write "sapientis enim est de nominibus non curare."[51] A first variation is had inasmuch as the term "operatio" is suggestive of efficient causality; hence the contrast between operation and movement is taken as ground for denying that divine activity presupposes an uncreated matter.[52] A second variation arises by a natural transition from the imperfection of the material continuum with its indefinite divisibility to the imperfection of anything that has not, as yet, attained its end; in this transferred sense the *Sentences* speak of an *actus imperfecti*,[53] where also one may read the more cautious statement that the act of hope is "quasi quidam motus" and "sicut actus imperfecti."[54] A third variation arises from the fact that what exists in act is a ground of efficient causality; thus, an angel moves locally by an application of his virtue to a continuous series of places; this local movement is described as "motus existentis in actu."[55] I believe that only poor judgment would desire to take such instances as these, not as incidental variations, but as key passages to the meaning of the repeated statement that sensation, understanding, and willing are *actus perfecti*.

---

[51] *In II Sent.*, d. 3, q. 1, a. 1 c. He is explaining the sense in which one might say that angels are composed of matter and form.

[52] *In I Sent.*, d. 7, q. 1, a. 1, ad 3m; cf. d. 42, q. 1, a. 1, ad 3m, which solves the same problem differently.

[53] *In II Sent.*, d. 11, q. 2, a. 1 c.

[54] *In III Sent.*, d. 31, q. 2, a. 1, sol 2 c. Cf. the use of "existentis in potentia inquantum huiusmodi" in *Sum. Theol.*, I-II, q. 27, a. 3 c.

[55] *Sum. Theol.*, I, q. 53, a. 1, ad 3m; ad 2m. On angelic local movement: *ibid.*, aa. 1-3; *In I Sent.*, d. 37, q. 4, aa. 1-3; *Quodlib.* I, a. 9; IX, a. 9; XI, a. 4.

Pati

There is no difficulty in thinking of movement in the strict sense of *actus imperfecti* as a *pati*. But there appears to be enormous difficulty in thinking of movement in the broad sense, which includes the *actus perfecti*, as a *pati*. Since that difficulty necessarily tends to the substitution of what someone else thinks for what Aquinas said, we must endeavor to surmount it at once. We begin from the variety of meanings of the term, *pati*, in Aquinas' source.

In the *Ethics* Aristotle recognizes in the soul three things: potencies, habits, and πάθη. The last are illustrated by desire, anger, fear, boldness, envy, joy, friendliness, hate, longing, rivalry, pity, and in general the feelings accompanied by pleasure or pain.[56] Secondly, in a logical context Aristotle will speak of ἴδια πάθη which are attributes or properties, even of ideal numbers.[57] Thirdly, and this is the fundamental usage, πάθος is connected with the species of movement called alteration. In general, alteration is defined as change of quality,[58] but the quality subject to such change is restricted to the *sensibilia per se et propria* such as the white and black, the heavy and light, the hot and cold, the hard and soft, and so forth.[59] Πάθη are such qualities as such; they are also the process of change of such qualities; especially, they are such change when it is for the worse.[60] Fourthly, in close connection with the foregoing there is the account of the affective qualities in the *Categories*,[61] though the feelings of the *Ethics* are also relevant here.[62] Fifthly, with reference to any movement in the strict sense Aristotle distinguishes the passive process (πάθησις) and the received term (πάθος) of the incomplete act, and these he maintains to be really identical with the production (ποίησις) and the effected term (ποίημα) respectively of the same

---

[56] *Eth.*, II, 4, 1105b, 20 ff.

[57] E.g., *Met.*, Γ, 2, 1004b, 6, 10.

[58] *Phys.*, V, 2, 226a, 26; lect. 4, §2. Cf. *Met.*, Δ, 1022b, 15; Λ 1069b, 12; N 1088a, 32 ; but the apparent circle in defining (cf. Ross on 1022b, 15) is solved by appeal to the *sensibilia propria*.

[59] *In VII Phys.*, lect. 4, §2; lect. 5 & 6; *In I de Gen. et Corr.*, lect. 10, §2, §7.

[60] *Met.*, Δ, 21, 1022b, 15 ff; V, lect. 20, §1065 ff; note definition of predicament.

[61] *Cat.*, 8, 8b, 28—10a, 10.

[62] Cf. *ibid.*, 9b 27 ff.

incomplete act.[63] Sixthly, in an extended sense already noted, πάσχειν is employed to denote sensation which is an act of the completed;[64] it is to be observed that the theorem of the identity of action and passion is extended to this usage on the ground that without such an identity it would be necessary for every mover to be moved.[65]

The complexity of Aristotelian usage pours into the writings of Aquinas. In the *Sentences* some nine meanings of *pati* are distinguished; the basic meaning is considered to be "alteration for the worse," and other meanings are allowed greater or less propriety according to their approximation to what is considered basic.[66] In later works this jungle growth is cut through with a distinction between *pati proprie* and *pati communiter*.[67] To *pati proprie* is assigned the province of Aristotelian physics and, as well, the linguistic associations of *pati* with suffering and of *passio* with human passions. On the other hand, *pati communiter* is a purely metaphysical idea; it is somewhat less general than "being an effect," for it presupposes a subject; it is described as *recipere*, as something found in every creature, as something following necessarily from the potentiality involved in every creature.[68] However, there seems to be a concentration on the moment of reception,[69] and it is pointed out that, since this *pati* involves no diminution of the recipient, it might be better named a *perfici*.[70]

---

[63] *Phys.*, III, 3, 202a, 23 ff. Aquinas had only two terms to correspond to Aristotle's four.

[64] *De An.*, II, 5, 416b, 33; 417a, 14; 417b 2; cf. III, 5 430a, 10 ff.

[65] *De An.*, III, 2, 426a, 4 ff; lect. 2, §592; cf. II, 2, 414a, 11; lect. 4, §272; *De Unit. Int.*, III (ed. Keeler, §74); hence *De An.*, III, 430a, 3, 20; 431a, 1; 431b, 17 & 22. The application of "actio in passo" to knowledge becomes complicated with the doctrine of *species*; cf. *Sum. Theol.*, I, q. 14, a. 2 c; q. 87, a. 1, ad 3m.

[66] *In III Sent.*, d. 15, q. 2, a. 1, sol. 1 & 2.

[67] *De Ver.*, q. 26, a. 1 c; *Sum. Theol.*, I, q. 79, a. 2 c; I-II, q. 22, a. 1 c.

[68] *De Ver.*, q. 26, a. 1 c.

[69] *Sum. Theol.*, I, q. 79, a. 2 c.

[70] *Ibid.*, I-II, q. 22, a. 1 c. Also of interest are: *In III Sent.*, d. 26, q. 1, a. 1 sol.; IV, d. 44, q. 3, a. 1, sol. 3; *De Ver.*, q. 26, aa. 2 & 3; *Sum. Theol.*, III, q. 15, a. 4 c; *In I de An.*, lect. 10, §157-62; II, lect. 10, §350; lect. 11, §365-72; lect. 12, §382, III, lect. 7, §676 ; §687 f.; lect. 9, §720 & 722; lect. 12, §765 f.

The question before us is whether operation or action as *actus perfecti* can be called a *pati* in the sense of a received perfection. The difficulty here, in so far as I have been able to grasp it, lies in distinguishing between the grammatical subject of a transitive verb in the active voice and, on the other hand, the ontological subject of the exercise of efficient causality. When it is true that "I see," it is also true that "I" is the grammatical subject of a transitive verb in the active voice. But it is mere confusion to conclude immediately that "I" also denotes the ontological subject of the exercise of efficient causality. Further, it may or may not be true that one must conclude mediately from the transitive verb to the efficient cause; with such abstract questions I am not concerned. But it is false to suppose that either Aristotle or Aquinas acknowledged or drew such a conclusion. I quote:

> Videbatur enim repugnare, quod sentire dicitur in actu, eo quod dictum est, quod sentire est quoddam pati et moveri. Esse enim in actu videtur magis pertinere ad agere. Et ideo ad hoc exponendum dicit [Aristoteles], quod ita dicimus sentire in actu, ac si dicamus, quod pati et moveri sint quoddam agere, idest quoddam esse in actu. Nam motus est quidam actus, sed imperfectus, ut dictum est in tertio Physicorum. Est enim actus existentis in potentia, scilicet mobilis. Sicut igitur motus est actus, ita moveri et sentire est quoddam agere, vel esse secundum actum.[71]

The question is, how can one speak of sensing in act, when one has maintained that sensing is a matter of undergoing change and being moved? For sensing in act seems to be just the opposite of being changed and being moved, namely, acting. The answer is that there is an acting which is simply being in act, and simply being in act is not opposed to being changed and being moved. On the contrary, movement itself is defined as an act. If there is no difficulty about defining movement as an act, though it is an imperfect one, there is no difficulty in saying that the *pati* of sensation is an act and in that sense an acting.

Next, one may ask whether this Aristotelian view-point is to be found in Aquinas' independent writings. Let us begin by noting two senses of the term "operatio." In many contexts it denotes the exercise of efficient causality, for example, "Deus

---

[71] *In II de An.*, lect. 10, §356.

operatur in omni operante." But such usage certainly is not exclusive and, I believe, it is not the most fundamental. For *operatio* also means simply "being in act," as does the etymologically
parallel ἐνέργεια; and in this sense it is a perfection which, in
a creature, is received and so is a *pati* or a *passio* of the operating
subject. Thus, Aquinas spoke of an "operatio non activa sed
receptiva."[72] He urged that the fact that sense had an operation
did not make sense an active potency; for all powers of the soul
have operations but most of them are passive potencies.[73] He
pointed out that nature provides suitable principles for operations;
when the operation is an action, the principle is an active potency;
and when the operation consists in a passion, the principle is a
passive potency.[74] He distinguished the operation of a mover,
such as heating or cutting, the operation of what is moved, such
as being heated or being cut, and the operation of what exists
in act without tending to effect change.[75] He defined potency
as just the principle of operation, whether that be action or passion.[76] Finally, so familiar to Aquinas was the notion of operation
as passive, as something to be predicated not of the mover but
cf the moved, that in speaking of operative grace he found it
necessary to explain that in this instance operation was to be attributed to the mover because it was the operation of an effect:
"operatio enim alicuius effectus attribuitur non mobili sed mo-
venti."[77] That explanation would seem to be rather superfluous
today when people think it a contradiction in terms to speak of
the operating subjects as being moved.

What is true of *operatio*, also is true of *actio*. In an early period
these terms are contrasted,[78] but later they are juxtaposed in op-
postion to *factio*,[79] and such equivalence subsequently seems to
be maintained. Frequently enough, then, *actio* means the exercise

---

[72] *In I Sent.*, d. 15, q. 5, a. 3, ad 4m.
[73] *De Ver.*, q. 16, a. 1, ad 13m; q. 26, a. 3, ad 4m; cf. *De Virt. in Comm.*,
a. 3, ad 5m.
[74] *C. Gent.*, II, 76, §15.
[75] *Ibid.*, III, 22, §2.
[76] *Q. D. de An.*, a. 12 c.
[77] *Sum. Theol.*, I-II, q. 111, a. 2 c.
[78] *In I Sent.*, d. 40, q. 1, a. 1, ad 1m; *De Ver.*, q. 8, a. 6 c.
[79] *C. Gent.*, II, 1, §4.

of efficient causality. But this meaning is not the only meaning. It also means simply *actus*. It is *actio* in the sense of *actus* that is the actuality of virtue, as being is the actuality of substance.[80] It is *actio* in the sense of *actus* that is the complement of potency and stands to potency as second act to first.[81] It is *actio* in the sense of *actus* that pertains to an active potency or to a passive potency.[82] It is *actio* in the sense of *actus* that makes it possible to define passion as the *actio* of alterable quality,[83] and as the *actio* of the patient.[84] Finally, the action that goes forth into external matter would seem to have a prescriptive claim to denoting the exercise of efficient causality; but in an earlier work one may read that transient action is the act and perfection of the patient;[85] and in later works one may read that transient action is the action and perfection of the patient,[86] and the action and perfection of the transformed matter.[87] Presumably, passive potencies and patients and transformed matter have an *actio* not in the sense that they are exercising efficient causality but in the sense that they are in act.

To conclude, the influence of Aristotle did lead Aquinas to use *operatio* and *actio* in the sense of act or of being in act; and in that sense there is no absurdity—on the contrary, there is a necessity—in saying that such act in a creature is a *pati communiter*. However, before making any applications to the act, the action, the operation of understanding, it will be necessary to consider the notion of active potency.

---

[80] *Sum. Theol.*, I, q. 54, a. 1 c.

[81] *C. Gent.*, II, 9, §3. It may be objected that shortly in §5 Aquinas mentions *actio* as predicament. But this does not show that it is not an *actus* that is the complement of potency and stands to potency as second act to first. It may show, perhaps, that *actio* in the sense of act and *actio* in the sense of exercising efficient causality were not, at least on the verbal level, very sharply differentiated by Aquinas. But that happens to be what we are proving. Elsewhere we have discussed "*actio in agente*" and "*actio in passio*": see *Theological Studies*, III (1942), 375-81.

[82] *Sum. Theol.*, I, q. 77, a. 3 c.

[83] *In V Met.*, lect. 20, §1066.

[84] *Sum. Theol.*, I, q. 79, a. 4, ob. 5a.

[85] *De Pot.*, q. 3, a. 15 c.

[86] *Sum. Theol.*, I-II, q. 3, a. 2, ad 3m; *In IX Met.*, lect. 8, §1864.

[87] *Sum. Theol.*, I-II, q. 31, a. 5 c.

Potentia Activa

The ambiguity we have just noted in connection with *operatio* and *actio* becomes clear and systematic when we turn to the parallel ambiguity of the term "potentia activa." P. Stufler has remarked that, while early works make the *forma gravitatis* an active principle, later works make the same form with the same functions in the context of the same theory a passive principle.[88] The shift observed by P. Stufler is but a particular case in a far more fundamental ambiguity. For in the writings of Aquinas there are two distinct definitions of *potentia activa*. There is an Aristotelian definition, "principium transmutationis in aliud inquantum aliud," which attains a certain dominance in later works. There is what may be called, though with diffidence, an Avicennist definition, "principium operationis" or "principium actionis," which is dominant in earlier works and far from disappears in later ones. Since these definitions are not equivalent, it will be convenient to translate *potentia activa*, used in an Aristotelian sense, by "efficent potency," with the corresponding *potentia passiva* translated by "receptive potency"; further, it will be convenient to translate *potentia activa*, used in the Avicennist sense, by "active potency," with the corresponding *potentia passiva* translated by "passive potency." Finally, there is to be noted a "principium effectus," which is concomitant with Avicennist active potency, is distinguished from it, and amounts to a generalization of Aristotelian efficient potency. These distinctions have now to be verified.

In his account of relations in the *Metaphysics* Aristotle recognized three types of ground, namely, quantity, action and passion, measure and measured. The second type included a sub-division

---

[88] J. Stufler, *Gott, der erste Beweger aller Dinge*, (Innsbruck 1936), p. 34. Form is an active principle : *In III Sent.*, d. 3, q. 2, a. 1, ad 6m; d. 22, q. 3, a. 2, sol. 1; IV, d. 43, q. 1, a. 1, sol. 3; *De Ver.*, q. 12, a. 3 c; *C. Gent.*, III, 23, §9; *De Pot.*, q. 5, a. 5 c. Form is passive principle: *In II Phys.*, lect. 1, § 4; VIII, lect. 8, §7; *In V Met.*, lect. 14, §955; *In I de Caelo et Mundo*, lect. 3, §4; *Sum. Theol.*, III, q. 32, a 4 c. The early active principle is a *principium motus* but not a *motor*: *In II Sent.*, d. 14, q. 1, a. 3 c; *De Ver.*, q. 22, a. 3 c; a. 5, ad 8m; *C. Gent.*, III, 23, §§4, 7, 8.

according to potency and act. What can heat and what can be heated are related according to efficient and receptive potency; what is heating or cutting and what is being heated or being cut are related according to (efficient and receptive) act.[89] This passage is noteworthy in two respects. First, it speaks not merely of δύναμις but of δύναμις ποιητικὴ καὶ παθητική. Secondly, it makes quite clear the relational element in the Aristotelian concept of efficient potency and receptive potency: efficient potency is not conceived apart from a corresponding receptive potency; and receptive potency is not conceived apart from a corresponding efficient potency; to have either, one must have both.

More explicit definitions respect this viewpoint. Efficient potency was defined as the principle of movement or of change in the other or, if in self, then in self as other.[90] Receptive potency was defined as the principle of movement or of change by the other or, if by self, then by self as other.[91] Clearly these definitions presuppose an objective duality; they do not exclude the occurrence of both efficient and receptive potency in the same subject, provided that subject has two parts, one to move and the other to be moved; but they do exclude the one subject as one from being both efficient and receptive.

Complementary to these concepts of efficient and receptive potency, which necessarily involve some "other," was the concept of nature. Nature was the "principium motus et quietis in eo in quo est primo et per se et non secundum accidens."[92] Nature is not the thing but a principle in it; it is the matter of the thing, or its form, and its form rather than its matter.[93] But above all, from our viewpoint, nature is a principle in the thing of movement in the thing; it is "principium motus in eo in quo est motus." It follows that nature is neither efficient potency nor receptive potency. It is not efficient potency; for that is the principle of movement, not in self as self, but in the other or in self as other. It is not receptive potency; for that is the principle of movement, not in self as self, but by the other or by self as other. To this

---

[89] *Met.*, Δ, 15, 1021a, 14 ff; V, lect. 17, §1023 ff.
[90] *Ibid.*, 12, 1019a, 15 ff; lect. 14, §955, Θ, 1, 1046a, 9 ff; IX, lect. 1, § 1776 f.
[91] *Loc. cit.*
[92] *Phys.*, II, 1, 192b, 24 ff; lect. 1, §5.
[93] *In II Phys.*, lect. 2.

differentiation Aristotle adverted more than once. The doctor that cures himself is mentioned, from opposite viewpoints, in both the *Physics* and the *Metaphysics*.[94] The *De Caelo* contrasts potency and nature.[95] The ninth book of the *Metaphysics*, after defining efficient and receptive potency, goes on to employ the term "potency" in a still broader sense to include nature as well.[96]

In his *Metaphysics* Avicenna distinguished a large number of meanings of what was translated by *potentia* but would seem better rendered by "power." They may be indicated as follows: (1) power, as an intensive form of strength, the opposite of weakness, the source of mighty actions within the genus of movement; (2) power as ease of performance with some immunity from suffering; (3) power simply as a notable immunity from suffering without an implication of performance; (4) power as complete immunity from suffering; (5) strength as capcity to act, though without action, on the ground that it is "principium effectus"; (6) any disposition of a subject that is a "principium variationis ab illo in aliud inquantum illud est aliud"; from the context this is clearly the Aristotelian efficient potency; (7) the possibility of receiving; the perfection of this possibility is named "*actus*," though it is said to be not an *actus* but a *passio* or else an *acquisitio essendi*; (8) various modal variations of the foregoing and, as well, power in the sense of mathematical exponent; (9) the divisions of passive potency, i. e., the possibility of receiving, into perfect and imperfect, proximate and remote; (10) the principle of action. This last is propounded separately in the form of a theorem. Provided the action of a body is neither violent nor *per accidens*, then it must be ascribed to a potency in the body; this is clear when the action is due to will and choice; it is no less true when the action is due to some other body or to some separate substance; for there must be in the thing some property that accounts for the action, else the action will be either accidental or violent.[97]

Phys., II, 1, 192b, 23; Met., Δ, 12, 1019 a, 17.
[95] *De Caelo et Mundo*, III, 2, 301b, 17 f.
[96] *Met.* Θ, 8, 1049b, 5 ff; IX, lect. 7, §1844 f.
[97] Avicenna, *Metaphysica vel Philosophia Prima*, (Opera [Venice, 1508] fol. 84ᵛ-85ᵛ). I am indebted to Fr. Francis Firth, C.S.B., for a copy of these

In the *Sentences* there is a discussion of the potency of God. Aquinas begins by referring to Avicenna: the name "potentia" initially referred to powerful men and then was transferred to natural things; it means not only power to act but also immunity from suffering; on both counts it is to be attributed to God in a supreme degree.[98] The first solution specifies more precisely the initial meaning of potency as "principium actionis"; opposed to this active potency which has its complement in operation or action, there is a passive potency which receives action.[99] The second solution repeats that potency is the principle of action and of acting; any such principle is termed "potency"; even the divine essence, inasmuch as it is principle of operation, involves a potency, though not a potency distinct from the essence.[100] The fourth solution identifies divine essence, existence, and operation; it then points out that, just as the divine essence is taken as a "principium essendi," so divine potency is taken as "principium operandi et praeter hoc ut principium operati."[101] The fifth solution admits the real identity of divine potency and divine operation but denies eternal operation to involve eternal effects.[102] We may observe at once that such contrasts between divine operation or action and, on the other hand, its *operatum*, effect, or term, are quite common. To confine our illustration to the *Sentences*, we find that the operation is necessary but the effects contingent;[103] the operation is eternal but the effects temporal;[104] the operation is one but the effects are many;[105] the operation has no ulterior end but the effects have;[106] that omnipotence, which is the active potency of God, regards both operation and

---

pages from the photostat reproduction of this edition in the library of the Medieval Institute, Toronto.

[98] *In I Sent.*, d. 42, q. 1, a. 1 sol.

[99] *Ibid.*, ad 1m.

[100] *Ibid.*, ad 2m; cf. a. 2 sol.

[101] *Ibid.*, ad 4m.

[102] *Ibid.*, ad 5m.

[103] *Ibid.*, d. 43, q. 2, a. 1, ad 3m.

[104] *Ibid.*, d. 8, q. 3, a. 1, ad 4m; d. 14, q. 1, a. 1, ad 3m; d. 35, q. 1, a. 5, ad 3m.

[105] *Ibid.*, d. 42, q. 1, a. 2 sol.

[106] *In II Sent.*, d. 1, q. 2, a. 1, ad 4m.

effects but, in the latter case, regards only creatures;[107] that God
rests by a cessation, not of his operation, but of fresh effects.[108]

It is now necessary to turn to the third objection and solution
which were omitted above. The objection stems from the fifth
book of Aristotle's *Metaphysics*; it argues that potency is either
active or passive; that divine potency cannot be passive, for God
cannot suffer change; not can it be active for, according to Aristotle,
that is the principle of change in the other as other, but divine
activity does not presuppose any "other."[109] This lack of generality
in the Aristotelian concept of efficient potency had given rise to
difficulty on a previous occasion. Then Aquinas had met the
problem by admitting that divine potency was neither active
nor passive and by claiming that it was *superactiva*, i.e., not by
way of movement but by way of operation.[110] Now, however,
he prefers to generalize the Aristotelian definition and, incidentally,
to modify it into conformity with his own terminological preference: "potentia activa est principium operationis in aliud sicut
in effectum productum, non sicut in materiam transmutatam."[111]

The nature of divine potency was examined again in the opening
article of the *De Potentia*. The Aristotelian definition of efficient
potency appears in the third objection· and in the fifteenth; but
it has no influence either on the body of the article or on the so-
lutions. The body of the article begins by pointing out that there
are two distinct types of act—a first act which is form, and a second
act which is operation. Corresponding to these two types of act,
there are two types of potency—passive potency is the potency
to receive form; active potency is the "principium operationis"
or, without' apparent difference, the "principium actionis."[112] In
the context there is no mention of Avicenna, but a rather close
parallel may be found in Aristotle's *Metaphysics* where the analogy
of act is explained. Aristotle remarked that when A is in B as C
is in D, the proportion is that of matter to essence (οὐσία), but
when E is to F as G is to H, the proportion is that of potency to

[107] *In I Sent.*, d. 20, q. 1, a. 1, ad 4m.
[108] *In II Sent.*, d. 15, q. 3, a. 1, ad 3m; a. 2 sol.
[109] *In I Sent.*, d. 42, q. 1, a. 1, ob. 3a.
[110] *Ibid.*, d. 7, q. 1, a. 1, ad 3m.
[111] *Ibid.*, d. 42, q. 1, a. 1, ad 3m.
[112] *De Pot.*, q. 1, a. 1 c.

movement.[113] This gives a twofold potency and a twofold act, and it does so without any mention of the "other"; on both counts it resembles the analysis of the *De Potentia*.

As in the *Sentences*, so here active potency, besides being "principium operationis vel actionis," also is "principium effectus."[114] But it is far clearer in the *De Potentia* than in *Sentences* that active potency is "principium effectus" only by an accidental concomitance; one could have inferred as much from the earlier work; but one has only to read if one is to learn it from the latter. I quote:

> Potentia autem, licet sit principium quandoque et actionis et eius quod est per actionem productum; tamen unum accidit ei, alterum vero competit ei per se: non enim potentia activa semper, per suam actionem, aliquam rem producit quae sit terminus actionis, cum sint multae operationes quae non habent aliquid operatum, ut Philosophus dicit; semper enim potentia est actionis vel operationis principium.[115]

It would have been impossible to make the foregoing assertion of Aristotle's efficient potency; that, by definition, is principle of movement or change in the other, and so *per se* it looks towards an effect even though it may not actually produce one. But the active potency, with which Aquinas is dealing, is primarily principle of operation or action; such operation or action may involve an ulterior effect, as is the case when action goes forth into external matter; on the other hand, it may not involve anything over and above itself, as is the case when actions remain in the agent.[116] Thus, active potency in the *De Potentia* is at once both Aristotle's natural potency to an act in the subject and Aristotle's efficient

---

[113] *Met.*, Θ, 6, 1048b, 6-9. Aquinas' illustration is of sight in the eyes and of seeing to sight (*In IX Met.*, lect. 5, §1828 f.). Compare the standard Aristotelian contrast of the learner to science and of the scientist to consideration: *Phys.*, VIII, 4, 255a, 30—b, 31 (VIII, lect. 8) ; *De An.*, II, 1, 412a, 10, 22 ff. (II, lect. 1, §216; lect. 2, §239); *De An.*, II, 5, 417a, 21-418a, 6 (II, lect. 11 & 12). The parallel in artefacts is of raw materials to product, and of product to use (*In II Phys.*, lect. 4, §8), e.g. of materials to motorcar, and of car in garage to car on the road. However, the division of *De Pot.*, q. 1, a. 1 c. is not purely Aristotelian; cf. *In I Sent.*, d. 42, q. 1, a. 1, ad 1m.

[114] *De Pot.*, q. 1, a. 1, ad 1m; cf. *supra*, footnotes 101-108; also *C. Gent.*, II, 10; and *Sum. Theol.*, I, q. 25, a. 1, ad 3m.

[115] *De Pot.*, q. 2, a. 2 c.

[116] Cf. *C. Gent.*, II, 30, §§12, 13, and *infra* on *duplex actio*.

potency of a change in the other; spontaneously this ambivalence leads to Aquinas' repeated distinction of two kinds of action.

The *Contra Gentiles* introduces us to a reversal of roles. Hitherto we have noticed Aristotelian definitions only in objections. But now we find *potentia activa* defined not as principle of action but as "principium agendi in aliud secundum quod est aliud."[117] Further, we read that potency in God is not a principle of action but a principle of a product, because the very definition of active potency involves a relation to some "other."[118] It would seem to be a recognition of this relational element that underlies the statement, "sicut potentia passiva sequitur ens in potentia, ita potentia activa sequitur ens in actu";[119] for, while Aristotle's natural potency, like the active and passive potency of the *De Potentia*, pertains to the thing considered in itself, Aristotle's efficient and receptive potencies pertain to the thing considered, not merely in itself, but also in its relation to the "other" or to self as other; accordingly, it is not the *ens actu* but follows from it.

The treatment of divine active potency in the *Summa* maintains this reversal of roles. The Aristotelian definitions of efficient and of receptive potency are the basis of argument in the body of the article.[120] On the other hand, the Avicennist definition of principle of operation occurs only in the third objection.[121]

As when the waters of two rivers join to flow along side by side, so the two sets of definitions persist in the writings of Aquinas. He uses whichever suits his immediate purpose and, as is the way with intelligent men, he does not allow a common name for different things to confuse his thinking. However, open conflict between the two systems does break out at least once, and naturally enough this occurs in commenting the Aristotelian definition of efficient potency, namely, "principium motus vel mutationis in alio inquantum est aliud." Aquinas points out that in the thing

---

[117] *C. Gent.*, II, 7, §2.

[118] *Ibid.*, II, 10, §1.

[119] *Ibid.*, II, 7, §3. Cf. *Sum. Theol.*, I, q. 25, a. 1, ad 1m: "potentia activa non dividitur contra actum sed fundatur in eo"; a relation is suggested by "fundatur" even more than by "sequitur."

[120] *Sum. Theol.*, I, q. 25, a. 1 c.

[121] *Ibid.*, ob. 3a.

that is changed there are two principles of movement—its matter and also the formal principle on which movement follows. Neither of these principles is *potentia activa*, for whatever is moved is moved by the other, and nothing moves itself unless it has two parts, one moving and the other moved; accordingly, in so far as potency is a principle of movement in what is moved, it pertains to *potentia passiva* rather than *potentia activa*.[122] This passage brings into the open the latent ambiguity with which we have been dealing. But the tension is not maintained, for when later in the same work Aquinas has to characterize the potency of sight to seeing, he does not say that this potency is active and he does not say that it is passive; he introduces the terms, *potentia motiva* and *potentia operativa*;[123] it is a neat verbal solution to a merely verbal difficulty, and it must have pleased him; for we find *potentia operativa* employed in the *Prima Pars*[124] and in the *De Spiritualibus Creaturis*.[125]

Duplex Actio

Frequently Aquinas distinguished two types of *actio*, one which remains in its subject, another which goes forth into external matter to effect its transformation. This distinction has led subsequent writers to make metaphysical ultimates of what they term immanent and transient action and, as not rarely happens, such speculative constructions are a barrier rather than a help to a grasp of St. Thomas' thought, for they give an air of finality and completeness to what, in point of fact, contained not a little of the incidental and was not complete.

[122] *In V Met.*, lect. 14, §955. Note that the shift is only terminological: what before was called active, here is called passive; but what before was called active, then was not intended to mean efficient; and the present use of "passive" does not deny natural potency but only efficient potency. Early writings explicitly distinguish between *principium operationis vel actionis* and *principium operati vel effectus* (cf. footnotes 101-108, 115); similarly they distinguish between *principium motus* and the *movens* or *motor* (cf. *footnote* 88).
[123] *In IX Met.*, lect. 5, §1829. Cf. ἀρχὴ κινητική (*Met.*, 1049b, 9); contrast κινητικόν (*Phys.*, 202a, 13).
[124] *Sum. Theol.*, I, q. 54, a. 3 c.
[125] *De Sp. Cr.*, a. 11 c.

Aquinas alleges two different sources in Aristotle for his *duplex actio*. Contrasts between *actio* and *factio*, and so between *agere* and *facere*, *activum* and *factivum*, *agibile* and *factibile* stem from Aristotle's *Ethics*.[126] In the relevant passage Aristotle was distinguishing art, science, prudence, wisdom, and intellect; three of these, science, wisdom, and intellect, regard the necessary; the other pair, art and prudence, regard the contingent; the distinction between them is set forth by a parallel distinction between production (ποίησις) and moral conduct (πρᾶξις).[127] Now in medieval Latin both ποίησις and πρᾶξις might be rendered by *actio*, and in such cases Aquinas' distinction was between the *actio* of moral conduct, which is a perfection of the agent, and the *actio*, more proprerly *factio*, which transforms external matter.

A corollary may be noted. When Aquinas restricts *actio* to beings that have dominion over their acts, *actio* has at least an association with moral conduct. "Bruta aguntur et non agunt," because St. John Damascene said so;[128] but also because Aristotle remarked that sense is not a principle of moral conduct, since brutes have senses yet have no part in moral conduct.[129] The "non agunt" does not mean that brutes do not act in the sense of "aliquam actionem exercere," which may mean simply being in act;[130] it does not even deny that brutes move themselves locally inasmuch as one part in act moves another part in potency.

Evidently this source in the *Ethics* lacks generality.[131] But the other source in the ninth book of the *Metaphysics* is so general that it deals not with action but with act. The problem under discussion is the essential priority of act over potency, because act is the end of potency, the end is a cause, and a cause is prior.[132] The point was evident in cases in which only potency and act

---

[126] *In II Sent.*, d. 12, expositio textus; III, d. 23, q. 1, a. 4, sol. 1, ad 4m; III, d. 33, q. 2, a. 2, sol. 1; III, d. 35, q. 1, a. 1 sol.; *De Ver.*, q. 5, a. 1 c.

[127] *Eth.*, VI, 3, 1139b, 14 ff; cf. 1140a, 1 ff; 1140 b, 2 ff; *In VI Eth.*, *lect.* 3 (ed. Vives, XXV, 491); cf. lect. 2 (488a) ; lect. 4 (494a).

[128] *De Ver.*, q. 5, a. 9, ad 4m.

[129] *Eth.*, VI, 2, 1139a, 19; referred to in *De Unione Verbi*, a. 5 c. Cf. C. *Gent.*, III, c. 111; c. 112, §1; *In II Phys.*, lect., 10 §4.

[130] Cf. *supra*, footnotes 128 and 71.

[131] The contrast really is threefold : speculative, active, and productive. *Met.*, E. 1, 1025b, 19-26; VI, lect. 1, §1152; IX, lect. 2, §1788; XI, lect. 7, §2253.

[132] *Met.*, Θ, 8, 1050a, 3 ff.

existed; but when besides potency and act there was also an ulterior product, the apparent difficulty was met by noting that
then the act was in the thing produced and that it emerged simultaneously with the product.[133] There followed the familar
corollary on the twofold subject of the act (ἐνέργεια).[134]

The medieval translator laid no stress on *actio*: the ἐνέργεια
that is in the agent was translated by *actio*; the one that is in
the product was translated by *actus*.[135] The opposite usage may
be found in the *Prima Pars*.[136] General Thomist usage is variable. In the *Sentences* and in the *De Veritate* an attempt is
made to reserve *operatio* for the act that remains and *actio* for
the act that goes forth.[137] In the *Contra Gentiles, factio* is proposed for the act that goes forth and *operatio* or even *actio* for
the act that remains.[138]

In *De Potentia*, the *Contra Gentiles*, and the *Prima Pars*, the
distinction is drawn with respect to a *duplex operatio*.[139] However, it is *duplex actio* that is regular in the *Prima Pars*.[140] Still,
in the *De Potentia* mention was made of a *duplex actus secundus*,[141]
and this viewpoint returns in the *Prima Secundae*,[142] where also
one may find an identification of the act that goes forth with
the *actio in passio* of the *Physics*.[143] As a final observation, one
may note that Aquinas did not keep his two sources distinct;
in both the *Contra Gentiles* and the *Prima Secundae* he refers
to the ninth book of the *Metaphysics* and proceeds to speak of

[133] *Ibid.*, lines 23 ff.

[134] *Ibid.*, lines 30-37.

[135] Cf. téxt to *In IX Met.*, lect. 8 (ed. Cathala) and as quoted by Aquinas,
De Unit. Intel., III (ed. Keeler, §71).

[136] *Sum. Theol.*, I, q. 87, a. 3 c.

[137] *In I Sent.*, d. 40, q. 1, a. 1, ad 1m; *De Ver.*, q. 8, a. 6 c.

[138] *C. Gent.*, II, 1, §5.

[139] *De Pot.*, q. 10, a. 1 c; q. 9, a. 9, ad 4m (1a ser.); *C. Gent.*, II, 1, §3; *Sum.
Theol.*, I, q. 14, a. 2 c; cf. I-II, q. 3, a. 2, ad 3m.

[140] *Sum. Theol.*, I, q. 18, a. 3, ad 1m; q. 23, a. 2, ad 1m; q. 27, a. 1 c; a. 3 c;
a. 5 c; q. 28, a. 4 c; q. 54, a. 1, ad 3m; a. 2 c; q. 56, a. 1 c; q. 85, a. 2 c. Also
In I Sent., d. 40, q. 1, a. 1, ad 1m; *De Ver.*, q. 8, a. 6 c; q. 14, a, 3c; *De Pot.*,
q. 3, a. 15 c; q. 8, a. 1 c; *C. Gent.*, II, 23, §5; *Sum. Theol.*, I-II, q. 3, a. 2, ad 3m;
De Unit. Intel., III (ed. Keeler, §71).

[141] *De Pot.*, q. 5 a. 5, ad 14 m.

[142] *Sum. Theol.*, I-II, q. 57, a. 4 c; q. 74, a. 1 c; cf. q. 31, a. 5 c.

[143] *Ibid.*, q. 74, a. 1 c.

factio, a term that implicitly is present in the *Metaphysics* but explicitly only in the *Ethics*.[144]

This fluidity of terminology is not surprising unless one indulges in an anachronistic projection of present usage upon the past. On the other hand, the meaning of these passages and their significance are quite clear. There is an act that remains in the agent and is the perfection of the agent; there is another act that goes forth into external matter and effects a change of it. The pair spontaneously come together in thought—grammatically, because both are expressed by transitive verbs in the active voice, historically, because both proceed from the "principium actionis" that was Aquinas' initial definition of active potency. Even though later Aquinas did manifest a preference for a different definition of *potentia activa*, there was a deeper root in Aristotle himself to keep the two types of act associated; for it is a form that is the principle both of the act remaining in the agent and of the act that goes forth. In the *Physics* it was pointed out that the mover possesses a form which is principle of movement; for it is a man in act that makes a man out of what is a man only in potency.[145] In his *Sentences* Aquinas refers to this passage and applies it both to transient and to immanent acts: "causa autem actionis est species, ut dicitur in III Phys., quia unumquodque agit ratione formae alicuius quam habet ... sicut ignis qui desiccat et calefacit per caliditatem et siccitatem, et homo audit et videt per auditum et visum."[146] Even in his latest works Aquinas will speak of active potency as pertaining to things because of their forms,[147] and will explain differences of efficacy because of differences in the perfection of forms; thus, fire heats and illuminates; what is so heated or illuminated can do the same but only in a less degree, while merely intentional forms cannot have natural effects.[148] But form is not only the ground of efficiency but also the principle of operation: "propria forma uniuscuiusque faciens ipsum esse in actu, est principium operationis propriae

---

[144] *C. Gent.*, II, 1, §3, *Sum. Theol.*, I-II, q. 57, a. 4 c.

[145] *Phys.*, III, 2, 202a, 9; lect. 4, §6.

[146] *In III Sent.*, d. 18, q. 1, a. 1 c.

[147] *Sum. Theol.*, III, q. 13, a. 1 c.; *In III Phys.*, lect. 4, §6; VIII, lect. 21, §9.

[148] *Sum. Theol.*, I-II, q. 5, a. 6, ad 2m; cf. *In II de An.*, lect. 14, §425.

ipsius."[149] Such operation is the end of the operator and more
perfect than his form;[150] it is what is last and most perfect in each
thing, and so it is compared to form as act to potency, as second
act to first act.[151]

But however germane to Aquinas' thought as it actually developed, *duplex actio* is not a capsule of metaphysical ultimates.
The act that goes forth into external matter corresponds to the
predicament of action as defined in the *Sentences*: "actio secundum
quod est praedicamentum dicit aliquid fluens ab agente et cum
motu."[152] But later Aquinas wrote that there are two actions,
one that involves movement (in the sense of incomplete act),
and another that does not, as when God causes grace in the soul.
On the latter he remarked, "Quod quidem difficile est ad intelligendum non valentibus abstrahere considerationem suam ab
actionibus quae sunt cum motu."[153] This tart observation would
seem to be relevant to the passage in the *Commentary on the Physics* where, after explaining Aristotle's concept of action and passion,[154] he goes on to give his own quite different and quite universal definitions of the predicament of action and passion.[155]
As causal efficiency does not require external matter and movement, so also it need not go forth: there is a "processio operati"

[149] *Sum. Theol.*, II-II, q. 179, a. 1, ad 1m.
[150] *De Pot.*, q. 5, a. 5, ad 14m: "... obiectio illa procedit de actu secundo, qui est
operatio manens in operante, qui est finis operantis, et per consequens ex-
cellentior quam forma operantis."
[151] *In IV Sent.*, d. 49, q. 3, a. 2 sol: "Ultimum autem et perfectissimum quod
est in unoquoque est sua operatio; unde omnis forma inhaerens comparatur
ad operationem quodammodo ut potentia ad actum; propter quod forma dicitur
actus primus ut scientia; et operatio, actus secundus, ut considerare, ut patet
in II de Anima." Cf. also *In I Sent.*, q. 35, q. 1, a. 5, ad 4m; *De Malo*, q. 1,
a. 5 c; *Sum. Theol.*, I-II, q. 3, a. 2; q. 49, a. 3, ad 1m; III, q. 9, a. 1 c; a. 4 c.
Cf. *supra*, footnote 113.
[152] *In I Sent.*, d. 8, q. 4, a. 3, ad 3m.
[153] *Quodlib. IV*, a. 9 c; cf. *Sum. Theol.*, I, q. 41, a. 1, ad 2m.
[154] *In III Phys.*, lect. 5, §13.
[155] *Ibid.*, §15: "Sic igitur secûndum quod aliquid denominatur a causa agente,
est praedicamentum passionis, nam pati nihil est aliud quam suscipere aliquid
ab agente: secundum autem quod e converso denominatur causa agens ab effectu,
est praedicamentum actionis, nam actio est actus ab agente in aliud, ut supra
dictum est."

of the inner word within the intellect.[156] On the other hand, *actio*
that remains in the agent does not involve efficient causality
inasmuch as it proceeds from form, *species*, or informed potency;
for that procession is not "processio operati" but "processio operationis";[157] as we have just seen, operation is more perfect than
form, and only an instrument is less perfect than its effect. The
idea that efficient causality occurs in this type of *actio* has, I fear,
little more basis than a failure to distinguish between the two
different ways in which Aquinas defined his *potentia activa*.

Species, Intelligere

The Latin term, *species*, translates Aristotle's term, εἶδος,
and shares its ambiguity. It may mean a form and then it includes neither common nor individual matter; and it may mean
a universal and then it includes common but not individual
matter.[158] In cognitional contexts *species* occurs in both senses:
"similitudo rei intellectae, quae est species intelligibilis, est forma
secundum quam intellectus intelligit";[159] "intellectus igitur ab-
strahit speciem rei naturalis a materia sensibili individuali, non
autem a materia sensibili communi."[160] The former *species* is
a form; the latter is a universal. To determine in which sense
the term "species" is employed is not always as easy as in the
above cases. However, our criteria may be extended: a form
is known only by metaphysical analysis; but the universal enters
into the knowledge of everyone. To the objection that intellect
does not abstract *species* because, according to Aristotle, intellect
knows *species* in the phantasm, Aquinas answered:

> Dicendum quod intellectus noster et abstrahit species in-
> telligibiles a phantasmatibus, inquantum considerat naturas
> rerum in universali ; tamen intelligit eas in phantasmatibus,
> quia non potest intelligere ea quorum species abstrahit, nisi
> convertendo se ad phantasmata, ut supra dictum est.[161]

[156] *De Ver.*, q. 4, a. 2, ad 7m.
[157] *Ibid*. For parallels to this distinction, cf. *supra*, footnotes 101-108, 114,
and 115.
[158] *In VII Met.*, lect. 9, §1473.
[159] *Sum. Theol.*, I, q. 85, a. 2c.
[160] *Ibid.*, a. 1; ad 2m.
[161] *Ibid.*, ad 5m.

The generality of this statement, the fact that universals are being considered, the fact that the *species* are known in the phantasm, all favor taking *species* in the sense of a universal. On the other hand, to the objection that names signify things known and that, according to Aristotle, names are signs of the passions of the soul so that the things known are passions of the soul, Aquinas anwered:

> ... Et utraque haec operatio [i. e. of external sense and of imagination] coniungitur in intellectu. Nam primo quidem consideratur passio intellectus possibilis, secundum quod informatur specie intelligibili. Qua quidem formatus format secundo vel definitionem vel divisionem vel compositionem, quae per vocem significatur. Unde ratio quam significat nomen est definitio; et enuntiatio significat compositionem et divisionem intellectus. Non ergo voces significant ipsas species intelligibiles, sed ea quae intellectus sibi format ad iudicandum de rebus exterioribus.[162]

Here we have metaphysical analysis revealing the passion of the possible intellect being informed by species and its activity in forming definitions and judgments; *species* means form, and though the universal is referred to as the "ratio quam significat nomen," it is not here called a *species*.

Our present purpose is to discuss the relation between *species* as form and the act, *intelligere*. Our view is that this relation is expressed by Aquinas in two different manners—one according to what we have ventured to name the Avicennist definition of active potency, the other according to the Aristotelian concept of form as natural potency.

First, then, just as the *De Potentia* conceives active potency as the principle of operation or action which takes place in virtue of form,[163] so one may read that (intellect actuated by) *species* is the "principium actus intelligendi,"[164] the "principium actionis,"[165]

---

[162] *Ibid.*, a. 2, ad 3m.

[163] *De Pot.*, q. 1, a. 1 c.

[164] *De Ver.*, q. 3, a. 2 c.

[165] *De Pot.*, q. 8, a. 1 c; q. 9, a. 5 c; *Sum. Theol.*, I, q. 14, a. 5, ad 3m.

[166] *C. Gent.*, I, 46, §2; cf. *Sum. Theol.*, I, q. 56, a. 1 c; q. 85, a. 2 c; note the introduction of "principium formale," *In V Met.*, lect. 14, §955; *In II Phys.*, lect. 1, §4, where it is opposed to "potentia activa." On the other hand, the "principium formale" of act in the other, of heating in the heated, of specifica-

the "principium formale actionis,"[166] the "principium formale quo intellectus intelligit."[167] Again, just as the *De Potentia* conceives passive potency as potency to the reception of form,[168] and contrasts this passive potency with the active potency to operation and action, so one may read a parallel contrast between the reception of *species*, which is named a *passio*, and the subsequent *operatio*, which is an *actus perfecti*.[169] Thirdly, just as the *De Potentia* distinguishes between "principium actionis" and "principium effectus,"[170] and again between action and the term of action,[171] so there is a contrast between the form which is the principle of the act of understanding and the thought-out form of a house which is the term of the act of understanding and, as it were, its effect;[172] similarly contrasted are the *species* which is the form that actuates the intellect and is its principle of action, the action of the intellect, and the inner word which is term to the action and, as it were, something constituted by it.[173] Finally, while we have seen that the terms, *operatio* and *actio*, sometimes mean simply act or being in act and sometimes mean the exercise of efficient causality, we now find that the precision of trinitarian theory led Aquinas to distinguish exactly between

tion of the act of will by the intellect, would correspond not to Aristotle's natural potency but to his efficient potency; cf. *Sum. Theol.*, I-II, q. 9, a. 1 c; the distinction between exercise and specification is parallel to the distinction between applying agent and form in I, q. 105, a. 5 c; this triple distinction of end, applying agent, and form surpasses the twofold distinction of I, q. 82, a. 4 c; *C. Gent.*, I, 72, §7; III, 88, §5; which derives from *In XII Met.*, lect. 7, §2519 f. "Finis operantis" is somehow efficient: *In Lib. de Causis*, lect. 1. Cf. *infra*, footnote 209.

[167] *De Sp. Cr.*, a. 9, ad 6m.

[168] *De Pot.*, q. 1, a. 1 c; cf. *In I Sent.*, d. 3, q. 4, a. 2, ad 4m; d. 42, q. 1, a. 1 ad 1m.

[169] *In I Sent.*, d. 40, q. 1, a. 1, ad 1m. Though doubt is cast upon the authenticity of this part of the response (see ed. Mandonnet, I, 943), other pas-, sages are sufficiently similar, though perhaps not quite so explicit.

[170] *De Pot.*, q. 1, a. 1, ad 1m.

[171] *Ibid.*, q. 2, a. 2 c. Cited *supra*, footnote 115.

[172] *De Ver.*, q. 3, a. 2 c. The term, "form," is applied to the inner word here, not as form that is principle of the act of understanding, but as form that is principle of the artefact; cf. *Quodlib. V*, a. 9 c., and "idea operati," *Sum. Theol.*, I, q. 15, a. 2 c.

[173] *De Pot.*, q. 8, a. 1 c; cf. q. 9, a. 5 c.

these two meanings with regard to the operation or action of intellect; when that operation is meant in the sense of act, it is termed *intelligere*; but when by operation is meant that one act is grounding another, it is termed *dicere*.[174]

So much for a sketch of one scheme of metaphysical analysis applied by Aquinas to intellect. For it is only to be expected that there should be in his writings some evidence of another scheme of analysis that stands in more immediate conformity with Aristotelian thought. The most impressive example of such conformity occurs in the following incidental statement.

> ... forma recepta in aliquo non movet illud in quo recipitur; sed ipsum habere talem formam, est ipsum motum esse; sed movetur ab exteriori agente; sicut corpus quod calefit per ignem, non movetur a calore recepto, sed ab igne. Ita intellectus non movetur a specie iam recepta, vel a vero quod consequitur ipsam speciem; sed ab aliqua re exteriori quae imprimit in intellectum, sicut est intellectus agens, vel phantasia, vel aliquid huiusmodi.[175]

It may not be out of place to note how exactly this fits in both with general doctrine and with intellectual theory. It is in accord with the general doctrine that the efficient cause not merely produces the form but also produces the movement consequent to the form,[176] that what produces the *species* should also produce the consequent *intelligere*. It is in accord with the general doctrine that form is less perfect than operation,[177] and so not its proportionate cause, that the *species* should not move intellect to the act, *intelligere*. It is in accord with the general doctrine, "quidquid movetur ab alio movetur,"[178] that intellect actuated by *species* should not produce its acts of understanding, just as the will actuated by a habit does not produce its act of willing the end; on the other hand, just as will actually willing the end moves

---

[174] *De Ver.*, q. 4, a. 2, ad 4m; "...dicere autem nihil est aliud quam ex se emittere verbum"; cf. *ibid.*, ad 5m; *De Pot.*, q. 9, a. 9, ad 8m (ser. lae); *Sum. Theol.*, I, q. 34, a. 1. ad 3m; *ibid.*, ad 2m.

[175] *De Ver.*, q. 22, a. 5, ad 8m.

[176] *C. Gent.*, IV, 59, §4; *Sum. Theol.*, I-II, q. 23, a. 4 c; q. 26, a. 2 c. Cf. any account of the theorem "generans movet gravia et levia quoad locum."

[177] Cf. *supra*, footnotes 150 & 151.

[178] *In I Sent.*, d. 8, q. 3, a. 1, ad 3m; and *passim*.

itself to willing the means,[179] so intellect actually understanding is able to utter, constitute, produce its inner word of definition or judgment. Further, the passage before us accords with specific intellectual doctrines. It makes it quite clear why the procession of the act of understanding is only a "processio operationis," while the procession of the act of defining or of judging is a "processio operati."[180] It is quite in harmony with the statement, "sicut enim esse consequitur formam, ita intelligere sequitur speciem intelligibilem,"[181] for no form is efficient cause of its *esse* and similarly *species* is not the efficient cause of *intelligere*. Again, it harmonizes with the parallel statement that "... intelligere, quod ita se habet ad intellectum in actu, sicut esse ad ens in actu";[182] for the *ens in actu* is not the efficient cause of its *esse*. Finally, of course, there is no opposition between this scheme of analysis and the preceding; when (intellect actuated by) *species* is said to be the principle of action or the principle of operation, it is not said to be the principle of an effect; as we have seen, these two are repeatedly distinguished by St. Thomas.

OBJECT

The importance of recognizing the Aristotelian, as well as the Avicennist, scheme of analysis becomes fully apparent, however, only when one turns to the Thomist theory of the object. For this theory is Aristotelian. After defining soul generically, Aristotle had raised the problem of differentiating between the souls of plants, animals, and men.[183] The distinction of these essences, he maintained, depended on the distinction of their respective potencies; the distinction of the potencies depended on the distinction of their acts; the distinction of the acts depended on the distinction of their objects.[184] This series of dependences provided

---

[179] *De Malo* q. 6, a. 1 c; *Sum. Theol.*, I-II, q. 9, a. 3 c. This is a "processio operati" within the will but it is not relevant to trinitarian theory.
[180] *De Ver.*, q. 4, a. 2, ad 7m.
[181] *Sum. Theol.*, I, q. 14, a. 4 c.
[182] *Ibid.*, q. 34, a. 1, ad 2m.
[183] *De An.*, II, 3, 414b, 32 ff; lect. 6, §299.
[184] *Ibid.*, II, 4, 415a, 14-22; lect. 6, §§304-306.

Aquinas with his method to determine the nature of the human soul.[185]

The precise relation between object and act was described by Aquinas in terms of efficient causality. There were two opposite cases. On the one hand, the potency in question may be receptive, and then the object produces the act. On the other hand, the potency in question may be efficient, and then the act produces the objects as its term. Since the former of these alternatives has been forced into oblivion by neglect of the Aristotelian scheme of analysis with a consequent misinterpretation of the implications of the Avicennist scheme, I had best quote.

> Omnis enim animae operatio, vel est actus potentiae activae, vel passivae. Obiecta quidem potentiarum passivarum comparantur ad operationes earum ut activa, quia reducunt potentias in actum, sicut visibile visum, et omne sensibile sensum. Obiecta vero potentiarum activarum comparantur ad operationes ipsarum ut fines. Obiecta enim potentiarum activarum sunt operata ipsarum.[186]
>
> ... non enim distinguitur potentia activa a passiva ex hoc quod habet operationem: quia, cum cuiuslibet potentiae animae tam activae quam passivae sit operatio aliqua, quaelibet potentia animae esset activa. Cognoscitur autem eorum distintio per comparationem potentiae ad obiectum. Si enim obiectum se habeat ad potentiam ut patiens et transmutatum, sic erit potentia activa; si autem e converso se habet ut agens et movens, sic erit potentia passiva....[187]
>
> Actus autem ex obiectis speciem habent: nam si sint actus passivarum potentiarum, obiecta sunt activa; si autem sunt activarum potentiarum, obiecta sunt ut fines.[188]
>
> Ratio autem actus diversificatur secundum diversam rationem obiecti. Omnis enim actio vel est potentiae activae vel passivae. Obiectum autem comparatur ad actum potentiae passivae, sicut principium et causa movens; color enim inquantum movet visum, est principium visionis. Ad actum autem potentiae activae comparatur obiectum ut terminus et finis; sicut augmentativae virtutis obiectum est quantum perfectum, quod est finis augmenti.[189]

---

[185] *In III Sent.*, d. 23, q. 1, a. 2, ad 3m; *Sum. Theol.*, I, q. 87, a. 3 c.

[186] *In II de An.*, lect. 6, §305.

[187] *De Ver.*, q. 16, a. 1, ad 13m; cf. *Sum. Theol.*, I-II, q. 18, a. 2, ad 3m.

[188] *Q. D. de An.*, a. 13 c.

[189] *Sum. Theol.*, I, q. 77, a. 3 c. Observe that these definitions of "object" do not contain the word, "attingere," which is as much in need of definition

Equipped only with the Avicennist scheme of analysis, an interpreter will "explain" these passages right up to the point where
he debates whether Aquinas conceived the operation of sensation to
terminate immanently at some *species sensibilis expressa* or else,
without any such immanent product, to terminate with magnificent
realism at the present external real thing. No doubt such a debate
must arise if the object is always a term. No doubt the object
must always be a term, if the potency can be passive only with
respect to the reception of *species*, for then the active object can
be active and so can be object only with respect to the *species*
and not with respect to the subsequent act, action, or operation.
No doubt, finally, one arrives at these conclusions when one proceeds in the light of general principles formulated by attending
only to the Avicennist scheme of analysis. But I would submit
that taking into consideration the Aristotelian scheme of analysis,
one can omit such explanation and accept what Aquinas wrote
as a satisfactory account of what Aquinas thought.

In the passages quoted Aquinas states that the object of the
passive potency is active, not with respect to the *species* alone,
but with respect to the act, the action, the operation of the potency.
The coherence of this position with general Thomist doctrine
has engaged us through considerations of *actus perfecti*, *pati*,
potentia activa, and *duplex actio*. We may perhaps be permitted,
after this somewhat lenghty preamble, to point out that Aquinas
as a matter of fact actually does say that *sentire* is a *pati* and
that *intelligere* is a *pati*, and then to present our daring hypothesis

as is "object." They are in terms of the elementary concepts, active and passive
potency, agent, effect, and end. Since receptive potency can be actuated
only by agents of a given kind and since limited efficient potency can produce
effects only of a given kind, there is a "ratio formalis obiecti" (*Sum. Theol.*
I, q. 1, a. 3 c), an "obiectum... sub cuius ratione omnia referuntur ad po-
tentiam vel habitum" (*ibid.*, a. 7 c), a "propria ratio obiecti" (*ibid.*, q. 45, a. 4,
ad 1m), a "ratio obiecti quam per se respicit... potentia..." (*ibid.*, q. 77, a. 3,
ad 4m; cf. ad 2m), a "communis ratio obiecti" (*ibid.*, q. 82, a. 4, ad 1m) which
defines the specific function relating object, act, and potency or habit. Detailed application of this analysis is made to the external senses: *Sum. Theol.*,
I, q. 78, a. 3 c & ad 2m; *In II de An.*, lect. 13, §394. Though Aquinas employs
the term, "object," in a general and metaphysically defined sense, I am not
aware of any instance of "object" being employed in a cognitional context
and not meaning "known object."

that perhaps Aquinas meant what he said. In the following passages the reader will note that Aquinas is speaking not of some prior condition of sensation but of sensation itself and that Aquinas does not say that sensation has a prior condition or cause in some change but that it consists in a change and is completed in a change. I quote:

> ... sentire consistit in moveri et pati.[190] ... sentire consistit in quodam alterari et pati.[191] ... cognitio sensus perficitur in hoc ipso quod sensus a sensibili movetur.[192] Anima igitur sensitiva non se habet in sentiendo sicut movens et agens, sed sicut id quo patiens patitur.[193] ... si vero operatio illa consistit in passione, adest ei principium passivum, sicut patet de principiis sensitivis in animalibus.[194] ... sensum affici est ipsum eius sentire.[195] ... sentire perficitur per actionem sensibilis in sensum.[196] ... duplex operatio. Una secundum solam immutationem, et sic perficitur operatio sensus per hoc quod immutatur a sensibili.[197] ... cognito sensus exterioris perficitur per solam immutationem sensus a sensibili.[198]

With regard to external sense it would seem that the object is active, not merely inasmuch as it causes the *species*, but also inasmuch as it causes the act, action, operation of the sensitive potency.

Aquinas had the habit of quoting Aristotle to the effect that "intelligere est quoddam pati." In the *Sentences*, discussing the mutability proper to creatures, he concludes that creatures are mutable both inasmuch as they can lose what they possess and inasmuch as they can acquire what they do not possess; the latter is a true mutability, though in a broad sense, as when all reception is said to be a *pati* and *moveri*, for example, "intelligere quoddam pati est."[199] Again, discussing the meanings of *pati*, he urges that there

---

[190] *In II de An.*, lect. 10, § 350
[191] *Ibid.*, lect. 13, §393.
[192] *In IV Sent.*, d. 50, q. 1, a. 4 sol.
[193] *C. Gent.*, II, 57, §8.
[194] *Ibid.*, II, 76, §15.
[195] *Sum. Theol.*, I, q. 17, a. 2, ad 1m.
[196] *Ibid.*, q. 27, a. 5 c.
[197] *Ibid.*, q. 85, a. 2, ad 3m.
[198] *Quodlib. V*, a. 9, ad 2m.
[199] *In I Sent.*, d. 8, q. 3, a. 2 c. Cf. *De An.*, III, 4, 429a, 13-15 (lect. 7, §675 f.); 429b, 22-25 (lect. 9, §720, 722).

is no *pati proprie* in the intellect because it is immaterial, but still there is there an element of passion inasmuch as there is reception; and that is the meaning of "intelligere est pati quoddam."[200] Again, meeting the objection that the divine essence cannot be the object of created knowledge because the judged is to the judge as passive, he answered that on the contrary the sensible and intelligible objects are to sense and intellect as agent inasmuch as *sentire* and *intelligere* are a *pati quoddam.*[201] Arguing against Averroes, he made an antithesis of *agere* and *pati* and then urged, "Posse autem intelligere est posse pati: cum 'intelligere quoddam pati sit.'"[202] Proving that the possible intellect was a passive potency, he concluded, "Sic igitur patet quod intellegere nostrum est quoddam pati, secundum tertium modum passionis. Et per consequens intellectus est potentia passiva."[203] In these passages it is quite clear that Aquinas said that the act of understanding itself, *intelligere*, was a *pati.* Such statements fit in perfectly with the general doctrine of agent object and passive potency; they fit in perfectly with the general Aristotelian scheme of analysis that distinguishes neatly between nature, which is a principle of movement in the thing moved, and efficient potency, which is a principle of movement in the other or, if in self, then in self as other; nor is there any incompatibility between them and the Avicennist scheme of analysis except the merely apparent incompatibility that arises from the blunder of confusing what Aquinas distinguished—active potency as the principle of an operation and active potency as the principle of an effect.

But this, the reader will perhaps say, is all impossible. I am afraid I have not here the space to discuss abstract impossibilities. I am concerned with matters of fact, with what Aquinas said; and lest there be any misapprehension about Aquinas' ideas on the *actio manens in agente,* I proceed to observe that not only *sentire* and *intelligere* but also *velle* can be a *pati.* For with respect to the interior act of the will, the grace of God is operative and the will of man is "mota et non movens."[204] Though not stated

---

[200] *In III Sent.*, d. 15, q. 2, a. 1, sol. 2.
[201] *De Ver.*, q. 8, a. 1, ad 14m.
[202] *C. Gent.*, II, 60, §8.
[203] *Sum. Theol.*, I, q. 79, a. 2 c.
[204] *Ibid.*, I-II, q. 111, a. 2 c.

so explicitly, the same is true with respect to the act of willing the end as conceived in the *De Malo* and the *Prima Secundae*; for in these works the will moves itself only inasmuch as it is in act with respect to the end, but to that act it is moved by an external principle, God.[205] Finally, what is true of these later works with respect to willing the end, is true more generally in earlier works in which there appears no mention of self-movement in the will.[206]

NATURE AND EFFICIENCY

It has been seen that one of the difficulties Aquinas had in accepting Aristotle's definition of efficent potency was its lack of generality: it presupposed some "other" to receive the effect. The same difficulty, in a more acute form, arose with Aristotle's concept of an efficient cause; in its general formulation it was "unde principium motus";[207] but in the concrete it is moving, a matter of pushing, pulling, twirling, or carrying;[208] it is making, a matter of one contrary prevailing over its opposite—heat over cold, the wet over the dry, or vice versa;[209] it is generation, which is the term of such alterations, and the *generans* is the *per se* mover of the heavy and light,[210] just as the counsellor was of the actions of anyone following his advice.[211] It is in the light of such conceptions that one can understand why Aquinas considered only one of his five ways of proving God's existence to be an argument from the efficient cause.[212]

---

[205] *De Malo*, q. 6, a. 1 c; *Sum. Theol.*, I-II, q. 9, aa. 3, 4, 6.

[206] Cf. *Theological Studies*, III (1942), 534 f.

[207] *Phys.*, II, 3, 194b, 29 ff. (lect. 5, §7); *Met.*, A, 3, 983a, 30; 984a, 27; Δ, 2, 1013a, 29 ff. (V, lect. 2, § 765 ff.; cf. Λ, 4, 1070b, 22 & 28 (XII, lect. 4, §2468ff.).

[208] *Phys.*, VII, 2, 243a, 16 ff. (lect. 3, §4 ff.); cf. push and pull of heart in *In III de An.*, lect. 15, §835.

[209] *De Gen. et Corr.*, I, 7, 323b, 17—324a, 24. Aquinas' commentary does not go beyond chapter 5. However, this is the principal source of the idea of causality as the victory of the agent over the patient; e.g. *C. Gent.*, II, 30, §13. It also is the context of the statement that the end is only metaphorically ποιητικόν (324b, 15).

[210] *In VIII Phys.*, lect. 8.

[211] *In II Phys.*, lect. 5, §5.

[212] *Sum. Theol.*, I, q. 2, a. 3 c, Secunda via....

Aristotelian influence gave formal causality a preponderant role. A cause is that on which the being of something else follows. Absolutely, the form is the cause, for it is the *causa essendi*. In considering the *immobilia*, only formal causality is relevant. But insofar as things become, three other causes are to be taken into account, the matter, the agent which reduces potency to act, and the end to which the action of the agent tends.[213] It is this viewpoint that explains such statements as that form gives being, simply to substance, qualifiedly to accident,[214] that form keeps things in being,[215] that form has two effects with *esse* as its first effect and operation as its second effect.[216] It is in this sense of formal cause and formal effect that one has to understand the statement in the *De Veritate*: action and passion are confined to the production and reception of *species*; the act of understanding follows upon that action or passion as effect follows cause.[217]

A more complex problem arises from the proof that potency is distinct from substance. In the *Sentences* it is argued that a proper and immediate effect must be proportionate to its cause; therefore, since operation is an accident, potency must also be an accident.[218] Are cause and effect formal or efficient? In favor of the latter view is the fact that a response speaks of "forma accidentalis ... per quam producitur operatio."[219] On the other hand, one may insist on the preposition "per" and add that Aquinas shortly affirms "quidquid movetur, ab alio movetur."[220] But that is not all. In the *Summa* and in the *De Spiritualibus Creaturis*, the potency to an accidental operation must itself be an accident because of the very Aristotelian rule[221] that "proprius actus fit in propria potentia."[222] There is, then, some evolution or at least clarification

---

[213] *In II Phys.*, lect. 10, §15.
[214] *Sum. Theol.*, I, q. 76, a. 4 c.
[215] *Ibid.*, q. 59, a. 2 c; q. 9, a. 2 c.
[216] *Ibid.*, q. 42, a. 1, ad 1m; I-II, q. 111, a. 2 c.
[217] *De Ver.*, q. 8, a. 6 c.
[218] *In I Sent.*, d. 3, q. 4, a. 2 sol.
[219] *Ibid.*, ad 3m. Cf. *Sum. Theol.*, I, q. 77, a. 1, ad 4m.
[220] *In I Sent.*, d. 8, q. 3, a. 1, ad 3m.
[221] *De An.*, II, 2, 414a, 25 (lect. 4, §277); cf. II, lect. 11, §366; lect. 19, §483 ff.
[222] *Sum. Theol.*, I, q. 54, a. 3 c; q. 77, a. 1 c; q. 79, a. 1 c; *De Sp. Cr.*, a. 11 c.

of thought. None the less, one can read in the *Summa* that the substance is productive of its proper accidents.[223] Does this *productivum* mean efficient causality? Hardly, for in answering the objection, "quidquid movetur, ab alio movetur," Aquinas stated that the emanation of proper accidents from substance was not a transmutation—the term regularly employed in translating Aristotle's definition of efficient potency—but a natural resultance.[224] To attempt to determine to just what extent the doctrine of the *Summa* revises the doctrine of the *Sentences* and, again, to what extent differences are merely verbal, is too nice a question to be undertaken here.

The *De Virtutibus* commonly is considered to pertain to the second Paris period, but it has been noted to contain views not found outside the *Sentences*.[225] It affirms that subject is to accident as cause to effect, because the subject is the *per se* principle of the accidents.[226] This is quite compatible with natural resultance. But it also states that habits are the *causae effectivae* of acts, and the context parallels this relation with that of medicine to its effect, health.[227] The passage is more than reminiscent of the statement in the *Sentences* that operation is produced through accidental form; but really it can hardly mean anything very different from the statement of the *Prima Secundae* that habit is a *principium operationis*.[228]

It probably will occur to the reader that Aquinas would not have used the terms "cause" and "effect," "productive" and "effective," if he had not meant something very much like efficient causality. That is quite true. The difference between the efficient potency and the natural potency, if I may use that term, is not that the former is ontologically perfect while the latter is not; it is not that the former is a principle while the latter is not; it is not that the

An intermediate position is given in *Quodlib. X*, a. 5, and perhaps also in *Q. D. de An.*, a. 12 c.

223 *Sum. Theol.*, I, q. 77, a. 6 c.

224 *Ibid.*, ad 3m.

225 See de Guibert, *Les doublets de S. Thomas d'Aquin*, p. 108, on *De Caritate*, a. 2, ad 17m; also Simonin, "Du problème de l'amour," *Arch. d'hist. litt. doct. M. A.*, VI (1931), 179, on *De Spe*, a. 3, and on *De Caritate*, a. 3.

226 *De Virt. in Comm.*, a. 3 c.

227 *Ibid.*, a. 12, ad 5m; cf. a. 1, ad 14m.

228 *Sum. Theol.*, I-II, q. 49, a. 3, ad 1m.

former is a principle of movement, in all or any of the senses of the word, movement, while the latter is not. The one difference is that efficient potency is a principle of movement in the other or in self as other, while natural potency is a principle of movement in the selfsame.[229]

That the greater ontological perfection and the greater contribution to the effect can pertain to the recipient is clear enough from sensation; for sensation is what it is because it is immaterial, and it is immaterial because of the mode of reception of the patient.[230] Hence, in dealing with an Augustinian text that contained the Augustinian view of the activity of soul, Aquinas can concede that the *species sensibilis* as sensed is not due to the object but to the virtue of soul.[231] With regard to intellect, unambiguous illustrations are hard to find because man possesses not only an *intellectus possibilis* but also an *intellectus agens*. On the other hand, as soon as the theory of God moving the will to the act of willing the end was proposed, Aquinas immediately perceived a difficulty; that difficulty to a modern Scholastic would be in all probability that man must be the efficient cause of his own operation, action, act, willing; but to Aquinas the difficulty was that the act must be not violent but natural; he noticed it both in the *De Malo* and in the *Prima Secundae*, and his answers run as follows:

> ... voluntas aliquid confert cum a Deo movetur; ipsa enim est quae operatur sed mota a Deo; et ideo motus eius quamvis sit ab extrinseco sicut a primo principio non tamen est violentus.[232]
> ... hoc non sufficit ad rationem violenti, quod principium sit extra, sed oportet addere quod nullam conferat vim patiens. Quod non contingit dum voluntas ab exteriori movetur; nam ipsa est quae vult, ab alio tamen mota.[233]

Now what does the patient, the will moved by God, when it is moved by God, while it is moved by God, confer or contribute? It operates. It wills. In this case the operation is an *operatio receptiva*, just as *sentire* is a *pati* of sense and just as *intelligere*

---

[229] *Met.*, Θ, 8, 1049b, 5-10 (IX, lect. 7, §1844 f).

[230] *In II de An.*, lect. 24, §§551-54.

[231] *De Malo*, q. 16, a. 12, ad 2m.

[232] *Ibid.*, q. 6, a. 1, ad 4m.

[233] *Sum. Theol.*, I-II, q. 9, a. 4, ad 2m; cf. ad 1m, 3m; cf. also q. 6, aa. 4 & 5 (esp. a. 4, ad 2m).

is a *pati* of the possible intellect. The will operates inasmuch as it is the will that is actuated. The will contributes inasmuch as an act received in the will has to be a "willing," not because it is act, nor merely because of the extrinsic mover, but proximately because act is limited by the potency in which it is received.

It is the reality of such and similar contributions that underlies the conception of *potentia activa* as principle of action and as formal principle of action; as well, it underlies the usage of cause and effect, productive and effective, that we have noted. Just as form is principle of action and formal principle of action, so too we may read that the substance or subject with respect to its accidents is a "causa ... quodammodo activa" and a "principium activum."[234] Just as the principle of action or operation is distinguished from the principle of an effect, so too the activity of the subject with respect to the emanation of its accidents is no efficiency but natural resultance.[235] To complete the parallel, one need only add that the necessity of action proceeding from form is like the necessity of accidents proceeding from substance.[236] But the necessity of an accident that emanates from substance does not make superfluous an efficient cause to produce the accident: there cannot be a creature without the dependence named "creatio passiva";[237] but that relation is "quoddam ... concreatum."[238] In like manner the necessity of an operation or action emanating from form, from its active principle, from its formal principle, from active potency, does not dispense with the necessity of an efficient potency.

CONCLUSIONS

First, there seem to be no notable variations in the concept of procession and, in particular, there seems no reason for supposing that the doctrine of *De Ver.*, q. 4, a. 2, ad 7m was retracted or revised later: the act of love with respect to an end is, as proceeding

---

[234] *Ibid.*, I, q. 77, a. 6, ad 2m.
[235] *Ibid.*, ad 3m. Cf. *De An.*, II, 4, 415b, 8-28 (lect. 7, §§319-23). See J. de Finance, *Être et Agir* (Paris, 1945) p. 212.
[236] *C. Gent.*, II, 30, §12.
[237] *Quodlib. VII*, a. 10, ad 4m.
[238] *De Pot.*, q. 3, a. 3, ad 2m.

from the will, "processio operationis," but as proceeding from the inner word, "processio operati." Second, the *actio manens in agente* is act and perfection; as act, it admits no further description; for description is of limitation, and limitation is due not to act but to potency; but as act of someone, it has the characteristic of being an ulterior actuation of what already is completed and perfected by the specific essence of the act; it is act beyond essence and so is contrasted with the act of the incomplete, which is act as process towards essence. Incidentally, it was Scotus who affirmed immanent action to lie in the first species of the predicament, quality.[239] I have not noticed such a statement in Aquinas, but I suggest that it would be Thomistic to affirm that, as *esse* is substantial, so immanent act is qualitative;[240] for the essence that *esse* actuates is substance and the essence that immanent act actuates is a quality. Thirdly, among the various meanings of *passio, pati*, many are opposed to immanent act; but *pati* in the metaphysical sense of receiving is opposed only to the exercise of efficient causality in an equally strict metaphysical sense; hence *pati* is not incompatible with immanent act or with *actio* or *operatio* in the sense of immanent act; on the contrary, inasmuch as immanent act is a perfection received in a creature, necessarily it is a *pati*. Fourthly, a distinction is necessary between efficient potency, principle of act in the other or in self as other, and natural potency, principle of act in the selfsame; the active and passive potencies of *De Potentia* q. 1, a. 1 and the active and passive principles of *Contra Gentiles* III, 23 are sub-divisions of natural potency and so both are receptive potencies and principles; hence the apparent paradox that an active potency or principle is also receptive. This paradox is only apparent: what is opposed to receptive potency is efficient potency and not some sub-division of natural potency. On the other hand, the appearances are impressive: just as Aristotle was handicapped in writing his *De Anima* by the technical elaborations of his *Physics*, so Aquinas was handicapped both by Aristotle's lack of generality in conceiving the efficient cause and by the initial strong influence of Avicenna; for him to clarify the notion of *potentia activa* by appealing to

---

[239] Scotus, *In I Sent.* (*Op. Ox.*), d. 3, q. 6 (ed. Vives, IX, 304 ff.).
[240] Cf. footnotes 181 and 182 above.

the notion of causal efficiency was impossible, for the latter notion was just as much in need of clarification; hence only indirectly can we observe differences that are crucial, inasmuch as "principium motus" and even "principium activum motus" is not the "movens" or the "motor"; inasmuch as "principium operationis vel actionis" does not mean the same thing as "principium effectus, operati, termini producti" and does not even necessarily imply it; inasmuch as form is cause of *esse* and operation; inasmuch as subject is cause, active principle, somehow active cause, and productive of accidents which none the less emanate by a natural resultance. Fifthly, the foregoing clarification of Thomist usage and principles is of paramount importance in grasping Thomist metaphysics as applied to psychology; a failure to distinguish between efficient and natural potency results in a negation of the division of objects into agent and terminal, and the elimination of the agent object provides a metaphysical scheme into which Thomist psychology does not fit; further, natural potency which, though receptive, none the less makes a most significant contribution to its act, tends to disappear to be replaced by efficient forms and habits in need of a divine *praemotio physica* which, I have argued elsewhere,[241] cannot be said to be a doctrine stated or implied by Aquinas; and incidentally, we may ask whether this neglect of natural potency has not some bearing on unsatisfactory conceptions of obediential potency.

The coherence of present conclusions with the psychological data already assembled may be noted briefly. The distinction between agent intellect and possible intellect is a distinction between an efficient potency that produces and a natural potency that receives. The distinction between the possible intellect of one that is learning and the possible intellect of one in possession of a science is a distinction between the *De Potentia's* passive potency to the reception of form and its active potency to the exercise of operation in virtue of form. The distinction between *intelligere* and *dicere* is a distinction between the two meanings of action, operation: *intelligere* is action in the sense of act; *dicere* is action in the sense of operating an effect. The distinction between agent object and terminal object is to be applied twice.

---

[241] *Theological Studies*, III (1942), 375-402, 533-78.

On the level of intellectual apprehension the agent object is the *quidditas rei materialis*, not τὸ τί ἐστιν but τὸ τί ἦν εἶναι, known in and through a phantasm illuminated by agent intellect; this agent object is the *objectum proprium intellectus humani*; it is the object of insight. Corresponding to this agent object there is the terminal object of the inner word; this is the concept, and the first of concepts is *ens*, the *objectum commune intellectus*. Again, on the level of judgment the agent object is the objective evidence provided by sense and/or empirical consciousness, ordered conceptually and logically in a *reductio ad principia*, and moving to the critical act of understanding. Corresponding to this agent object, there is the other terminal object, the inner word of judgment, the *verum*, in and through which is known the final object, the *ens reale*.

Here, as is apparent, metaphysics and psychology go hand in hand, and the metaphysical analysis is but the more general form of the psychological analysis. Souls are distinguished by their potencies, potencies by their acts, acts by their objects. The final object of intellect is the real; the real is known through an immanent object produced by intellect, the true; the true supposes a more elementary immanent object also produced by the intellect, the definition. This production is not merely utterance, *dicere*, but the utterance of intelligence in act, or rationally conscious disregard of the irrelevant, of critical evaluation of all that is relevant, of *intelligere*. This *intelligere* can be what it is only if there are objects to move it as well as the objects that it produces: the *intelligere* that expresses itself in judgment is moved by the relevant evidence; the *intelligere* that expresses itself in definition is moved by illuminated phantasm. But evidence as relevant and phantasm as illuminated are not mere sensible data; hence besides the sensitive potencies and the possible intellect there is needed an agent intellect. Finally, as the contrast between the labor of study and the ease of subsequent mastery manifests, there are forms or habits to be developed in the possible intellect—understanding for the grasp of principles, science for the grasp of implications, wisdom for right judgment on the validity both of principles and of conclusions; they come to us through acts of understanding; they stand to acts of understanding as first act to second; and like the second acts, they are produced by agent objects which themselves are instruments of agent intellect.

IV

VERBUM AND ABSTRACTION

Two general observations on Thomist trinitarian theory have
inspired this inquiry into the concept of *verbum*.[1] The first was
that the analogy to the procession of the Divine Word lies in the
analysis, not of knowledge in general, but of intellectual reflection,
of rational consciousness.[2] The second was that the analogy to
the procession of the Holy Spirit lies in the act of love, not as
within the will for that is *processio operationis*, but as grounded
in a perfect inner word, a judgment of value.[3] Now because rational consciousness has received remarkably little attention from
commentators and manual writers, not only in their trinitarian
thought but also in their psychology and its corresponding metaphysics, a rather lengthy investigation has been forced upon us.
The conclusions to which we have been brought may be summarized by stating: (1) that there exists an act of understanding
(*intelligere*), (2) that rational consciousness (*dicere*) is the act of
understanding as ground and origin of inner words of conceptualization and judgment, and (3) that inner words proceed from acts of
understanding, not on some obscure analogy of the emergence
of terminal states at the end of material processes,[4] but as *actus*

[1] See chapters I and II above.

[2] See chapter I.

[3] See chapter III.

[4] When insight into phantasm is overlooked, the *intelligere* has to produce
the *verbum* to have an object. It truly produces yet is not predicamental action
(material movement as from the mover) except eminently: it has the virtue
and actuality of producing without the potentiality, movement, imperfection
of action. As looking at its object, it is a quality which is a second act. See
John of St. Thomas, *Curs. Theol., In Im.*, q. 27, disp. 32, a. 5, nn. 18, 37;
ed. Desclée, 1946, vol. IV, fasc. 2, pp. 74, 80. On our analysis an *intelligere*
that is producing before being a knowing is merely spontaneous activity
and not the ground of an *emanatio intelligibilis*. The *intelligere* exercises
efficient causality; predicamental action, as defined, is the effect *in fieri* and
so, even *eminenter*, does not include the exercise of efficient causality. Finally,
a quality is an essence and a second act is beyond essence; quality is to second
act, as habit to operation or as substantial essence to existence.

ex actu.[5] Thus, the center of Thomist[6] analysis of intellect is held, not by such products of intelligence in act as concepts, nexus, judgments, syllogisms, but by intelligence in act itself. Even reasoning for Aquinas is not simply a matter of concepts and judgments but principally a progress from a less to a more complete act of understanding.[7] Again, the speculative habits of *intellectus, scientia, sapientia,* stand to acts of understanding as first acts to second; and this relation is the same as that of species to *intelligere,* of form to *esse,* of *principium actionis* to *actio manens in agente.*[8] Finally, the objects of Thomist intellect are the objects of understanding: first, there is the moving object of direct understanding, namely, the actuated intelligibility of what is presented by imagination; secondly, there is the terminal object of direct understanding, the essence expressed in a definition; thirdly, there is the moving object of reflective understanding, the aggregate of what is called the evidence on an issue; fourthly, there is the terminal object of reflective understanding, the *verum* expressed in a judgment; fifthly, there is the transcendent object, reality, known imperfectly in prior acts but perfectly only through the truth of judgment.[9]

This intellectualist interpretation of Thomist thought runs counter throughout to the currently accepted conceptualist view, but the point of most apparent conflict lies in the issue to which conceptualists attend almost exclusively, the abstraction of concepts. To this issue we may now direct our attention, asking: first, what is the matter from which intellect abstracts; secondly, what is the immateriality by which it knows; thirdly, what is the formative abstraction of the concept; fourthly, what is the prior apprehensive abstraction of insight into phantasm; and fifthly, what is intellectual knowledge of the singular.

---

[5] *C. Gent.,* IV, 14, §3 (i.e., the third paragraph in the Leonine manual edition).

[6] I wish to employ the distinction whereby "Thomist" means "of St. Thomas," and "Thomistic" means "of his school."

[7] *Sum. Theol.,* I, q. 79, a. 8 c.

[8] See pages 112 ff, 124 ff above.

[9] *Ibid.,* 433 ff.

THE ANALOGY OF MATTER

The old naturalists had concluded, not only from beds and tables to an underlying subject, wood, but also from wood and bones to an element, earth, and from gold and bronze (they could be melted) to an element, water. Aristotle accepted the principle of such analysis: any change is defined for thought by stating the underlying subject and the variable determination or form; and what holds for defining thought, also holds for the real thing.[10] But while he accepted the principle, he corrected the conclusion. The ultimate subject of change in the older philosophies had always been some sensible body; that was the stuff of the universe; it alone was substantial and permanent; all else was accidental and mutable.[11] Against this materialism Aristotle argued that every assignable object was subject to change; the element, air, could be changed into the element, water; and so he concluded that the ultimate subject of change could not be an assignable object; it could be neither *quid* nor *quantum* nor *quale* nor any other determinate type of reality;[12] it could not, of itself, be knowable;[13] its nature could be stated only by recourse to analogy.

> Quod igitur se habet ad ipsas substantias naturales, sicut se habet aes ad statuam, et lignum ad lectum, et quodlibet materiale et informe ad formam, hoc dicimus esse materiam primam.[14]
>
> ... materia prima... se habet ad formas substantiales, sicut materiae sensibiles ad formas accidentales.[15]
>
> (materia prima) ita se habet ad omnes formas et privationes, sicut se habet subjectum alterabile ad qualitates contrarias.[16]

Such is the defining analogy of matter. In its limit it defines prime matter which is proportionate to substantial form. And as prime matter of itself is not knowable, so substantial form has the complementary distinction of being knowable by intellect alone.[17]

[10] *In I Phys.*, lect. 13 §2: Ea in quae resolvitur definitio rei sunt componentia rem illam.

[11] *In II Phys.*, lect. 2 §1.

[12] *Met.* Z, 3, 1029a 20; *VII*, lect. 2 §1285.

[13] *Ibid.*, 10, 1036a 8; lect.- 10 §1496.

[14] *In I Phys.*, lect. 13 §9.

[15] *Ibid.*, lect. 15 §10.

[16] *In VIII Met.*, lect. 1 §1689.

[17] *In II de An.*, lect. 14 §420; lect. 13 §395 ff.

The full significance of this analogy is not easy to measure. It eliminates the materialism of the old naturalists for whom the real was the sensible.[18] It corrects the misguided intellectualism of Plato for whom the intelligible was real but not of this world. One might even say that by anticipation it puts in its proper place and perspective, that of prime matter, what Kant thought was the thing-in-itself. It does all this because it places in the most material of assignable material things an intelligible component known by our intellects and identifiable in our knowledge; that intelligible component, form, species, quiddity, has as much title to being named "cause" and "nature" as has matter itself; and what it is, is fixed by its relation to the *ratio rei*, the *ratio definitiva rei*, the *ratio quidditativa rei*.[19] Conversely, it is only because Aristotle's real thing is not the materialists' real thing that Aristotle was able to satisfy his own epistemological law: unless particulars are identical, at least inadequately, with their quiddities, then the former cannot be objects of scientific knowledge and the latter cannot be realities.[20]

But the significance of the analogy is not confined to its metaphysical limit of prime matter and substantial form. Besides prime matter, there are sensible and intelligible matter, common and individual matter, appendages of matter, parts of the matter, material and individual conditions. What are all these? The answer is simple if one grasps that natural form stands to natural matter as the object of insight (*forma intelligibilis*) stands to the object of sense (*materia sensibilis*).[21] But to convince conceptualists, a more detailed approach is necessary. Just as the correspondence between definitions and things was the ultimate ground of the analysis of change into subject, privation, and form,[22] whence proceeded the notion of prime matter, so the more detailed correspondence between parts of the definition and parts of the thing should bring to light the other elements in the analogy. Accordingly we proceed to sample a lengthy and complex Aristotelian discussion.[23]

---

18 *In VII Met.*, lect. 2 §1284.

19 *In II Phys.*, lect. 2 §3; lect. 5 §3 f.

20 *Met.*, Z, 6, 1031b 3 ff.; *VII*, lect. 5 §1363.

21 *De Ver.*, q. 10, a. 8, ad 1m (1ae ser.).

22 Cf. *sup.* note 10.

23 *Met.*, Z, 10 and 11; cf. *In Boet. de Trin.*, q. 5, a. 3.

Segments are parts of circles and letters are parts of syllables. Why is it that the definition of the circle makes no mention of segments, while the definition of the syllable must mention letters? A typical solution is found in the contrast between "curvature" and "snubness": curvature is curvature whether in a nose or not; but snubness is snubness only in a nose. In general one may say that as without proportionate matter there cannot be the corresponding material form (just as without a proportionate phantasm there cannot be the corresponding insight), so for different forms different measures of matter are necessary. There must be letters if there are to be syllables; but the necessary letters are not necessarily in wax or in ink or in stone; hence letters are *de ratione speciei* or *partes speciei*; but letters as in wax or as in ink or as in stone are *partes materiae*. Similarly, one cannot have a particular circle without having potential segments; but the notion of circle is prior to the notion of segment, since the latter cannot be defined without presupposing the notion of the former; and so one can appeal either to the potentiality of the segments or to the priority of the definition of circle to conclude that segments are, with respect to the circle, *partes materiae*.[24]

The notion of priority is of wide and nuanced application. The right angle is prior to the acute; the circle to the semi-circle; and man to hand or finger. In each of these instances the former is a whole and the latter a part; in each the definition of the former must be presupposed by a definition of the latter; in each, accordingly, the latter does not enter into the definition of the former and so is a *pars materiae*. But complex cases are not to be solved so simply. Parts of a living body cannot be defined without reference to their function in the whole; again, the whole itself cannot be defined without reference to its formal principle which constitutes it as a whole; accordingly, the soul and its potencies must be prior to the body and its parts. Still it does not follow that parts of the body are mere *partes materiae*, that "man" can be defined without bothering about corporal parts just as "circle" can be defined without bothering whether it be made of wood or of bronze. The difference arises because the principle of priority must here be complemented by the principle of proportion between

[24] *Met.*, Z, 10, 1034b 20 ff.; *VII*, lect. 9 §1461-63, 1474 ff.

form and matter; a circle requires no more than intelligible matter; man requires sensible matter;[25] and so while bronze and wood are not *de ratione speciei circuli* still flesh and bones are *de ratione speciei hominis.*[26]

A sufficient sample has been taken from Aristotle's involved discussion to make it plain that matter is not merely prime matter but also the matter that is sensibly perceived and imaginatively represented. If further one wishes to understand why the discussion is so complex, why Aristotle warned against simple rules of solution,[27] even perhaps a conceptualist might consider the hypothesis that the real principle of solution is neither one rule nor any set of rules but rather the fashioner of all rules, intelligence itself in act, determining what it takes as relevant to itself and so *de ratione speciei* and what it dismisses as irrelevant to itself and so pertaining to the *partes materiae.*

In any case let us close this section with a summary account of the analogy of matter. In the first instance matter is the matter of common sense, the wood of the table and the bronze in a statue. But unless corrected, that notion easily leads to materialism, whether the crude materialism of the old naturalists or the elaborate materialism of the nineteenth-century atomists who equally considered the real to be the sensible. On the other hand, the material world is neither sheer flux, as for Plato, nor unknowable in itself, as for Kant. The higher synthesis of these opposites lies in defining matter as what is known by intellect indirectly. Directly intellect knows forms, species, quiddities; but these knowns have antecedent suppositions, simultaneous suppositions, and consequents, all of which, as such, are indirectly known. Antecedent suppositions are matter in the sense that genus is named matter and specific difference is named form, and again in the sense that substance is named matter and accident is named form; such usage is Aristotelian and Thomist but still somewhat improper. Simultaneous suppositions fall into two classes: if they pertain to the intelligible unity of the form, as letters to syllable, they are parts of the form, *de ratione speciei,* and in Thomist usage

---

25 *Ibid.,* 1035b 2 ff.; 14 ff.; 1036b 24 ff.; lect. 10 and 11, §1483 ff., 1519.
26 Cf. *Sum. Theol.,* I, q. 85, a. 1 ad 2m.
27 *Met.,* Z, 10, 1036a 13 ff.

common matter; if they do not pertain to the intelligible unity of the form yet are ever included in some fashion in the concrete presentation, they are *partes materiae* or material conditions or individual matter. Finally, consequents that are contingent and potential, as segments to circles, are again *partes materiae*. Clearly, it is the second of these three types of indirectly knowns that offer the principal meaning of the term, matter, and it is this meaning that the analogy of matter considers chiefly. The general analogy is the proportion of wood to tables and bronze to statues; but the specifically Aristotelian analogy is that natural form is to natural matter as intelligible form is to sensible matter,[28] that is, as the object of insight is to the object of sense.

THE IMMATERIALITY OF KNOWING

It will be most convenient to begin from the theorem that knowing involves an identity in act of knower and known. This identity is an extension of the theorem in the *Physics* that affirms the identity of action and passion; one and the same real movement as from the agent is action and as in the patient is passion.[29] Now in the *De Anima* it is seen that this theorem holds no less with regard to operations (*actus perfecti*) than with regard to movements (*actus imperfecti*).[30] The one operation, sensation, is effected by the sensible object and received in the sensitive potency; as from the object, it is action; as in the subject, it is passion; thus, sounding is the action of the object and hearing the passion of the subject and so, by the theorem of identity, sounding and hearing are not two realities but one and the same.[31] From this theorem Aristotle immediately deduced, first, an alternative account of sensitive empirical consciousness,[32] secondly, a solution to the question whether unseen things are colored[33] and, thirdly, an explanation of the fact that excessive stimuli destroy senses.[34] Aquinas fails

---

[28] *De Ver.*, q. 10, a. 8 ad 1m (lae ser.).

[29] *Phys.*, III, 3, 202 a22-b29; lect. 4 and 5; cf. *Theological Studies*, III (1942), 377 ff.

[30] See pages 101 ff above.

[31] *De An.*, III, 2, 425b 26-426a 26; lect. 2 §591-96.

[32] *Ibid.*, §591.

[33] *Ibid.*, §594-96.

[34] *Ibid.*, §597 f.

to manifest the slightest difficulty concerning this theorem in his *Commentary*, yet rarely if ever does he employ it in his independent writings. There one may read repeatedly that "sensible in actu est sensus in actu, et intelligibile in actu est intellectus in actu." But the meaning is not the original Aristotelian identity in second act[35] but rather assimilation on the level of species.[36] Quite probably the cause of this shift from identity to assimilation was the terminological embroglio of "action" to which we have referred already.[37]

That knowing is by assimilation is a theorem offering no special difficulty. It was a matter of common consent: "hoc enim animis omnium communiter inditum fuit, quod simile simili cognoscitur."[38] Its grounds in specifically Aristotelian theory are reached easily: as the thing is the thing it is in virtue of its form or species, so too the knowing is the ontological reality it is in virtue of its own form or species; further, unless the form of the thing and the form of the knowing were similar, there would be no ground for affirming that the knowing was knowing the thing.

It is a short step from a theorem of assimilation to a theorem of immaterial assimilation. If knower and known must be similar on the level of form, there is no necessity, indeed no possibility, of assimilation on the level of matter. The contrary view had been advanced by Empedocles and against it Aristotle marshalled no less than ten arguments.[39] His own view was in terms of potency and act, action and passion: the sense in potency is unlike the sensible in potency;[40] but the sense in act is like the sensible object

---

[35] *Ibid.*, §592: unus et idem est actus sensibilis et sentientis.

[36] *Sum. Theol.*, I, q. 87, a. 1 ad 3m: Dicendum quod verbum illud Philosophi universaliter verum est in omni intellectu. Sicut enim sensus in actu est sensibile propter similitudinem sensibilis, quae est forma sensus in actu; ita intellectus in actu est intellectum in actu propter similitudinem rei intellectae, quae est forma intellectus in actu.

[37] *Theological Studies*, III (1942), 375-81; see pages 112-129 above.

[38] *Sum. Theol.*, I, q. 84, a. 2 c.

[39] *De An.*, I, 5, 409a 19-411a 7.

[40] *In II de An.*, lect. 12 §382. None the less there must be a proportion and, in that sense, a similitude between object and potency, else eyes would hear and ears see. Cf. *ibid.*, lect. 11 §366; *Sum. Theol.*, I, q. 12, aa. 2 and 5 applies this to the beatific vision.

on the general ground that effects are similar to their causes;[41] it followed that the senses were receptive of sensible forms without the matter natural to those forms, much as wax is receptive of the imprint of a seal without being receptive of the gold of which the seal is made.[42] In human intellect immaterial assimilation reaches its fulness in immaterial reception: not only is the matter of the agent not transferred to the recipient, as the gold of the seal is not transferred to the wax; not only is the form of the agent not reproduced in matter natural to it, as in sensation; but the form of the agent object is received in a strictly immaterial potency, the possible intellect. Thus, the structures of sense and intellect differ radically. The sensitive potency, such as sight, is form of the sensitive organ, the eye; just as soul is the form of the body.[43] Sensation itself is the operation not merely of the organ nor merely of the potency but of the compound of organ and potency.[44] Directly, the sensible object acts on the sensitive organ;[45] but since matter and form, organ and potency are one, the movement of the organ immediately involves the operation of its form, the sense.[46] On the other hand, the possible intellect is not the form of any organ;[47] it has no other nature but ability to receive;[48] it stands to all intelligible forms as prime matter stands to all sensible forms;[49] and precisely because it is in act none of the things to be known, it offers no subjective resistance

[41] *De An.*, 416a 35 ff; 417a 18; lect. 10 §351 and 357.

[42] *De An.*, II, 12, 424a 17 ff; lect. 24 §551.

[43] *Ibid.*, lect. 2 §239, 241; *Sum. Theol.*, I, q. 85, a. 1 c.

[44] *De Pot.*, q. 3, a. 9 ad 22m; *Sum. Theol.*, I, q. 75, a. 2 ad 3m; a. 3; q. 77, a. 5 ad 3m; q. 84, a. 6; q. 89, a. 1 ad 1m; *In I de An.*, lect. 2 §19 f.; lect. 10 §159; *II*, lect. 2 §241; lect. 12 §377; *III*, lect. 7 §684-88, cf. 679-82; *C. Gent.*, II, 57, 82; cf. 49 §8, 50, §4.

[45] *De Unitate Int.*, cap. I, ed. Keeler, §24: Sensitiva enim pars non recipit in se species sed in organo; pars autem intellectiva non recipit eas in organo sed in se ipsa....

[46] *Ibid.*, §23: Sensus enim proportionatur suo organo et trahitur quodam modo ad suam naturam; unde etiam secundum immutationem organi immutatur operatio sensus. Cf. §35, 37, 38, 46. See the account of Cajetan's position in Yves Simon. *Rev. de Phil.*, IV (1933), 228-58. Also see pages 130-131 above.

[47] *Sum. Theol.*, I, q. 75, a. 2 et *passim*.

[48] *De An.*, III, 4, 429a 21; cf. 429b 30 ff.

[49] *Sum. Theol.*, I, q. 87, a. 1 c.

to objective knowing.[50] Thus, possible intellect stands to its first
act, which is science, as the sensitive organ stands to its first act,
which is the sensitive potency;[51] both sensation and understanding
are the operations of compounds, but sensation is the operation
of a material compound, while understanding is the operation of
an immaterial compound; since, then, *operari sequitur esse*, the
substantial form of man must be subsistent but the substantial
form of a brute cannot be subsistent.[52]

We have considered immaterial assimilation and immaterial
reception; beyond these there is a general theorem that knowledge
is by immateriality. If this general theorem is taken out of its
historical context and made the premise of merely dialectical
deductions, endless difficulties arise. But obviously the general
theorem cannot have a different meaning than its particular applications. It does not mean, then, that other patients receive
both matter and form from agents, but cognoscitive potencies
receive only form: the wax does not receive the matter of the seal.[53]
It does not mean that other recipients are material but cognoscitive
potencies are immaterial: both outer and inner senses are forms
of corporeal organs; and they know the particular because the
species they receive are individuated by the matter and the determinate dimensions of the organs they inform.[54] It does not mean
that objects have to be material to be really distinct from the
subjects that know them: angels are immaterial and really distinct from the similitudes by which other angels know them.[55]
But if the object does not have to be material, nor the subject
immaterial, and the action of the object on the subject has no
particular claim to immateriality, what can be the meaning of the
general theorem? In the first place, its meaning is negative;
the knower need not be the known; assimilation indeed is necessary
but it is on the level of form and not that of matter; complete
assimilation, both material and formal, would make the knower

[50] *Ibid.*, q. 75, a. 2 c.
[51] *De An.*, II, 5, 417 b 16 ff.; lect. 12 §373 f.
[52] *C. Gent.*, II, 57, 82; *Sum. Theol.*, I, q. 75, aa. 3 and 6; *De Unit. Int.*, cap.
1, ed. Keeler §35ff.
[53] *In II de An.*, lect. 24 §551 ff.
[54] *De Ver.*, q. 10, a. 5 c; q. 8, a. 11 c.
[55] *Sum. Theol.*, I, q. 56, a. 2 ad 3m; *De Sp. Cr.*, a. 8 ad 14m.

be the known but would give no guarantee of knowledge. Out of this negative and anti-Empedoclean meaning there arises a positive meaning. The form of the knowing must be similar to the form of the known, but also it must be different; it must be similar essentially for the known to be known; but it must differ modally for the knower to know and not merely be the known. Modal difference of forms results from difference in recipients: the form of color exists naturally in the wall but intentionally in the eye because wall and eye are different kinds of recipient;[56] similarly, angels have a natural existence on their own but an intentional existence in the intellects of other angels.[57] Thus, the negative concept, immateriality, acquires a positive content of intentional existence; and intentional existence is a modal difference resulting from difference in the recipient. There remains a still further step to be taken. Why have forms two different modes of existence, natural or intentional, according to difference in recipients? It is because Thomist system conceives perfection as totality: if finite things which cannot be the totality are somehow to approximate towards perfection which is totality, they must somehow be capable not only of being themselves but also in some manner the others as others; but being themselves is natural existence and being the others as others is intentional existence. Moreover, if potency and especially matter are the principles of limitation, tying things down to being merely the things they are, it follows that the intentional mode of existence results from the negation of potency and specifically from the negation of matter.[58] It is only in the perspective of such systematic principles that the general theorem, knowledge is by immateriality, can be understood.

FORMATIVE ABSTRACTION

We have been considering the matter from which intellect abstracts, and we turn to abstraction itself. In this section we consider the abstraction that supposes the formation of an inner word and yields knowledge of "rem ut separatam a conditionibus

---

[56] *In II de An.*, lect. 24 §551-54; cf. *C. Gent.*, II, 50, §5.

[57] *Sum. Theol.*, I, q. 56, a. 2 ad 3m.

[58] *Ibid.*, q. 84, a. 2 c; *De Ver.*, q. 2, a. 2 c.

materialibus sine quibus in rerum natura non existit."⁵⁹ In the
next section we shall consider a prior apprehensive abstraction,
already described as insight into phantasm;⁶⁰ its object differs modally from the object of formative abstraction, for by it man knows
not the abstract object of thought, the universal that is common
to many, but the universal existing in the particular,⁶¹ the "quidditas sive natura in materia corporali existens."⁶² On the conceptualist interpretation of Aquinas, formative abstraction is unconscious and non-rational; it precedes apprehensive abstraction.
On the intellectualist interpretation, which we find more in accord
with the text of Aquinas, the apprehensive abstraction precedes
and the consequent formative abstraction is an act of rational
consciousness. In dealing with this issue we begin from the more
obvious and proceed towards the more fundamental aspects of
Thomist thought.

Elementary reflection on abstraction is concerned with common
names, the corresponding concepts, and the relation of concepts to
reality. Two samples of Thomist treatment of these matters are
given. In the *Sentences* it is explained that a *ratio* is what intellect
apprehends of the meaning of a name. No ultimate difference
arises whether the meaning be primitive or derived. In either
case to attribute a *ratio* to a reality is to attribute not the active
meaning (which it an act of the mind or the intention of an act)
but the passive meant; it is to affirm that in the thing there is
what corresponds to the concept, as what is signified or meant
corresponds to sign or meaning.⁶³ The same issue is treated more
expeditiously in the *Summa*. Names are signs of meanings, and
meanings are similitudes of things; it follows that names refer to
things through concepts in our intellects; and so the measure of
the use of names is the knowledge in our intellects. Because we
know the essence of man, the name "man" signifies the definition
which expresses the essence of man. But we do not know the

⁵⁹ *C. Gent.*, I, 53 §3.
⁶⁰ See pages 10-32 above.
⁶¹ *Sum. Theol.*, I, q. 85, a. 3 ad 1m; a. 2 ad 2m.
⁶² *Ibid.*, q. 84, a. 7 c.
⁶³ *In I Sent.*, d. 2, q. 1, a. 3 sol.

essence of God, and so since meaning is consequent to knowledge we cannot use names to express the essence of God.[64]

This clear reduction of meaning to knowledge suggests that one had better approach the problem of abstraction on a profounder level, namely, that of knowledge and especially that of science. Now science is of the necessary and universal; but all material things are contingent and particular. A man is composed not of this sort of form and this sort of matter but of this form and this matter.[65] What then is the possibility of science? It was, we read, this very problem that forced Plato to posit his separate ideas. Since he accepted the opinion of Cratylus and Heraclitus that everything sensible was in a perpetual flux, he had to choose between denying the objectivity of definitions and of science and, on the other hand, positing universal and necessary objects. He chose the latter, but his choice was not really inevitable. It is true that all sensible things are subject to change, but such change is not absolute; one may distinguish between the composite thing and its *ratio* or form; the thing changes *per se*, but the form changes only *per accidens*. Since, then, intellect can prescind from all that does not *per se* pertain to a thing, it follows that intellect can define universally and deduce with necessity on the basis of the changeless forms of changing things.[66] But one may ask what is the changeless form or *ratio* of a changing thing; the answer is to be had by working out the conditions of change. On Aristotelian physics every other change supposes local movement; in turn, local movement supposes a thing to be in a given place at a given time; and a thing is in a given place at a given time inasmuch as it is individuated by matter existing under assigned (as opposed to merely specified) dimensions. It follows that one considers the changeless *ratio* of a thing, inasmuch as one considers the thing apart from assigned matter and so apart from the consequents of assigned matter, namely, determinate place, determinate time, and mobility. On the other hand, one is not to prescind

---

[64] *Sum. Theol.*, I, q. 13, a. 1 c.

[65] *Met.*, Z, 10, 1035b 27 ff; *VII*, lect. 10 §1490.

[66] *In Boet. de Trin.*, q. 5, a. 2 c. See the excellent text and annotations of QQ. 5 and 6 put out by P. Wyser, O.P., *Div. Thom. Freiburg*, XXV (1947), 437-85; XXVI (1948), 74-98. (Now supplemented by the edition of Bruno Decker, Leiden, Brill, 1959—editor's note.)

from more than assigned matter; to do so would be to prescind
from matter relevant to the form which by its proportion determines a measure of matter proper to itself; thus, the definition
of man and, as well, scientific knowledge of man prescind from
these bones and this flesh but not from bones and flesh.[67]

After the problem of necessary science of contingent things,
there comes the problem of universal science of particular things.
The abstract *rationes* are considered and employed in two different
manners. They may be considered in themselves and employed
as objects of thought, and this is their first and principal use.
But also, with the aid of sensitive potencies, they may be considered
relatively, used as instrumental means of knowledge, and so applied with the aid of sense to particular things; this use is secondary
and involves a measure of reflection.[68] In this quite clear passage
Aquinas settles a recurrent antinomy of Aristotelian thought:
science is of the universal;[69] all reality is particular;[70] therefore
science is not of reality. To this problem Aristotle adverted in his
list of basic questions in *Metaphysics B*,[71] and again in similar
terms in books K and *M*.[72] The last of these is his fullest treatment:
it distinguishes between science in potency and science in act;
it affirms that science in potency is indeterminate and so of the
indeterminate and universal, but science in act is determinate
and of the determinate and particular; it concludes that in one
manner science is of the universal and in another manner it is of
the particular.[73] Aquinas specified what these two manners were:
primarily science is concerned with universal objects of thought;
secondarily, with the help of sense, intellect uses these universal
objects as instrumental means and applies them to particular things.
Nor is this solution of the *In Boetium de Trinitate* out of harmony
with, much less contradicted by, later writings. The *Contra Gentiles* has it that by the use of inner words intellect is able to know

---

[67] *In Boet. de Trin.*, q. 5, a. 2c.

[68] *Ibid.*, and ad 4m.

[69] *Met.*, Z, 15, 1039b 27; K, 1, 1059b 26; *De An.*, II, 5, 417b 22; cf. *Post.
Anal.*, I, 31, 87b 27 ff.

[70] *Met.*, Z, 13, 1038b 35.

[71] *Ibid.*, B, 6, 1003a 6-17, esp. 14-17.

[72] *Ibid.*, K, 2, 1060b 20-23; M, 10, 1087a 10-25.

[73] *Ibid.* Cf. Ross, *Aristotle's Metaphysics*, Introd. cviii-cx.

"rem ut separatam a conditionibus materialibus sine quibus in rerum natura non existit."[74] The *Pars Prima* affirms "ideam operati esse in mente operantis sicut quod intelligitur; non autem sicut species qua intelligitur."[75] The fifth of the *Quodlibeta*, of Christmas, 1271, advances that intellect understands in two manners: formally by the species actuating it; instrumentally by the inner word it employs to know the thing.[76] Finally, it is plain that without instrumental objects of thought Aquinas could not have accounted as he did for the meaning of common names and false propositions.[77] However, since an accusation of an implication of idealism has been tossed at me, some explanation may not be out of place. First, the universal *ratio* or object of thought known by means of the inner word is not subjective but objective; it is not the thinking, meaning, defining, but the thought, meant, defined; but though it is objective, still it is universal and all reality is particular; accordingly its immediate reference is not to the thing except potentially, inasmuch as reflection and the use of sense enable one to apply the universal *ratio* to particular things. Secondly, before anyone may quote such a passage as *Summa Theol.*, I, q. 85, a. 1, ad 1m., against the clear statements of the *In Boetium de Trinitate*, he must show that both deal with formative abstraction; in fact, as will appear, the above cited passage from the *Summa* deals not with formative abstraction but with the prior apprehensive abstraction. Thirdly, it may be quite true that if the clear statements of the *In Boetium de Trinitate* are given the current conceptualist interpretation, then they do imply idealism. If formative abstraction is not preceded by apprehensive abstraction, by insight into phantasm, then the application of universal *rationes* to particular things must be blind; but that is a point against conceptualist interpretation. The intellectualist interpretation finds no implication of idealism in the *In Boetium de Trinitate* because for it formative abstraction is not the only abstraction just as the universal common to many is not the only universal;[78] prior to knowledge of essences without

[74] *C. Gent.*, I, 53 §3.
[75] *Sum. Theol.*, I, q. 15, a. 2 c.
[76] *Quodl.* V, a. 9 ad 1m.
[77] *In I Peri Herm.*, lect. 2 and 4; see page 3 above.
[78] *Sum. Theol.*, I, q. 85, a. 3 ad 1m; a. 2 ad 2m.

existence through definitions, there are insights into phantasm in which are known universals, natures, quiddities existing in corporal matter; and as such insight governs the formation of meanings and definitions, so also it governs the application of them to particular things.

Two approaches to Thomist thought on formative abstraction have been considered, namely, through the meanings of common names and through the possibility of necessary and universal knowledge of contingent and particular reality. A third approach is through the possibility of abstraction itself.[79] The two operations of intellect are distinguished: the first is knowledge of quiddity; the second is knowledge of existence. To the latter operation are assigned distinctions that regard separate things, such as man and stone, and, further, abstractions (more accurately separations) on the level of metaphysical or theological thought.[80] But to the first operation, knowledge of quiddities, are assigned physical and mathematical abstractions. Their general possibility is accounted for by the nature of intelligibility and the laws of its unity. A thing is intelligible inasmuch as it is in act: accordingly we must understand the natures of things in one or more of three ways; for the thing itself may be act, as is the separate substance; or it may possess a constituent act, as the composite substance; or it may be related to act, as matter to form and a vacuum to what it might contain. Now inasmuch as the nature of a thing is constituted intelligibly by its relation to or dependence on something else, it is impossible to abstract from the something else; on the other hand, inasmuch as the nature of a thing is not dependent intelligibly on something else, in that measure it is possible to abstract from the something else. Thus, one can abstract "animal" from "foot" but not "foot" from "animal"; one can abstract "whiteness" from "man" and "man" from "whiteness"; one can abstract neither "son" from "father" nor "father" from "son," and neither "substantial form" from "matter" nor "matter" from "substantial form." Evidently, intelligibility governs abstraction on the level

[79] *In Boet. de Trin.*, q. 5, a. 3 c; ed. Wyser, p. 472 line 1 ff. (ed. Decker, p. 182).

[80] *Ibid.*, p. 472; p. 473 lines 8-16; p. 474 lines 42-44 (ed. Decker, p. 182; p. 183 lines 22-32; p. 186 lines 13-16); on the formation of metaphysical concepts, see pages 42-45, 85-89 above.

of the *intelligentia indivisibilium*; precisely because of intelligible unity, intelligence in act knows what intelligibly is indivisible and abstracts from all that does not pertain to that intelligible indivisibility. By this general principle, in a passage that more than recalls the complications of its parallel in the *Metaphysics* of Aristotle,[81] both physical and mathematical abstraction are explained. In the order of intelligible priority, a thing is constituted, first, by substance, secondly, by quantity, thirdly, by quality, fourthly, by passions and movements. Now one cannot conceive the intelligibly posterior and prescind from the prior: substance enters into the definition of accident; similarly, sensible qualities presuppose quantity, and changes presuppose sensible qualities; it follows that one cannot abstract accident from substance, sensible quality from quantity, change from sensible quality. On the other hand, one can conceive the intelligibly prior and prescind from the posterior. As we have seen, to abstract from assigned matter eliminates the possibility of change but leaves substance, quantity, and sensible quality; it leaves flesh and bones but not these bones nor this flesh. But one may go a step further to abstract not only from assigned matter but also from sensible quality or, as it is named, sensible matter.[82] This leaves substance and quantity and the necessary consequents of quantity such as figure; it is the abstraction of the mathematician; and when it is named the abstraction of form from matter, what is meant is not the impossible abstraction of substantial form from its corresponding matter (the two are correlative) but the abstraction of the form of quantity and its consequent, figure, from sensible qualities such as the hard and soft, hot and cold.[83] Finally, to advance beyond mathematical abstraction and prescind from quantity as well as sensible quality and the conditions of change is, Aquinas stated explicitly, not so much abstraction as separation; it pertains to the level of judgment and the fields of metaphysics and theology.[84]

[81] *Met.*, Z, 10 and 11.
[82] *Met.*, K, 3, 1061a 28 ff; cf. M, 3, 1077b 17 ff; *De An.*, III, 7, 431b 15 f.
[83] *In Boet. de Trin.*, q. 5, a. 3 c; cf. *Sum. Theol.*, I, q. 85, a. 1 ad 2m.
[84] *In Boet. de Trin.*, ed. Wyser, p. 474, lines 38-44 (ed. Decker, p. 186, lines 10-16).

APPREHENSIVE ABSTRACTION

Repeatedly in the neat treatise on human intellect in the *Pars Prima*[85] one reads that the proper object of human intellect is the *quidditas rei materialis.*[86] This proper object is also the proportionate object of our intellects,[87] their first object,[88] their *primo et per se cognitum,*[89] their object according to the state of the present life,[90] and finally an object that can be known only by the conversion of intellect to phantasm.[91] Reasons on a cosmic scale are assigned for this position. In the universal hierarchy of cognoscitive potencies human intellect holds an intermediate place. Sense is the first act of a material organ, and so its object is a form existing in matter as it exists in matter. Angelic intellect is the potency of a pure form, and so its object is a pure form. But human intellect is neither the act of an organ, as sense, nor the potency of a pure form, as angelic intellect; it is the potency of a form that actuates matter, and so its object must be a form, existing indeed in matter, but not as it exists in matter.[92] Less striking reasons for the position are to be had in the historical order. In the incessantly quoted third book of Aristotle's *De Anima* there is recalled the distinction of *Metaphysics Z,* 6, between water and the quiddity of water, magnitude and the quiddity of magnitude, Socrates and the quiddity of Socrates; then it is advanced that directly by sense we know water, magnitude, flesh, that directly by intellect we know the quiddities of water, magnitude, flesh, and that indirectly by intellect we know what directly we know by sense.[93] From this passage Aquinas drew three conclusions and of them the first regarded the proper object of human intellect. That object is the *quidditas rei* which is not separate from the thing, as the Platonists held, nor apart from sensible things, even

---

[85] *Sum. Theol.,* I, qq. 79, 84-89.

[86] *Ibid.,* q. 84, a. 7; a. 8; q. 85, a. 5 ad 3m; a. 8; q. 86, a. 2; q. 87, a. 2 ad 2m; a. 3; q. 88, a. 3; cf. q. 12, a. 4; q. 85, a. 1.

[87] *Ibid.,* q. 84, a. 8 c.

[88] *Ibid.,* q. 87, a. 3; q. 88, a. 3 c.

[89] *Ibid.,* q. 85, a. 8 c.

[90] *Ibid.,* and q. 88, a. 3 c.

[91] *Ibid.,* q. 84, a. 7 c.

[92] *Ibid.,* q. 85, a. 1 c.; cf. q. 12, a. 4 c.

[93] *De An.,* III, 4, 429b 10-21; lect. 8 §705-16.

though intellect apprehends it without apprehending the individual conditions it possesses in sensible things.[94] It is perhaps clear enough that this proper object of human intellect is the same as the proper object defined in the *Pars Prima*; equally clearly, its source is Aristotle and its ultimate ground is the Aristotelian principle that quiddities and particulars must be identical (at least inadequately) if the former are to be realities and the latter are to be objects of science.[95]

It remains that there is an anomaly that must be removed. According to the *De Anima* intellect "directe apprehendit quidditatem carnis; per reflexionem autem, ipsam carnem."[96] According to the *Pars Prima* intellect must convert to phantasm to know its proper object which still is the quiddity.[97] It seems that direct apprehension is by conversion! Again, we read that the first object and the first known of intellect is the quiddity of a material thing.[98] How can what is known not only directly but also first, none the less be known only by a conversion to phantasm? To solve this difficulty one must first distinguish conversion to phantasm from reflection on phantasm and, secondly, settle precisely what is meant by conversion. Now conversion and reflection are quite distinct both in themselves and in their consequents. They are distinct in themselves: conversion to phantasm is necessary to know the quiddity, the proper object of human intellect;[99] but reflection on phantasm presupposes not only conversion to phantasm but also knowledge of the quiddity; it is needed, not for knowledge of the proper object, but only for knowledge of the indirect object, the singular.[100] This distinction between objects

---

[94] *Ibid.*, §717.

[95] *Met.*, Z, 6, 1031b 3 ff; *VII*, lect. 5 §1363.

[96] *In III de An.*, lect. 8 §713.

[97] *Sum. Theol.*, I, q. 84, a. 7 c. In this context and in general Aquinas' *quidditas* or *quod quid est* is objective; it is of the thing as intelligible, just as color is of the thing as visible. *In I Sent.*, d. 19, q. 5, a. 1 ad 7m: "quidditatis esse est quoddam esse rationis" is exceptional; it refers to the act of defining and explains "verum est in mente"; but the context also speaks of the *quidditas* and *esse* as components of the thing. When I wrote pages 23-25 above, I had not sufficiently adverted to this, nor to the nature of conversion to phantasm.

[98] *Sum. Theol.*, I, q. 85, a. 8; q. 87, a. 3; q. 88, a. 3 c.

[99] *Ibid.*, q. 84, a. 7 c.

[100] *Ibid.*, q. 86, a. 1 c.

and so between acts results in a further distinction of problems
regarding the separate soul: because the separate soul has no body
and so no imagination, it might seem that it could not know the
proper object of human intellect which requires conversion to
phantasm; for this reason Aquinas regularly asks whether the
separate soul understands anything at all;[101] again, because the
separate soul has no imagination and so cannot reflect on phantasm,
it might seem that even if it knew the proper object still it might
not know the singular; and for this reason Aquinas regularly
asks in a separate article whether the departed souls can know
the singular.[102] At least, then, conversion to phantasm is not the
kind of reflection involved in knowing the singular. But is it in
any manner a reflection? Certainly, there is an etymological
suggestion of reflection in the name, conversion; on the other hand,
there is a notable measure of Thomist usage which excludes from
conversion what is the essential implication of reflection, namely,
the existence of other knowledge or activity prior to or supposed
by the reflection. Thus, when Avicenna's possible intellect *converts* to his separate agent intellect for the reception of species,[103]
one cannot say that, prior to this conversion and reception, the
possible intellect was engaged in any activity. Again, when Aquinas spoke of his own immanent agent intellect *converting* upon
phantasms,[104] there is no need to wonder what is converted from.
More specifically, the conversion of possible intellect to phantasm is described by Aquinas neither as an activity nor as a shift in
activity but as a natural orientation of human intellect in this
life: it results from the perfection of the conjunction of soul to
body;[105] it consists in human intellect having its gaze (*aspectus*)
turned to phantasms[106] and to inferior things;[107] and this present
state of intellect is contrasted with that of the next life when
conversion is not to phantasms nor to bodies but to superior things

---

[101] *In I V Sent.*, d. 50, q. 1, a. 1 sol.; *De Ver.*, q. 19, 1 c; *Q.D. de An.*, a. 15;
Sum. Theol., I, q. 89, a. 1 c.

[102] *Ibid.*, a. 3; a. 2; a. 20; a. 4 respectively.

[103] *In I V Sent.*, d. 50, q. 1, a. 2 sol; *De Ver.*, q. 10, a. 2 c; *Q. D. de An.*,
a. 15 c; *Sum. Theol.*, I, q. 84, a. 4 c.

[104] *Sum. Theol.*, I, q. 85, a. 1 ad 3m.

[105] *In I V Sent.*, d. 50, q. 1, a. 2 sol.

[106] *Q.D. de An.*, a. 16 c.

[107] *Ibid.*, aa. 17 and 18 c.

and pure intelligibles.[108] It may or may not be surprising that the term, *conversio*, should be used to name what strictly is a natural orientation but the facts already noted remain and, if one finds abstract statements more convincing, there are Aquinas' own words:

> ... nulla potentia potest aliquid cognoscere non convertendo se ad obiectum suum, ut visus nihil cognoscit nisi convertendo se ad colorem. Unde cum phantasmata se habeant hoc modo ad intellectum possibilem sicut sensibilia ad sensum, ut patet per Philosophum in III de Anima, quantumcumque aliquam speciem intelligibilem apud se habeat, numquam tamen actu aliquid considerat secundum illam speciem nisi convertendo se ad phantasmata: et ideo, sicut intellectus noster secundum statum viae indiget phantasmatibus ad actu considerandum antequam accipiat habitum, ita et postquam acceperit.[109]

But plainly there is no difficulty in reconciling the necessity of sight converting to color with the fact that color is what sight first and directly knows; similarly, there is no difficulty in reconciling the necessity of possible intellect converting to phantasm to know the quiddity with the statement that possible intellect first and directly knows the quiddity in the phantasm.

This account of conversion throws a new light on such a passage as *Summa Theol.*, I, q. 84, a. 7. The influence of the doubtful *De Natura Verbi Intellectus*[110] forced older interpreters to take it as genuinely Thomist that the *verbum* was formed prior to any understanding; in consequence they held that intellect first knew the quiddity in the *verbum* and then converted to phantasm to know it again existing in corporeal matter. But once the *opusculum* is recognized as doubtful, the whole position falls to the ground. Thomist conversion does not mean reflecting nor turning back but simply a natural orientation; q. 84 of the *Pars Prima* does not seem to mention the *verbum*; indeed the whole treatise on human intellect in the *Pars Prima* mentions the *verbum* only in incidental

---

[108] *Sum. Theol.*, I, q. 89, a. 1 c and ad 2m. Note that Avicennist conversion is named simply conjunction, *C. Gent.*, II, 74 §3.

[109] *De Ver.*, q. 10, a. 2 ad 7m.

[110] *Ed. Mandonnet*, V, 369-75, esp. 372-74. For instance, John of St. Thomas appealed to this work, *In Im.*, q. 27, disp. 32, a. 5, n. 12, 27, 28 (ed. Desclée, 1946, IV², 72, 77).

fashion.[111] When, then, in *Summa Theol.*, I, q. 84, a. 7, Aquinas affirms the necessity of conversion to phantasm and of acts of imagination and other sensitive potencies both in the initial acquisition of science and in its subsequent use; when he argues both from the experimental fact that the lesion of a sensitive organ interferes with scientific knowledge, and again from the universal experience that whenever we try to understand we construct images in which, as it were, we inspect the solution; when he concludes that the proper object of human intellect in this life is the quiddity or nature existing in corporeal matter; when he maintains that true and complete knowledge of this object can be had only inasmuch as there is presupposed an act of imagination or sense apprehending the material singular and there supervenes an act of intellect apprehending the universal nature existing in that particular; then Aquinas is describing in his manner what from a concatenation of texts we already have described as insight into phantasm.[112]

Let us turn to another point. It is remarkable that the description of the object of intellect as "quidditas rei materialis" seems confined to the treatise on human intellect in the *Pars Prima*. Elsewhere one can read that the object of intellect, the proper object of intellect, the object according to the third book of the *De Anima*, is the "quid," or the "quod quid est," or the "quidditas rei."[113] Again, elsewhere when need arises, the peculiarity of human

---

[111] E.g., *Sum. Theol.*, I, q. 85, a. 2 ad 3m.

[112] *Ibid.*, q. 84, a. 7 c; see pages 10-32 above.

[113] *In I Sent.*, d. 19, q. 5, a. 1 ad 7m; *II*, d. 13, q. 1, a. 3 sol; *III*, d. 23, q. 1 a. 2 sol; d. 35, q. 2, a. 2, qc. 1 sol; *IV*, d. 12, q. 1, a. 1, sol. 2 ad 2m; d. 49, q. 2 a. 3 sol; a. 7 ad 6m; *De Ver.*, q. 1, a. 12 c; q. 8, a. 7 ad 4m (3ae ser.); q. 14, a. 1 c; q. 15, a. 2 ad 3m; a. 3 ad 1m; q. 25, a. 3 c; *In Boet. de Trin.*, q. 5, a. 2 ad 2m; *C. Gent.*, I, 58 §5; III, 41 §3; 56, §5; 108 §4; *Sum. Theol.*, I, q. 17, a. 3 ad 1m; q. 18, a. 2 c; q. 57, a. 1 ad 2m; q. 58, a. 5 c; q. 67, a. 3 c; q. 85, a. 5 c; a. 6 c; I-II, q. 3, a. 8 c; q. 10, a. 1 ad 3m; q. 31, a. 5 c; II-II, q. 8, a. 1 c; III, q. 10, a. 3 ad 2m; q. 76, a. 7 c; *In Libr. de Causis*, lect. 6 *ad fin*; *In I Peri Herm.*, lect. 10 §5; *In II Post Anal.*, lect. 5 §9. Twenty of these texts refer to Aristotle's *De Anima*; sixteen speak of the proper object of intellect; four name the object *quid*; one *quod quid*; twenty-one *quod quid est*; eight *quidditas*; the spread is random except for *quid* and *quod quid* which are confined to earliest writings. *Sum. Theol.*, III, q. 75, a. 5 ad 2m states that the proper object of intellect according to the *De Anima* is *substantia*.

intellect in this life is indicated by stating flatly that the object of human intellect is the phantasm.[114] But it is in the *Pars Prima* that one finds the synthesis of these two complementary streams of thought, for there we find that the proper object is not simply the "quidditas rei" but the "quidditas rei materialis" and at the same time we are informed of the necessary condition of conversion to phantasm. The duality in Thomist writings has its source in Aristotle, who not only enlarged upon τὸ τί ἐστιν and τό τί ἦν εἶναι,[115] but also insisted that the soul never understands without phantasms,[116] that phantasms are to the rational soul what sensible objects are to sense,[117] that intellect understands species (ἐίδη) in phantasms.[118]

It is natural enough that this Aristotelian duality should reappear in Aquinas; it is no less natural that there should be in Thomist writings a series of attempts to break it down. In the *Sentences* one may read that phantasm is intelligible only in potency and so cannot be the proper and proximate object of intellect which is the *species intellecta*.[119] In the *De Veritate* one finds a qualification of the Aristotelian parallel that phantasms are to intellect what sensible objects are to sense; for sense directly knows the sensible object, but intellect directly knows not phantasm but the thing that phantasm represents; accordingly, insight into phantasm is like looking *in*, not looking *at*, a mirror.[120] In the *Contra Gentiles* the actual intelligibility of phantasm is clarified:

---

[114] *In I Sent.*, d. 3, q. 4, a. 3 sol; *II*, d. 8, q. 1, a. 5 sol; d. 20, q. 2, a. 2 ad 3m; d. 23, q. 2, a. 2 ad 3m; *III*, d. 14, q. 1, a. 3 sol 2; d. 27, q. 3, a. 1 sol; *De Ver.*, q. 18, a. 8 ad 4m; *C. Gent.*, II, 73 §38; 80 §6; 8 §6; 96 §3; *Q.D. de An.*, a. 1 ad 11m; a. 15 c, ad 3 m, ad 8m; *Sum. Theol.*, I-II, q. 50, a. 4 ad 1m; *De Unitate Intel.*, c. 1, ed. Keeler §40; *In Boet. de Trin.*, q. 6, a. 2c et ad 5m. There are a large number of equivalent texts with the Aristotelian parallel of phantasm standing to intellect as sensible to sense.

[115] See pages 10-25 above.

[116] *De An.*, III, 7, 431a 16.

[117] *Ibid.*, 14.

[118] *Ibid.*, 431b 2.

[119] *In III Sent.*, d. 31, q. 2, a. 4 ad 5m; for similar modifications, see "quasi obiecta" *In IV Sent.*, d. 50, q. 1, a. 2 sol *ad fin*; *De Ver.*, q. 10, a. 11 c; also "species phantasmatum quae sunt obiecta intellectus nostri," *In II Sent.*, d. 24, q. 2, a. 2 ad 1m.

[120] *De Ver.*, q. 2, a. 6 c; cf. q. 10, a. 9 c.

in the dark colors are visible in potency; in daylight they are
visible in act but seen in potency; they are seen in act only inasmuch
as sight is in act; similarly, prior to the illumination of agent intellect, phantasms are intelligible in potency; by that illumination
they become intelligible in act but understood only in potency;
they are understood in act only inasmuch as the possible intellect is in act.[121] Moreover, there occurs a description of the intelligibility in act of phantasm: the *species intelligibilis* is said
to shine forth in phantasm as the exemplar does in the example
or image.[122]

As has been already explained, the object of insight into phantasm is pre-conceptual, so that any expression of it is as conceived
and not as such, just as any expression of the object of sight is
of it as conceived and not as such.[123] It is this fact that accounts
for the variety of the descriptions one finds. Most commonly
it is the intelligibility in act of phantasm. In the *Pars Prima*
it is the "quidditas sive natura rei materialis in materia corporali existens." But there it also is the "formam in materia quidem corporali individualiter existentem, non tamen prout est
in tali materia."[124] In the *In Boetium de Trinitate* there occurs an identification of 1) "forma intelligibilis," 2) "quidditas
rei," and 3) object of intellect.[125] Since "species" translates Aristotle's εἶδος which regularly means form,[126] it is not surprising
that the object of insight should be named not only "forma intelligibilis" but also "species intelligibilis." Thus, the species
that shines forth in phantasm[127] is an object of intellectual knowledge; again the species that intellect understands, knows, ap-

[121] *C. Gent.*, II, 59 §14.
[122] *Ibid.*, II, 73 §38; cf. *In II Sent.*, d. 20, q. 2, a. 2 ad 2m.
[123] See pages 24-25 above.
[124] *Sum. Theol.*, I, q. 85, a. 1 c.
[125] *In Boet. de Trin.*, q. 5, a. 2 ad 2m; ed. Wyser p. 469.
[126] A subsequent convention has tended to confine "species" to meaning
forms in the cognoscitive potencies. Aquinas can write, *In III Sent.*, d. 18,
a. 1 c: Causa autem actionis est species, e.g. the form of heat in fire; *De Ver.*,
q. 10, a. 8, ad 10m (2ae ser.): species lapidis non est in oculo sed similitudo
eius; *C. Gent.*, II, 93 §2: quidditates subsistentes sunt species subsistentes;
In III de An., lect. 8 §707: naturalia habent speciem in materia.
[127] *C. Gent.*, II, 73 §38.

prehends in phantasm,[128] plainly is an object; and in such statements not only the thought but so also the expression is Aristotelian.[129] Finally, the object of insight, besides being "quidditas
sive natura rei materialis," "forma intelligibilis," and "species
intelligibilis," also is the universal which is not posterior but prior,
not with, but without the "intentio universalitatis," and concretely though inadequately identical with the particular material
thing,[130] just as the Aristotelian quiddity is concretely though
inadequately identical with the particular.[131]

We have been characterizing the agent object[132] of apprehensive
abstraction (insight) and now we turn to the act itself. This act
is defined as a *cognoscere* or *considerare*.[133] Not only is it itself cognitional, but what it abstracts from is also known, namely, the
individual matter represented by the phantasm,[134] or again the
sensible matter of hot or cold, hard or soft,[135] which may be equally
imagined. But though apprehensive abstraction is itself cognitional and abstracts from sensibly known individual or sensible
matter, still it may be considered insofar as it enters under metaphysical categories. From that view-point it is an operation,
a second act, an *actus perfecti*.[136] Because it involves psychological
necessity and universality, metaphysically the form whence it
proceeds must be received universally, immaterially, and im-
movably; "modus enim actionis est secundum modum formae
agentis."[137] Such a form is not the essence itself of the soul but
an immaterial similitude of the form that is received materially
in the known thing.[138] It is not innate,[139] nor derived from sep-

---

[128] *Sum. Theol.*, I, q. 85, a. 1, ob. 5a et ad 5m; q. 86, a. 1 c; III, q. 11, a.2 ad 1m.
[129] *De An.*, III, 7, 431b 2; lect. 12 §777.
[130] *Sum. Theol.*, I, q. 85, a. 2 ad 2m; a. 3, ad 1m.
[131] *Met.*, Z, 6; *VII*, lect. 5.
[132] See pages 128-133 above.
[133] *Sum. Theol.*, I, q. 85, a. 1 c et ad 1m.
[134] *Ibid.*, c.
[135] *Ibid.*, ad 2m.
[136] See pages 101-106 above.
[137] *Sum. Theol.*, I, q. 84, a. 1 c; q. 76, a. 2 ad 3m; *De Unitate Intel.*, c. 5,
ed. Keeler §111.
[138] *Sum. Theol.*, I, q. 84, a. 2 c.
[139] *Ibid.*, a. 3 c.

arate substances out of this world,[140] nor consisting exclusively of intellectual light;[141] but it is received from material things inasmuch as phantasms are made intelligible in act by agent intellect;[142] hence neither the acquisition nor the use of science can occur without conversion to phantasm;[143] nor can we even judge properly unless sense is functioning freely.[144] Now this form also is called a "species intelligibilis"; obviously it is quite different from the species of our preceding paragraph which is an object. If the latter be named "species quae," then this form is "species qua intelligitur"; the "species quae" is one of various attempts to characterize the pre-conceptual object of insight; the "species qua" is not a direct object but a conclusion of metaphysical reflection.[145] When the possible intellect is actuated by the "species qua," it is constituted in the first act of apprehensive abstraction; this first act of apprehensive abstraction stands to the second act, as does form to *esse* and as principle of action to action.[146] Finally, on the sensitive level passive operations are found in the outer senses, constructive operations in the imagination; but on the level of intellect both the passive and constructive operations pertains to the same potency, possible intellect; the reception of the "species qua" is a passion,[147] and

---

[140] *Ibid.*, a. 4 c.

[141] *Ibid.*, a. 5 c.

[142] *Ibid.*,   a. 6 c.

[143] *Ibid.*, a. 7 c.

[144] *Ibid.*, a. 8 c. Observe that Q. 84 is titled wrongly in the editions. These titles do not pertain to the Thomist text but were picked out by an early editor from the summaries Aquinas placed prior to his questions (See B. Geyer, *S. Thomae de Aquino Quaestiones de Trinitate divina*, Bonn 1934, Florilegium Patristicum, fasc. XXXVII, p. 3). The printed title (Quomodo anima coniuncta intelligat corporalia quae sunt infra ipsam) refers not to Q. 84 but to QQ. 84-86. The correct title would be: Per quid ea cognoscit. Thus, the topic of Q. 84 is the species: existence, aa. 1, 2; origin, aa. 3-6; conditions of use, aa. 7-8.

[145] *Sum. Theol.*, I, q. 85, a. 2 c; cf. *De Ver.*, q. 10, a. 4 ad 1m; a. 8 ad 2m (2ae ser) ad 9m (1ae ser); a. 9 c, 1m, 3m, 5m, 10m; a. 11 ad 4m; in some of these passages the species is a medium to be known not directly but on reflection and so may be the same as the "species quae" though differently conceived; cf. the earlier formulation, *Quodl.*, VII, a. 1 c; *In IV Sent.*, d. 49, q. 2, a. 1 ad 15m.

[146] See pages 124-129 above.

[147] *Sum. Theol.*, I, q. 85, a. 2 c et ad 3m.

the consequent second act is similarly a *pati* in the general sense of that term;[148] by that second act the preconceptual "quidditas rei materialis" or "forma intelligibilis" or "species quae" or universal in the particular is known; but in virtue of that second act there is formed the definition, the act of defining thought, the act of meaning;[149] and this, at times, is said to be or to contain a third "species intelligibilis" which may be distinguished from the "species quae" and the "species qua" by being called a "species in qua."[150]

There remains the question: What is meant by the abstraction of species from phantasm? The principal meaning clearly is that

[148] See pages 107-111, 124-129 above.

[149] *Sum. Theol.*, I, q. 85, a. 2 ad 3m.

[150] In all but early writings the inner word is called a form or species only on the secondary ground that it is the form in virtue of which the artisan operates: cf. *De Ver.*, q. 3, a. 2 c; *Quodl.*, V, a. 9 c. As already noted, the early *verbum* is the later concept plus an ordination towards manifestation (*In II Sent.*, d. 11, q. 2, a. 3 sol; cf. I, d. 27, q. 2, a. 1 sol.); what is conceived, is the *species intelligibilis* (*In I Sent.*, d. 27, q. 2, a. 1 ob. 4a; a. 2 ob. 4a). *Quodl.* VIII, a. 4, describes the formation of a classificatory definition of charity and calls it knowledge of the quiddity of charity; apparently the formed definition is to be identified with *species intelligibilis*; knowledge of the *quid* of charity is affirmed (*In III Sent.*, d. 23, q. 1, a. 2 ad 1m) but denied on the ground that we do not know its object, God, quidditatively (*De Ver.*, q. 10, a. 10 c). *Quodl.* VII, a. 2 c, speaks of knowledge in alleged Augustinian terms as an *intentio coniungens*. P. Glorieux (*Rech. théol. anc. méd.*, XIII [1946], 282-301) raises the possibility of doubting the authenticity of these *Quodlibeta*. On the other hand, they perhaps throw some light on *In I Sent.*, d. 35, q. 1, a. 2 sol., which distinguishes the sensible species received in the pupil as a first seen and the external thing as a second seen and, similarly, a similitude received in the intellect as a first understood and the external thing itself as a second understood. Cf. sup. note 145. Finally, there is the *species intellecta* recurrent in the *Sentences* (especially *II*, d. 17, q. 2, a. 1 sol.) but later conspicuous only in discussions of Averroes (*C. Gent.*, II, 75 §3; cf. §7; hence *De unit. int.*, §110: De rebus enim est scientia naturalis et aliae scientiae et non de speciebus intellectis; *Sum. Theol.*, I, q. 85, a. 2 c: species intellecta secundario est id quod intelligitur). The early *species intellecta* may be a concept but it may also be the *species quae* as suggested by *In IV Sent.*, d. 49, q. 2, a. 6 ad 3m: Facultas enim intellectus nostri determinatur ad formas sensibiles quae per intellectum agentem fiunt *intellectae* in actu, eo quod phantasmata hoc modo se habent ad intellectum nostrum sicut sensibilia ad sensum, ut dicitur in III de anima. However, too great a precision in early thought would be contradicted by *Sum. Theol.*, I, q. 85, a. 3 c.

there is produced in the possible intellect a similitude of the thing
presented by phantasm; this similitude is similar to the thing,
not in all respects, but with regard only to its specific nature;[151]
it is to be identified with the "species qua."[152] Still this meaning
is not exclusive; Aquinas himself wrote that "hoc est abstrahere
universale a particulari, vel speciem intelligibilem a phantasmatibus, considerare scilicet naturam speciei absque consideratione
individualium principiorum, quae per phantasmata repraesen-
tantur";[153] and here the abstracting is the second act of considering,
and what is abstracted from is said, indeed, to be phantasm but
means the individual principles that the phantasm represents.
Now when the abstracting is considering, the abstracted species
would seem to be the considered species; the considered species
might be the "species in qua" as conceptualist interpretation
might prefer; but it is more plausible perhaps that the considered
species is the "species quae" which shines forth in phantasm;
certainly, this would seem to be so when Aquinas rewrote Aristotle's "species quidem igitur intellectivum in phantasmatibus
intelligit" as "pars animae intellectiva intelligit species a phantasmatibus abstractas."[154]

SENSE AND UNDERSTANDING

As the sensible is the object of sense, so the intelligible is the
object of intellect.[155] The sensible is confined to material reality,
but the intelligible is co-extensive with the universe: whatever
can be, can be understood.[156] The supreme intelligible is the divine substance which lies beyond the capacity of human intellect, not as sound lies outside the range of sight, but as excessive
light blinds it.[157] Further, there are two classes of intelligibles
and two modes of understanding: what is in itself intelligible,
is the direct object of the intellects of separate, spiritual sub-

---

[151] *Sum. Theol.*, I, q. 85, a. 1 ad 3m.
[152] *Ibid.*, a. 2 c; *De Sp. Cr.*, a. 9 ad 6m.
[153] *Sum. Theol.*, I, q. 85, a. 1 ad 1m.
[154] *In III de An.*, lect. 12, §777.
[155] *C. Gent.*, II, 55 §10.
[156] *Ibid.*, II, 98 §9.
[157] *Ibid.*, III, 54 §8.

stances; but what is not in itself actually intelligible but only made intelligible by agent intellect, namely the material and sensible, is understood by intellect directly only inasmuch as it first is apprehended by sense, and represented by imagination, and illuminated by agent intellect.[158] But while the difference between the two classes of intelligible is real and intrinsic, the difference between the two kinds of understanding is only a difference in mode; hence, whether the soul is in or out of the body, it is the same human intellect, specified by the same formal object, but operating under the modal difference that actual intelligibility is presented or is not presented in phantasms.[159] Again, just as understanding the actuated intelligibility of sensible things abstracts from space and time,[160] so the spiritual substances that are in themselves actually intelligible exist outside space and time.[161]

From this it does not follow that the spiritual substances are not individual but only that they are not material.[162] But it does follow that our direct intellectual knowledge of material things is incomplete: sense knows external accidents, and intellect knows the internal essence of quiddity;[163] knowing the essence, intellect knows all that the essence involves; but while such knowledge of God would be comprehensive,[164] it cannot include knowledge of contingent existence,[165] nor of contingent acts of will,[166] nor of material individuality. Thus, our science is of the universal and necessary, and to account for a contingent and particular judgment, such as that Socrates lived at Athens, one must appeal to understanding as reflecting on sensitive knowledge.[167]

This indirect and reflective intellectual knowledge of the singular and contingent is presented by Aquinas in two manners. Earlier

---

[158] Ibid., II, 91 § 8; 94 §5; 96 §3-5.
[159] De Ver., q. 19, a. 1 ob. 4 a et 4m; ob. 5a et 5m; Q. D. de An., a. 15 ad 8m, 10m.
[160] In Boet. de Trin., q. 5, a. 2 c; De Ver., q. 2, a. 6 ad 1m; Sum. Theol., I, q. 57, a. 2 c; q. 86, a. 4 c.
[161] C. Gent., II, 96 §9-10.
[162] De Sp. Cr., a. 9 ad 15m.
[163] De Ver., q. 8, a. 7 ad 4m (3ae ser.); q. 10, a. 4 ad 1m; In I Post. Anal., lect. 42 §5.
[164] De Ver., q. 20, a. 5 c.
[165] Ibid., q. 15, a. 2 ad 3m.
[166] C. Gent., III, 56 §5.
[167] Sum. Theol., I, q. 86, aa. 1 et 3.

writings assign a series of steps: first, intellects graps the universal; secondly, it reflects on the act by which it grasps the universal; thirdly, it comes to know the species that is the principle of that act; fourthly, it turns to the phantasm whence the species is derived; and, fifthly, it comes to know the singular thing that is represented by the phantasm.[168] At once one is struck with the parallel between this process of reflection and the reflection by which one arrives at scientific knowledge of the essence of the soul; as the reader will recall, that involved reflection first on the act, then on the potency, and finally on the essence of soul.[169]

Accordingly, I cannot agree with the contention of R. P. Wébert that Thomist reflection on phantasm for knowledge of the singular is reflection in a unique sense and without a parallel in other types of reflection; indeed, though one may grant that the sidelong glance (*regard dévié*) which he postulates would be unique, I think it also must be said that such a glance not only fails to meet theoretical requirements (intellect no more glances than sight smells) but also has no basis in the texts.[170] On the other hand, it is necessary to point out the difference between reflection that arrives merely at a general notion of singularity and reflection that arrives at this singular thing. Just as one can infer a universal notion of matter from the universal notion of form,[171] so also one can infer an abstract notion of singularity from the notion of quiddity or from any specific quiddity;[172] but the abstract notion of matter does not suffice for knowledge of individual matter,[173] and there is no apparent reason why an abstract notion of singularity should suffice for knowledge of concrete singular things. In any case the reflection that Aquinas

---

[168] *In IV Sent.*, d. 50, q. 1, a. 3 sol; *De Ver.*, q. 2, a. 6 c; q. 10, a. 5 c; *De An.*, a. 20 ad 1m (2ae ser).

[169] *In III Sent.*, d. 23, q. 1, a. 2 ad 3m; *De Ver.*, q. 10, a. 8 c; *Sum. Theol.*, 1, q. 87, aa.1-4; *In II de An.*, lect. 6 §308; III, lect. 9, §721, 724 ff.

[170] Except, of course, in so far as "regard dévié" is a devious manner of speaking of reflection on insight. See R. P. Wébert's article, "Reflexio," *Mélanges Mandonnet*, I, 307-10, Bibl. Thomiste XIII.

[171] *See De Ver.*, q. 10, a. 5 c.

[172] See Cajetan, In I, q. 86, a. 1 §VI-VIII; J. de Tonquédec, *La critique de la connaissance*, Paris, 1929, pp. 146 ff.

[173] *De Ver.*, q. 10, a. 5 ad 1m.

describes is not from knowledge of quiddity to knowledge of a proportionate singularity; it is a reflection that proceeds from knowledge of quiddity to knowledge of the act by which the quiddity is known; that act is an immaterial singular; it is known in empirical consciousness as singular; from that singular act is known the singular species that is its principle, and then the singular phantasm that is its source, and so finally the singular thing. The process Aquinas described is truly of the singular, truly reflective, and truly intellectual.

However, there is reason to believe that Aquinas later modified the above view. The reflection, involved in at least three of the four passages cited above,[174] is metaphysical in character; it introduces the "species qua" that is the principle of the act of understanding; it explains how a Thomist metaphysician might account for intellectual knowledge of the singular; but it does not explain how the mass of mankind is capable of affirming that Socrates lived in Athens. Whether Aquinas adverted to this difficulty or whether he was influenced by the *Paraphrases* of Themistius which do not suppose metaphysical knowledge,[175] can hardly be determined. But what is plain is that the *Pars Prima* presents a significant variation. It mentions not merely the item of metaphysical knowledge, the "species qua," but also the item of anyone's knowledge, the "species quae" that intellect understands in phantasm.[176] Evidently this change accounts for the substitution of "quasi quamdam reflexionem" for the elaborate process of reflection of earlier passages.

---

[174] Note 168. All but *De Ver.*, q. 2, a. 6 c, speak of the species which is principle of the act; knowledge of this species supposes metaphysical analysis and reflection; but notes 145 and 150 above, together with the complicated peculiarity of the agent object as object (see note 192 below), will supply the reader with materials for grasping why Aquinas should not have adverted to the obvious difficulty mentioned in the text above.

[175] Themistii *Paraphrases, In III de Anima,* 4, ed. L. Spengel, Teubner Lipsiae 1866, pp. 176, 18-178, 30. The date of the medieval Latin translation has been discovered recently in a Toledo MS. The translation was completed at Viterbo, Nov. 22, 1267. See G. Verbeke, *Rev. Phil. de Louvain*, XLV (1947), 317.

[176] *Sum. Theol.*, I, q. 86, a. 1 c. Cf. *ibid.*, q. 85, a. 1 ad 5m; III, q. 11, a. 2 ad 1m; etc.

Revert to the problem: man by his imagination knows a singular and by his intellect understands a universal nature; the
question raised is how can he know that the universal nature
he understands is the nature of the singular that he is imagining;
the very terms of the question involve reflection on one's acts
of understanding and imagining; and the very nature of understanding, which initially is insight into phantasm, supplies the
answer.

Intellectual knowledge of the contingent raises no further problem.[177] But there does remain a prior issue, namely, how can
the act existing in a material organ, such as the phantasm, be
the agent object of immaterial intellect. Now Aquinas himself
was concerned with this possibility. He pointed out that, since
the objects of Platonist science were immaterial ideas, Platonist
doctrine had no use for an agent intellect; on the other hand,
since the objects of Aristotelian science were material things and
only potentially intelligible, there had to be a power of the soul
to illuminate phantasms, make them intelligible in act, make them
objects in act,[178] produce the immaterial in act,[179] produce the
universal,[180] by way of abstracting species from individual matter
or from material conditions.[181] Such statements raise three questions: what precisely is illuminated, immaterialized, universalized;
in what does the illumination, immaterialization, universalization
consist; and how can that provide an object in act for the possible
intellect?

As to the first question, it is plain that phantasms are illuminated,
immaterialized, univeisalized, made intelligible in act. Aquinas
said so repeatedly. More precisely, it is phantasm, not in the
sense of act of the imagination, but in the sense of what is imagined,
that is illuminated; for what is illuminated is what will be known;
and, certainly, insights into phantasm are not insights into the
nature of acts of imagination but insights into the nature of what

---

[177] *Ibid.*, I, q. 86, a. 3 c. See pages 64 ff above.
[178] *Sum. Theol.*, I, q. 79, a. 4 ad 3m; a. 7 c.
[179] *Ibid.*, a. 4 ad 4m.
[180] *Ibid.*, a. 5 ad 2m; *De Sp. Cr.*, a. 10 ad 14m.
[181] *Sum. Theol.*, I, aa. 3 et 4; *In III de An.*, lect. 10; *De Sp. Cr.*, aa. 9 et 10;
C. Gent., II, 76-78.

imagination presents; as Aquinas put it, insight into phantasm is
like looking in, not looking at, a mirror.[182]

As to the second question, there is an interesting Thomist objection against a possible Averroist alternative that would account for our knowing by a separate possible intellect on the ground
that species in the separate intellect irradiate our phantasms.
The objection runs:

> Secundo, quod talis irradiatio phantasmatum non poterit
> facere quod phantasmata sunt intelligibilia actu: non enim
> fiunt phantasmata intelligibilia actu nisi per abstractionem;
> hoc autem magis erit receptio quam abstractio. Et iterum
> cum omnis receptio sit secundum naturam recepti, irradiatio
> specierum intelligibilium quae sunt in intellectu possibili, non
> erit in phantasmatibus quae sunt in nobis, intelligibiliter sed
> sensibiliter et materialiter....[183]

From this passage it would seem that Aquinas did not consider
his own theory to involve the reception in phantasm of some
virtue or quality; what he affirmed was an abstraction that is
opposed to reception.

The foregoing is negative. On the positive side there is a list
of four requirements: the presence of agent intellect; the presence
of phantasms; proper dispositions of the sensitive faculties; and,
inasmuch as understanding one thing depends on understanding
another, practice.[184] The first two requirements recur in a description of illumination of phantasm as a particular case of the
general increase of sensitive power resulting from the conjunction
of sense with intellect.[185] The third requirement is connected
with the work of the *cogitativa* which operates under the influence
of intellect[186] and prepares suitable phantasms;[187] the significance
of this preparation appears from the statement that different
intelligible species result from different arrangements of phantasms
just as different meanings result from different arrangements of

---

[182] *De Ver.*, q. 2, a. 6 c. Cf. q. 10, a. 9 c.
[183] *De Unitate Int.*, c. IV, ed. Keeler §98. The "irradiatio phantasmatum"
is an objective genitive; the "irradiatio specierum" seems to be a genitive
of origin.
[184] *Sum. Theol.*, I, q. 79, a. 4 ad 3m.
[185] *Ibid.*, q. 85, a. 1 ad 4m.
[186] *Ibid.*, q. 78, a. 4, ob. 5a et ad 5m.
[187] *C. Gent.*, II, 73 §14-16 and 26-28.

letters.[188] The fourth requirement is a matter of common experience: the expert can understand where the layman can be only puzzled; the expert sees problems where the layman can barely suspect them.

The third question is whether the foregoing really suffices. It suffices if it enables one to distinguish between intelligible in potency, intelligible in act but understood in potency, and understood in act, just as clearly and precisely as we distinguish between colors in the dark, colors in daylight but not actually seen, and colors actually seen. Moreover, since the work of the *cogitativa* and the influence of past experience regard particular instances of understanding, the main burden of accounting for the threefold distinction must rest upon the prior requirements, namely, the presence of agent intellect and the presence of phantasms.

Now I think that any reader who will recall what has been gathered from Aquinas' statements on intellectual light[189] will also see that Aquinas in affirming an abstractive illumination of phantasm has left us not a puzzle but a solution. The imagined object as merely imagined and as present to a merely sensitive consciousness (subject) is not, properly speaking, intelligible in potency;[190] but the same object present to a subject that is intelligent as well as sensitive may fairly be described as intelligible in potency. Thus, pure reverie, in which image succeeds image in the inner human cinema with never a care for the why or wherefore, illustrates the intelligible in potency. But let active intelligence intervene:[191] there is a care for the why and wherefore; there is wonder and inquiry; there is the alertness of the scientist or technician, the mathematician or philosopher, for whom the imagined object no longer is merely given but also a something-to-be-understood. It is the imagined object as present to intelligent consciousness as something-to-be-understood that con-

---

[188] *Sum. Theol.*, II-II, q. 173, a. 2 c.

[189] See pages 79-85 above.

[190] *De Pot.*, q. 7, a. 10 c: "ipsa res quae est extra animam, omnino est extra genus intelligibile." The meaning is that material entities of themselves are not related to intellectual knowledge; the context deals with the non-reciprocal real relation of *scientia ad scibile*.

[191] This intervention would be what is meant by *Sum. Theol.*, I, q. 85, a. 1 ad 3m: "... ex conversione intellectus agentis supra phantasmata...."

stitutes the intelligible in act. Further, this illumination of the imagined object, this reception of it within the field of intellectual light, has the characteristic of being abstractive; for it is not the imagined object in all respects that is regarded as a something-to-be-understood; no one spontaneously endeavors to understand why "here" is "here" and why "now" is not "then"; effort is confined to grasping natures, just as explanation is always in terms of the character of persons, the natures of things, the circumstances of events, but never in terms of their being then and there. Finally, inquiry and wonder give place to actual understanding; the imagined object no longer is something-to-be-understood but something actually understood; this involves no diffference in the phantasm but only in the possible intellect, just as the difference between colors in daylight and colors actually seen involves no difference in the colors but only in eyes and sight; accordingly, the intelligible "species quae," which is understood in phantasm, is like the actually seen color, which is seen in the colored thing.[192]

It remains that a note be added on the *per se* infallibility of intellect. In Aristotle as well as Aquinas it is described by pointing out that definitions are neither true nor false.[193] But infallibility seems to mean more than such a negation and, in fact, there is another element to be observed in the original Aristotelian statement and in the Thomist *Commentary*. It is that infallibility is with respect to the first object of intellect, the *quod quid est*, the τὸ τί ἦν εἶναι; further, infallibility in direct understanding is like the infallibility of sight. Plainly, this seems to suggest that one examine insight for its infallibility; moreover, what one

---

[192] "Actually seen" is predicated of color by extrinsic denomination; similarly the *actu intellectum* is not a reality received in the phantasm. Hence the accuracy of the expression (*C. Gent.*, II, 59 §14) that has phantasms *actu intellecta* inasmuch as they are one with the actuated possible intellect. This factor is to be born in mind in connection with the problems raised by notes 35, 36, 145, 150, 174. Though I have spoken throughout in terms of what the *species qua* ultimately proves to be, namely, a *principium formale quo* (*De Sp. Cr.*, a. 9 ad 6m), accurate interpretation must include awareness of a gradual process of clarification and, no less, of the economic survival in later works of less accurate modes of speech which do not affect the immediate issue.

[193] *In III de An.*, lect. 11 §762.

finds, seems to me to provide a desired positive complement to the negation that definitions are neither true or false. No one misunderstands things as he imagines them: for insight into phantasm to be erroneous either one must fancy what is not or else fail to imagine what is; of itself, *per se*, apart from errors in imagining, insight is infallible; and, were that not so, one would not expect to correct misunderstandings by pointing out what has been overlooked or by correcting what mistakenly has been fancied.

CONCLUSION

Abstraction is from matter, and matter is an analogous term. One makes an initial approximation to the analogy by considering the proportion of wood to tables and bronze to statues; this broad analogy makes matter the subject of change or of difference, and so substance and genus are instances of matter. But an observation made by Averroes and repeated by Aquinas[194] fixes the proximately relevant analogy: natural form stands to natural matter, as the object of insight (*forma intelligibilis*) stands to the object of imagination (*materia sensibilis*); the former part of this analogy supplies the basis for an account of the metaphysical conditions of abstraction; the latter part supplies the basis for its psychological description.

On the metaphysical side, because the material thing has an intelligible component, form, it follows that what is known by understanding is real and not merely ideal as materialists, idealists, and pseudo-realists are prone to assume. Again, because the thing is form and matter, there is a possible knowledge of the thing by abstraction of form from matter. Further, because matter is a principle of limitation, so that form of itself is universal,[195] this abstract knowledge will be universal. But the act of knowing is as much an ontological reality as the known: as the thing is constituted determinately by its form, so the knowing is constituted determinately by its form, which will be similar to the form of the known; on the other hand, there cannot be material as well as formal assimilation of knowing to known, else the knowing would be, but not know, the known; further,

---

[194] *De Ver.*, q. 10, a. 8 ad 1m (1ae ser).
[195] *Ibid.*, q. 10, a. 5 c.

where the knowing has the characteristics of necessity and universality, its form must be received immaterially; finally, a general theorem that knowledge is by immateriality may be constructed within the assumptions of the Thomist system.

On the psychological side, because the object of insight is the object of pre-conceptual knowing, there is a certain vacillation in its description. Primarily insight adds to our knowledge a grasp of intelligible unity in sensible multiplicity; as the grasp of this unity, it is *intelligentia indivisibilium*.[196] Still, it is not any unity or unity in general that is grasped, but the unity specific and proportionate to the sensible multiplicity presented; further, this intelligible unity divides the sensible multiplicity into a part necessary for the unity to be the unity it is and, on the other hand, a residue that also happens to be given; the former part is described as *partes speciei, de ratione speciei, materia communis*; the latter residual part is described as *partes materiae*. The dividing line does not always fall in the same place: physical abstraction is from individual or assigned matter with its consequents of determinate place and time and the possibility of change; mathematical abstraction is from sensible matter (hot and cold, wet and dry, bright and dark, etc.) as well. The so-called third degree of abstraction is more properly named a separation; it is different in kind from the preceding; because it is a separation, disputes about real distinctions are disputes about the validity of metaphysical concepts. *Forma intelligibilis* would seem to be, at least normally, the specific intelligible unity. *Quidditas rei materialis* is the intelligible unity plus common matter; primarily, it is the quiddity of substance;[197] but it is sound Aristotelian doctrine to speak of the quiddities of accidents.[198] *Species* has both the meaning of form and the meaning of quiddity.[199]

There are three stages to physical and mathematical abstraction: the objective, the apprehensive, the formative. Objective abstraction is the illumination of phantasm, the imagined object; it consists in treating the imagined object as something to be un-

---

[196] Aristotle's study of unity is a study of the ἀδιαιρετόν; *Met.*, I, 1, 1052a 36; b 15. Hence, *De An.*, III, 6, 430a 26; 430b 5; lect. 11.

[197] *Sum. Theol.*, I, q. 85, a. 5 c.

[198] *In VII Met.*, lect. 4.

[199] *Ibid.*, lect. 9 §1473.

derstood as far as its specific nature goes; like action and passion, it is one reality with two aspects; as effected by agent intellect, it may be named efficient; as effecting the imagined object, it may be named instrumental. Next, with regard to apprehensive abstraction, one has to distinguish between first act and second act: first act is the possible intellect informed and actuated by a species *qua*; second act proceeds from first as *esse* from form and action from principle of action; accordingly, the procession is *processio operationis*; the second act consists in grasping, knowing, considering an intelligible species *quae* in the imagined object. *Per se* this second act is infallible; consequent to it by a sort of reflection, there is indirect, intellectual knowledge of the singular, i.e. a reflective grasping that the universal nature understood is the nature of the particular imagined. Thirdly, there is the act of formative abstraction; this consists in an act of meaning or defining; but whenever there is an act of meaning or defining, by that very fact there is something meant or defined; accordingly, formative abstraction may also be described as positing a universal *ratio* or an *intentio intellecta*.

The principal efficient cause of apprehensive abstraction is agent intellect; the instrumental efficient cause is the illuminated phantasm; hence not only is the impression of the species *qua* a *passio* but also the consequent second act, *intelligere*, is a *pati*; again, the procession of species *qua* and *intelligere* from agent intellect and phantasm is a *processio operati*; but, as already noted, the procession of intelligere from species *qua* is *processio operationis*. Now formative abstraction proceeds from apprehensive abstraction just as the apprehensive abstraction proceeds from agent intellect and phantasm; hence its procession is *processio operati*; and, as ground of this procession, *intelligere* is named *dicere*. However, the procession of the formative abstraction has a special property; it is an *emanatio intelligibilis*, an activity of rational consciousness, the production of a product because and inasmuch as the sufficiency of the sufficient grounds for the product are known. Just as we affirm existence because and inasmuch as we know the sufficiency of sufficient grounds for affirming it, so also we mean and define essences because and inasmuch as we understand them. In similar fashion by *processio*

operati and *emanatio intelligibilis* a rational act of love proceeds from a judgment of value.

Let us now compare objects. Objective abstraction, the illumination of phantasm, constitutes the imagined object as something to be understood with regard to its specific nature. Apprehensive abstraction, insight into phantasm, actually understands what objective abstraction presented to be understood.
But what was presented to be understood was the imagined object, the phantasm; hence it was perfectly natural and no less
reasonable for Aquinas so repeatedly to affirm that the object
of human intellect in this life was the phantasm; if one cannot
see that, then it would seem that one has very little idea of what
Aquinas was talking about. But if what is understood is the phantasm, the imagined object, still what is added to knowledge, what
is known, precisely by understanding is the *forma intelligibilis*,
the quiddity, the *species intelligibilis quae*. This is known in
phantasm just as actually seen colors are seen in colored things.
It is not merely that there is the act of understanding and simultaneously the act of imagination, each with its respective object.
But the two objects are intrinsically related: the imagined object
is presented as something to be understood; and the insight or
apprehensive abstraction grasps the intelligibility of the imagined
object in the imagined object; thus, insight grasps imagined equal
radii in a plane surface as the necessary and sufficient condition of
an imagined uniform curve; imagination presents terms which
insight intelligibly relates or unifies.[200]

Thus, while apprehensive abstraction is not of material conditions still it is not of something apart from material conditions.
It is formative abstraction that sets up the object that is apart
from material conditions; it does so by meaning it or by defining it;
one can mean "circle" without meaning any particular instance
of circle; but one cannot grasp, intuit, know by inspection the

---

[200] This is the critical point in philosophy. For a materialist the terms are
real, the intelligible unification subjective; for an idealist the terms cannot
be reality and the intelligible unification subjective; for an idealist the terms
cannot be reality and the intelligible unification is not objective; for the Platonist the terms are not reality but the intelligible unifications are objective
in another world; for the Aristotelian both are objective in this world; Tho-
mism adds a third category, existence, to Aristotelian matter and form.

necessary and sufficient condition of circularity except in a diagram. In terms of the universal, apprehensive abstraction knows the universal in a particular instance; formative abstraction knows the universal that is common to many; and reflection on formative abstraction knows the universal as universal, the universal precisely as common to many. Again, the objects of apprehensive and of formative abstraction are essentially the same but modally different; they are essentially the same, for it is the same essence that is known; they are modally different, for what apprehensive abstraction knows only in the imagined instance, formative abstraction knows apart from any instances. On the other hand, though apprehensive abstraction must be with respect to an instance it must always be of a universal for always the individual is *pars materiae*; but while formative abstraction can posit the universal apart from any instance, still the act of meaning can mean the individual just as easily as it can mean the universal; but it means the universal in virtue of apprehensive abstraction and it means the particular in virtue of consequent indirect knowledge of the particular; and so while the particular can be meant, it cannot be defined explanatorily, quidditatively. Finally, there is the contrast between *quidditas* and *res*: apprehensive abstraction knows the *quidditas* such as *humanitas*; formative abstraction posits the *res* such as *homo*; again, apprehensive abstraction knows the *forma intelligibilis*, but formative abstraction posits the thing in which metaphysical analysis will uncover a *forma naturalis*.

Our plan of operations has been to investigate, first, the psychology relevant to an account of the Thomist concept of *verbum*; secondly, the relevant metaphysics; thirdly, issues in which the relevant psychology and metaphysics are inextricably joined together; and, fourthly, the application of this psychology and metaphysics to divine knowledge. The present article concludes the first three sections of the investigation. All that has been said so far and all that remains to be said can be reduced to a single proposition that, when Aquinas used the term, *intelligibile*, his primary meaning was not whatever can be conceived, such as matter, nothing, and sin, but whatever can be known by understanding. The proof of such a contention can only be inductive, i.e. it increases cumulatively as the correspondence between the contention with its implications and, on the other hand, the statements of Aquinas are found to exist exactly, extensively, and illuminatively. But, may it be noted, the proof of any opposed view cannot but have the same inductive character; insofar as such proofs of opposed views exist, perhaps some readers will agree with me in not finding their correspondence with the statements of Aquinas to offer a comparable measure of exactitude, extent, and light.

V

Imago Dei

... quia et illic intelligendo conspicimus tamquam dicentem, et verbum eius, id est, Patrem et Filium, atque inde procedentem charitatem utrique communem, scilicet Spiritum sanctum

     —St. Augustine, *De Trinitate*, XV, vi, 10.

... primo et principaliter attenditur imago Trinitatis in mente secundum actus, prout scilicet ex notitia quam habemus, cogitando interius verbum formamus, et ex hoc in amorem prorumpimus.

     —St. Thomas, *Sum. Theol.*, I, q. 93, a. 7 c.

Our inquiry began from the observation of a strange constrast.[1] St. Augustine restricted the image of God within us to the *ratio superior*.[2] St. Thomas restricted the image to the *principium verbi, verbum*, and *amor* of rational creatures.[3] But in prevalent theological opinion there is as good an analogy to the procession of the Word in human imagination as in human intellect, while the analogy to the procession of the Holy Spirit is wrapped in deepest obscurity.[4] It seemed possible to eliminate the obscurity connected with the second procession by eliminating the superficiality connected with opinions on the first. With this end in view we have devoted four articles to an exploration of related points in Thomist metaphysics and rational psychology. We now turn to the *imago Dei*,[5] which is the central issue both in Aquinas' thought on *verbum* and, as well, in our inquiry.

Ipsum intelligere

There are two radically opposed views of knowing.[6] For the Platonist, knowing is primarily a confrontation; it supposes the

---

[1] See chapters I-IV.

[2] St. Augustine, *De Trinitate*, XII, iv, 4; vii, 10 (*PL* XLII, 1000, 1003).

[3] *Sum. Theol.*, I, q. 93, a. 6 c.

[4] See chapter I.

[5] We refer to the *imago similitudinis* of trinitarian theory. On the *imago conformitatis*, see P. Paluscsák, *Xenia Thom.*, II (1925), 119-54.

[6] *C. Gent.*, II, 98 §19 f.

duality of knower and known; it consists in a consequent, added movement. The supposition of duality appears in Plato's inference that, because we know ideas, therefore ideas subsist. The conception of knowing as movement appears in Plato's dilemma that the subsistent idea of Being either must be in movement or else must be without knowing.[7] The same dilemma forced Plotinus to place the One beyond knowing; *Nous* could not be first, because *Nous* could not be simple. In St. Augustine the notion that knowing is by confrontation appears in the affirmation that we somehow see and consult the eternal reasons. In the medieval writers of the Augustinian reaction, knowing as confrontation reappears in the *species impressa* that is an object and in the doctrine of intuitive, intellectual cognition of material and singular existents. To cut a long story short, contemporary dogmatic realists escape the critical problem by asserting a confrontation of intellect with concrete reality.

For the Aristotelian, on the other hand, confrontation is secondary. Primarily and essentially knowing is perfection, act, identity. Sense in act is the sensible in act. Intellect in act is the intelligible in act. In this material world, of course, besides the knower in act and the known in act, there are also the knower in potency and the known in potency; and while the former are identical, still the latter are distinct. None the less, potency is not essential to knowing and therefore distinction is not essential to knowing. It follows that in immaterial substances, as one negates potency, so also one negates distinction: "In his quae sunt sine materia, idem est intelligens et intellectum."[8] A Platonist subsistent idea of Being would have to sacrifice immobility to have knowledge; but Aristotle, because he conceived knowing as primarily not confrontation but identity in act, was able to affirm the intelligence in act of his immovable mover.

As there are two radically opposed views of knowing, so there are two radically opposed views of intellect. All men are aware of their sensations. All educated men, at least, are aware of their thoughts and so of the division of thoughts into concepts, judgments, and inferences. But only Aristotelians are sufficiently

---

[7] Plato, *Sophistes*, 248e.
[8] Aristotle, *De Anima*, III, 4, 430a 3 ff; *Met.*, Λ, 9, 1075a 3 ff.

aware of their intellects to turn this awareness to philosophic
account. Between the activities of sense and, on the other hand,
the concepts, judgments, and inferences that constitute thought,
there stands the intellect itself. Unlike the natures of material
things, which can be known only by what they do, human intellect
can be known by what it is. Efficiently, it is the light of intelligence within us, the drive to wonder, to reflection, to criticism,
the source of all science and philosophy. Receptively, it offers
the three aspects of potency, habit, and act. As potency, human
intellect is the capacity to understand; it is common to all men,
for even the stupidest of men at least occasionnaly understand.
As habit, human intellect is fivefold: it is *nous*, grasping the point;
episteme, grasping its implications; reflective *sophia* and *phrone-
sis*, understanding what is and what is to be done, and finally,
tekhne, grasping how to do it.

These habits are not the habitual possession of concepts, judgments, syllogisms. A sergeant-major with his manual-at-arms
by rote knows his terms, his principles, his reasons; he expounds
them with ease, with promptitude, and perhaps with pleasure;
but he is exactly what is not meant by a man of developed intelligence. For intellectual habit is not possession of the book
but freedom from the book. It is the birth and life in us of the
light and evidence by which we operate on our own. It enables
us to recast definitions, to adjust principles, to throw chains of
reasoning into new perspectives according to variations of cir-
cumstance and exigencies of the occasion. As intellectual habit
is freedom from the book, so its genesis is not tied to the book.
In every first instance there were no books. In every second
instance what is needed is not a book but a teacher, a man who
understands, a man who can break down the book's explanation
into still more numerous steps for the tardy and, contrariwise,
for the intelligent reduce the book's excessive elaborateness to
essentials.

Intellectual habits, then, are not habits of concepts, judgments,
inferences; they are habits of understanding; from them with
promptitude, ease, pleasure, there results intelligence in act. Finally, it is intelligence in act that is the intellect, knowable and
known by what it is, and so the known sufficient ground and
cause of what it does. To define, not as a parrot but intelligently,

intelligence must be in act; for definition is but the expression of intelligence in act. To infer, not as a mere logical exercise but as learning, intelligence in act must be developing and expressing its development in an inference. To judge rationally and responsibly, intelligence must reach the reflective act that terminates a sweep through all relevant evidence, past as well as present, sensible as well as intellectual, to grasp the sufficiency of the evidence for the judgment.[9]

Against this view of intellect, there stands only its privation. Conceptualists conceive human intellect only in terms of what it does; but their neglect of what intellect is, prior to what it does, has a variety of causes. Most commonly they do not advert to the act of understanding. They take concepts for granted; they are busy working out arguments to produce certitudes; they prolong their spontaneous tendencies to extroversion into philosophy, where they concentrate on metaphysics and neglect gnoseology. Still, a conceptualist can advert to the fact of understanding, to the difference between intelligent men and stupid men, to opposed manners of systematic conception with consequent oppositions in judgments and inferences. But advertence falls short of analysis. It is one thing to be aware of one's intelligence in act; it is another to distinguish agent and possible intellect, to compare possible intellect in potency, in habit, and in act, to relate intelligence in act, on the one hand, to sensible and imagined data and, on the other hand, to concepts, judgments, and inferences. Finally, one can advert to intelligence and know how it is analysed and yet recoil from accepting the analysis. It is so much more difficult to do philosophy when's one's hands are tied by an array of facts; it is so much more easy to affirm an intellectual intuition of concrete reality, and thus eliminate so many problems, when the exact nature of the intellect is shrouded in obscurity.

Such are the basic positions. The Platonist conceives knowing as primarily confrontation, but the Aristotelian conceives knowing as primarily perfection, act, identity; again, the conceptualist knows human intellect only by what it does, but the intellectualist

---

[9] See chapters I and II.

knows and analyzes not only what intelligence in act does but also what it is.

It is not too surprising that conceptualists, who do not advert to their own acts of understanding, fail to observe such advertence in Aristotle and in Aquinas. The logical consequences of such a failure have, quite fortunately for my purpose, been put down in black and white.[10] Are not Aristotle's forms just Plato's ideas, plucked from their noetic heaven, and shoved into material things? Is not Aristotle's abstraction just a psychological fabrication, invented to provide us with knowledge of the Platonic ideas thrust into material things? Let us add a third question: Does there not seem to be a Rube Goldberg love of complexity in distinguishing between agent intellect, illuminated phantasm, possible intellect, intelligible species, intellection as production, inner word, and intellection as knowing, when all that results is the same spiritual look at a universal that John Duns Scotus and William of Ockham attained so much more simply and directly? I do hope that conceptualist interpreters of Aristotle and Aquinas will read and study Fr. Day's book and will be roused to something better than his and their suppositions.

For the intellectualist, obviously, it is impossible to confuse the Aristotelian form with the Platonic idea. Form is the *ousia* that is not a universal,[11] but a cause of being.[12] Ontologically it is intermediary between material multiplicity and flux and, on the other hand, that intelligible and determinate unity we call *ens*, *unum*, and *quid*. Form is what causes matter to be a thing. On the cognitional side, form is known in knowing the answer to the question: Why are the sensible data to be conceived as of one thing, of a man, of a house?[13] But knowing why and knowing the cause, like knowing the reason and knowing the real reason, are descriptions of the act of understanding. As then form mediates causally between matter and thing, so understanding mediates causally between sensible data and conception. By a stroke of genius Aristotle replaced mythical Platonic *anamnesis* by psychological

---

[10] S. Day, *Intuitive Cognition, A Key to the Significance of the Later Scholastics*, The Franciscan Institute, St. Bonaventure, N. Y., 1947, pp. 30 f.

[11] Aristotle, *Met.*, Z, 16, 1041a 4.

[12] *Met.*, Δ, 8, 1017b 14 ff.; Z, 17, 1041a 9 f.; 1041b 7 ff.; 25 ff.

[13] *Met.*, Z, 17, 1041a 9—1041b 9.

fact and, to describe the psychological fact, eliminated the subsistent ideas to introduce formal causes in material things. To complete the answer to Fr. Day, one need only note that primarily intellect is understanding and that understanding of the material is universal.[14]

As the Aristotelian form differs from the Platonic idea, so the Aristotelian separate substance differs from the Platonic separate idea. The separate idea is what is known by confrontation in conception. The separate substance is at once a pure form and a pure act of understanding. When we understand, we understand with respect to sensible data. But the separate substances understand, yet have no senses. As their understanding is not of this or that sensible presentation, so it is not potency but act and not by confrontation with the other, but by and in identity with the self. "In his quae sunt sine materia, idem est intelligens et intellectum." Aristotle did not anticipate Hegel to posit Absolute thinking relative thought. He extrapolated from insight into phantasm to posit pure understanding unlimited by sensible presentation. If you object that modern interpreters translate νόησις νοήσεως as "thinking thought," I readily grant what this implies, namely, that modern interpreters suppose Aristotle to have been a conceptualist. But also I retort that medieval translators did not write "cogitatio cogitationis" but "intelligentia intelligentiae."[15] It seems to follow that medieval translators did not regard Aristotle as a conceptualist.

Aquinas accepted and developed Aristotle. He took over the distinction between agent and possible intellect, the latter's dependence on phantasm, the account of its potency, habits, and acts, and the distinction between the two operations of intellect. From Augustinian speculation on the procession of the inner word, he was led to distinguish far more sharply than Aristotle did between intelligence in act and its products of definition and judgment. But his greater debt was to Augustinian theory of judgment with its appeal to the eternal reasons; Aquinas trans-

[14] See Fr. Day's argument, *op. cit.*, pp. 3-36. For corrections of W. Jaeger, see F. Nuyens, *L'évolution de la psychologie d'Aristote*, Louvain-The Hague-Paris, 1948.

[15] Aquinas, *In XII Met.*, lect. 11; *Sum. Theol.*, I, q. 79, a. 10; *De subst. sep.*, c. XII (Mandonnet ed., I, 117).

posed this appeal into his own "participatio creata lucis increatae" to secure for the Aristotelian theory of knowing by identity the possibility of self-transcendence in finite intellect.[16] On his own, Aquinas identified intelligible species with intellectual habit to relate species to *intelligere* as form to *esse*,[17] a parallel that supposes a grasp of the real distinction between finite essence and existence.[18] While Aristotle had only one kind of separate substance, Aquinas worked out distinct theories of God as *ipsum intelligere* and of angels in whom essence, existence, intellect, and *intelligere* are really distinct.[19] From the *Sentences* he appreciated the advantage of knowing as identity in reconciling divine simplicity with divine knowledge.[20] From the *Sentences* he appreciated the problem that knowing as identity creates for knowledge of the other.[21] Still, there is to be discerned an increasing Aristotelianism. In the *De Veritate* the appeal is to immateriality as principle of both knowing and being known;[22] in the *Contra Gentiles* immateriality is one argument out of many,[23] with Aristotelian considerations abundant;[24] in the *Summa Theologica* this exuberance is pruned. Sense differs from the sensible, intellect differs from the intelligible, only inasmuch as they are in potency. But in God there is no potency. Hence in God substance, essence,

---

[16] See pages 82 ff aboves. Cf. L. D'Izzalini, "Il principio intellettivo della ragione humana nelle opere di S. Tommaso d'Aquino," *Anal. Greg.*, XXXI, Rome, 1943.

[17] *De Ver.*, q. 10, a. 2 c., *ad fin. Sum. Theol.*, I, q. 14, a. 4 c.; q. 34, a. 1 ad 2m. Cajetan, *In I*, q. 12, a. 2, XVI (ed. Leon., IV, 119).

[18] It is not surprising that Siger of Brabant and Godfrey of Fontaines, who denied the real distinction, also should deny such a distinction between *species* and *intelligere*. Nor again is it surprising that Hervé de Nédellec who denied the real distinction (see E. Hocedez, *Aegidii Romani theoremata de esse et essentia*, Louvain, 1930, pp. [92]-[94]), conceived the *species* as a *movens* (*Durandi de S. Porciano, O.P., quaestio de natura cognitionis, etc.*, ed. J. Koch, Opuscula et Textus [Grabmann et Pelster], fasc. VI, Monasterii, 1935, p. 67) contrary to *De Ver.*, q. 22, a. 5, ad 8m.

[19] *Sum. Theol.*, I, q. 54, aa. 1-3, *et loc. par.*

[20] *In I Sent.*, d. 35, q. 1, a. 1 ad 3m.

[21] *Ibid.*, a. 2.

[22] *De Ver.*, q. 2, a. 2 c.

[23] *C. Gent.*, I, 44 §5.

[24] *Ibid.*, 45-48.

esse, intellect, species, *intelligere* are all one and the same.[25] Indeed, in divine self-knowledge it is impossible to say that knowing and known are similar, for similarity supposes duality and, until one reaches trinitarian doctrine, one knows nothing of more than one in God.[26]

When Aquinas spoke of God as *ipsum intelligere,* did he mean that God was a pure act of understanding? To that conclusion we have been working through four articles. But to cap that cumulative argument, there comes the impossibility of Aquinas having meant anything else. Either *ipsum intelligere* is analogous to sensation, or it is analogous to understanding, or it is analogous to conception, or it is analogous to nothing that we know. No one will affirm that *ipsum intelligere* is analogous to sensation. But is cannot be analogous to conception; for it is the *dicens, dicere, verbum* of trinitarian thery that is analogous to conception; and *ipsum intelligere* is demonstrable by the natural light of reason, while trinitarian doctrine is not. Further, in trinitarian theory *intelligere* is essential act common to Father, Son, and Spirit, while *dicere* is notional act and proper to the Father. Finally, there is a divine knowing prior in the order of our conception to the divine utterance of *verbum*: "Ipse autem conceptus cordis de ratione sua habet quod ab alio procedat, scilicet, a notitia concipientis";[27] and that prior knowing, that prior *notitia,* cannot be conceptual; it cannot be conceptual in potency, for in God there is no potency; it cannot be conceptual in habit, for in God there is no habit; it cannot be conceptual in act, for then conception in act would be prior to itself. But if *ipsum intelligere* is analogous neither to sensation nor to conception, it is not a solution to say that it is analogous to nothing that we know; for what is unknown cannot be meant or even named.[28] It remains

---

[25] *Sum. Theol.,* I, q. 14, aa. 2, 4.

[26] *Ibid.,* q. 16, a. 5 ad 2m.

[27] *Ibid.,* q. 34, a. 1 c.

[28] *Ibid.,* q. 13, a. 1 c.: Secundum igitur quod aliquid a nobis intellectu cognosci potest, sic a nobis potest nominari. It may be said that the prior *notitia* is analogus to consciousness. But consciousness is either concomitant, reflective, or rational. Concomitant consciousness is awareness of one's act and oneself in knowing something else; this has no place in God who knows first Himself and then other things. Reflective consciousness supposes con-

that *ipsum intelligere* is analogous to understanding, that God
is an infinite and substantial act of understanding, that as the
Father is God, the Son is God, the Holy Spirit is God, so also each
is one and the same infinite and substantial act of understanding,
finally that, though each is the pure act of understanding, still
only the Father understands as uttering the Word.[29]

THE NECESSITY OF *Verbum*

We began our inquiry by listing seven elements in the Thomist
concept of an inner word.[30] Six of these have been elucidated
sufficiently. It remains that the necessity of the inner word be
treated.

A few elementary points may be mentioned briefly. We are
not concerned with the concept of *verbum* in the *Commentary
on the Sentences*, in which Thomist thought on this issue had not
yet matured.[31] We are not concerned with the necessity of an
object for a cognitional act. If there is an *intelligere*, there must
be an *intellectum* as well as an *intelligens*; but this does not prove
the necessity of a *verbum*; for a *verbum* has two notes; it is not
only *intellectum* but also *expressum ab alio*.[32] We are not concerned with the necessity of the occurrence of *verbum* in our minds.
That is perfectly simple: Once one understands, the proportionate
cause for the inner word exists; once the proportionate cause
exists, the effect follows, unless some impediment intervenes;
but no impediment can intervene between understanding and its
inner word.[33] Hence, granted we understand, it necessarily follows

comitant consciousness. Rational consciousness pertains to the intelligible
procession of inner words, to the fact that they proceed from sufficient grounds
because they are known to be sufficient.

[29] *Ibid.*, q. 34, a. 1, ad 3m; a. 2 ad 4m.

[30] See pages 1-10 above.

[31] *Ibid.*, p. 360, note 51. Scripture speaks not only of the Word of God
(God the Son) but also of the word of God (God's revelation, manifestation).
Both elements are found in St. Augustine's account of *verbum* (M. Schmaus,
Die psychologische Trinitätslehre des hl. Augustinus, Münster i. W., 1927,
pp. 331 ff.). This perhaps lies behind the notion of the *Sentences* that *verbum*
is *species* as ordained to manifestation.

[32] *De Ver.*, q. 4, a. 2 c.

[33] The will can prevent the occurrence of *intelligere* by preventing the oc-

that we utter an inner word. We are not concerned with the necessity *quoad se* of the Word in God; whatever is in God is necessary.
But we are concerned with the essential necessity of the inner
word in us; why is our knowledge such that inner words are necessary in it? Next, we are concerned with the necessity *quoad
nos* of an inner word in divine self-knowledge and in divine knowledge of the other. Why cannot we establish by the light of natural
reason that there is a Word in God? Even if Aristotle's theorem
that knowing is by identity excludes our demonstrating the existence of the Word from divine self-knowledge, still why cannot
we demonstrate it from divine knowledge of the other?

The essential necessity of inner words in us appears as soon as
Aquinas got beyond the initial period of the *Sentences*. In the *De
Veritate* the Aristotelian parallel between nature and art was given
its complement by a parallel between speculative and practical
intellect. Practical intellect thinks out plans, designs, programs.
Such plans, say, of an architect, are the form whence external
operation proceeds. But they cannot be the form whence proceeds the "thinking out" that evolves the plans. There must be
a prior form, the intellectual habit of art, that stands to the thinking as the thought-out plan stands to the external operation.
But if nature and art are parallel, so that nature is but God's art-
istry, it follows that there will be a parallel between speculative
knowledge of nature and pratical knowledge of art. Just as the
habit of art results in the thinking out of plans whence artefacts
are produced, so speculative habit or form, by which we understand in act, results in the *quidditas formata* and the *compositio
vel divisio* by which we come to knowledge of external things.[34]
Needless to say, this intermediate role of the inner word between
our understanding and the external thing does not disappear
in later Thomist thought.[35]

---

currence of a corresponding phantasm. Again, the will is the cause of an act
of belief, but though the latter is a *verbum*, it is not a *verbum* proceeding directly from an *intelligere*. But we cannot permit the occurrence of *intelligere*
and yet prevent the procession of its immediate *verbum*.

[34] *De Ver.*, q. 3, a. 2 c.

[35] *Ibid.*, q. 4, a. 2 ad 3m; *De Pot.*, q. 8, a. 1 c; *Sum. Theol.*, q. 34, a. 1 ad
3m *ad fin.*; *Quodl.*, V, a 9 ad 1m; *In Ioan.*, c. 1, lect. 1.

Hence, to ask about the essential necessity of inner words in us, is to ask about the essential necessity of our complementing acts of understanding with inner words to obtain knowledge of external things. The answer will be had by comparing the object of understanding with the external things. Now the first and proper object of understanding, the "what is known inasmuch as one understands," must be simply intelligible; accordingly, the proportionate object of our intellects is the *quidditas rei materialis*.[36] This quiddity prescinds from individual matter, for individual matter is not intelligible in itself but only in its relation to the *per se* universality of forms which it individuates. Again the quiddity prescinds from contingent existence, for contingent existence is not intelligible in itself but only in its relation to the necessarily Existent which is final, exemplary, and efficient cause of contingent beings. The essential necessity of inner words in our intellects is the necessity of effecting the transition from the pre-conceptual *quidditas rei materialis*, first, to the *res*, secondly, to the *res particularis*, thirdly, to the *res particularis existens*. The transition from *quidditas rei* to *res*, say, from *humanitas* to *homo*, occurs in conception in which there emerges intellect's natural knowledge of *ens*.[37] In virtue of this step understanding moves from identity with its pre-conceptual object to confrontation with its conceived object; but as yet the object is only object of thought.[38] The second step is a reflection on phantasm that enables one to mean, though not understand nor explanatorily define the material singular.[39] In this step intellect moves from a universal to a particular object of thought. Finally, by a reflective act of understanding that sweeps through all relevant data, sensible and intelligible, present and remembered, and grasps understanding's proportion to the universe as well,[40] there is uttered the existential judgment through which one knows concrete reality.

We turn to our second question. Why cannot natural reason demonstrate the existence of the divine Word from the premise

[36] See pages 157-168 above.
[37] See chapter II.
[38] *Ibid.*, X (1949), 15 f.
[39] *Ibid.*, 29 ff.
[40] See pages 59-88 above.

of divine self-knowledge? First, the demonstration cannot be effected by contrasting the proper object of understanding with the divine essence. God is simply intelligible. He is pure form identical with existence. There is no distinction between His essence or His existence or His intellect or His understanding.[41] There is not even a distinction between His *esse naturale* and His *esse intelligibile*.[42] Secondly, the demonstration cannot be effected by arguing that without an inner word there would be no confrontation between subject and object. For one cannot demonstrate that such confrontation is essential to knowledge. Primarily and essentially, knowing is by identity. The natural light of reason will never get beyond that identity in demonstrating the nature of self-knowledge in the infinite simplicity of God.

We turn to the third question. If divine self-knowledge has no need of an inner word, as far as natural theology goes, because the knowing is pure understanding and the known is simply intelligible and knowledge is by identity, still divine knowledge of the other seems to require an inner word. For the other is not simply intelligible, nor always in act, nor identical with the knower. Further, in confirmation of this argument, there is the fact that Aquinas wrote some of his finest passages on *verbum* in the context of divine knowledge of the other.[42a] In additional confirmation there is the familiar doctrine that secondary elements in the beatific vision are known *in Verbo*.

Let us begin by considering the confirming arguments. The connection between the divine Word and the divine Ideas pertains to the whole Christian Platonist tradition,[43] and can be traced back to Philo's conception of the Logos as containing the ideas.[44] It follows that one cannot say that Aquinas by an intrinsic exigence of his own thought was led to treat *verbum* in the context of the divine ideas. There may exist such an exigence or there may exist no more than a traditional association. On the latter alternative the confirming arguments do not confirm, and we

[41] *Sum. Theol.*, I, q. 14, aa. 2, 4.
[42] *C. Gent.*, I, 47 §5.
[42a] *De Ver.*, q. 3, a. 2; *C. Gent.*, I, 53; *Sum. Theol.*, I, q. 15, a. 2.
[43] R. Arnou, "Platonisme des Pères," *DTC* XII, 2338 ff.; *De Platonismo Patrum, Textus et Documenta*, ser. theol. 21, Rome, 1935, p. 19.
[44] H. A. Wolfson, *Philo*, Cambridge, 1948, I, 204 ff., 229 ff.

may expect the latter alternative to be the correct one. The Platonist assumption that knowledge involves confrontation led later Scholastics to attribute to the ideas an *esse objectivum*.[45] Certainly Aquinas was free from that error and so he can be expected to apply the Aristotelian theorem of knowledge by identity to reconcile divine simplicity with divine knowledge of the other.

To handle the issue as expeditiously as possible,[46] let us proceed in two steps: first, we draw distinctions with respect to our knowledge; secondly, we proceed from the finite model to God. With regard to our knowledge distinguish (1) the thing with its virtualities, (2) the act of understanding with its primary and its secondary objects, (3) the expression of both primary and secondary objects in inner words. For example, the human soul formally is an intellective soul, subsistent, immortal; it is not formally a sensitive soul nor a vegetative soul; but virtually it does possess the perfection without the imperfection of sensitive and vegetative souls. When, however, we understand the human soul, we understand as primary object an intellective soul and as secondary object the sensitive soul and the vegetative soul; both objects are understood formally and actually, but the secondary object is understood in the primary and in virtue of understanding the primary. Further, once understanding of the human soul has developed, there are not two acts of understanding but one, which primarily is of intellective soul and secondarily, in the perfection of intellective soul, is of the sensitive and vegetative souls. Finally, our one act of understanding expresses itself in many inner words in which are defined intellective, sensitive, and vegetative souls and the relations between them; further, these inner words are the *esse intelligibile* or the *esse intentionale* of soul as distinct both from the *esse naturale* of soul itself and from the *esse intellectum* which is an extrinsic denomination from an *intelligere* of soul whether real or intentional.

Now on Thomist analysis the divine essence formally is itself but eminently it contains all perfection. The divine act of under-

---

[45] Guillelmi Alnwick, *Quaestiones disputatae de esse intelligibili et de Quodlibet*, Ad Claras Aquas, 1937, p. 1 gives the basic references. C. Michalski, *Les courants philosophiques à Oxford et à Paris*, Cracovie, 1921, is hard to obtain.

[46] *Sum. Theol.*, I, q. 15, aa. 1, 2; q. 14, aa. 5, 6; q. 12, aa. 8-10; *et loc. par.* especially *C. Gent.*, I, 48-55; *De Ver.*, q. 2, a. 3; q. 3, a. 2.

standing primarily is of the divine essence but secondarily of its virtualities.[47] The divine Word that is uttered is one, but what is uttered in the one Word is all that God knows.[48] Moreover, the divine essence, the divine act of understanding, and the divine Word considered absolutely are one and the same reality; hence there can be no real distinction between "contained eminently in the essence" and "secondary object of the understanding" or between either of these and "uttered in the one Word." Further, utterance in the one Word does not confer on the ideas an *esse intelligibile* that otherwise they would not possess; for in God *esse naturale* and *esse intelligibile* are identical.[49] It remains, then, that divine knowledge of the other provides no premise whence the procession of the divine Word could be established by natural reason. The plurality of divine ideas within divine simplicity is accounted for by an infinite act of understanding grasping as secondary objects the perfections eminently contained in the divine essence and virtually in divine omnipotence.[50] As we can understand *multa per unum*,[51] all the more so can God.

Hence, though our *intelligere* is always a *dicere*, this cannot be demonstrated of God's.[52] Though we can demonstrate that God understands, for undestanding is pure perfection, still we can no more than conjecture the mode of divine understanding and so cannot prove that there is a divine Word.[53] Psychological trinitarian theory is not a conclusion that can be demonstrated but an hypothesis that squares with divine revelation without excluding the possibility of alternative hypotheses.[54] Finally, Aquinas regularly writes as a theologian and not as a philosopher; hence regularly he simply states what simply is true, that in all intellects there is a procession of inner word.[55]

---

[47] *Sum. Theol.*, I, q. 14, a. 5 ad 3m.
[48] *Ibid.*, q. 34, a. 1 ad 3m.
[49] *C. Gent.*, I, 47 §5.
[50] *Sum. Theol.*, I, q. 14, aa. 5, 6.
[51] *Ibid.*, q. 85, a. 4 c.
[52] *De Ver.*, q. 4, a. 2 ad 5m.
[53] *De Pot.*, q. 8, a. 1 ad 12m.
[54] *Sum. Theol.*, I, q. 32, a. 1 ad 2m.
[55] *Ibid.*, q. 27, a. 1 c.

Eo Magis Unum

Scotus seems to have had no qualms in referring to the divine processions as productions.[56] Aquinas is much more restrained. In the *Summa* one will find *dicere* and *notionaliter diligere* defined in terms of causality;[57] one will find incidental statements in which a person that proceeds is said to be produced;[58] but it seems clear that the movement of Thomist thought is definitely away from conceiving the divine processions as productions.[59] Thus, the errors of Arius and Sabellius are reduced to the mistake of conceiving the divine processions in terms of agent and effect;[60] and the Aristotelian efficient cause, "principium agendi in aliud," is regarded as relevant, not to the divine processions, but only to the production of creatures.[61] But this is puzzling. Is it true or is it false that *dicere* is *producere verbum*? Or is it true in us but not in God? In that case what is the divine procession? We attempt an answer in three steps which, because of previous discussion,[62] may be brief.

Aristotle conceived the efficient cause as "principium motus vel mutationis in alio vel qua aliud." He conceived nature as "principium motus in eo in quo est primo et per se et non secundum accidens." Plainly, efficient cause and nature are complementary and opposed. An efficient cause cannot be nature; nature cannot be an efficient cause; for inasmuch as movement proceeds *per se* from a principle in the subject in which the movement occurs, the principle is nature; but inasmuch as movement proceeds from a principle in another subject, the principle is an efficient cause; and inasmuch as movement proceeds *per accidens* from a principle in the subject in which the movement occurs, the principle again is an efficient cause. Now, these defi-

---

[56] *In I Sent.* (*Op. Oxon.*), d. 2, qq. 4-7, aa. 2-3; ed. Fernandez, Quaracchi, 1912, pp. 240-72 (ed. Balić, Vatican, 1950, Vol. II, pp. 259-335).

[57] *Sum. Theol.* I, q. 37, a. 2 ad 2m.

[58] *Ibid.*, ad 3m.

[59] See pages 98 ff above. I wish to note that when I wrote p. 99, I had not yet adverted to the relation between *emanatio intelligibilis* and the disappearance in later works of *processio operati*. This will be corrected presently.

[60] *Sum. Theol.*, I, q. 27, a. 1 c.

[61] *Ibid.*, a. 5, ad 1m.

[62] See chapter III.

nitions are not ultimately satisfactory;[63] it remains that they are Aristotle's definitions; and they fully explain Aquinas' refusal to conceive the divine processions as instances of efficient causality. The proceeding Word and the proceeding Love are not from a principle outside God; nor are they *per accidens* from a principle within God; therefore, they are not from an efficient cause as conceived by Aristotle.

Secondly, Aquinas developed a more general notion of efficient causality than that defined by Aristotle. Thus, *principium operati, principium effectus, processio operati* include the idea of production but do not include the Aristotelian restrictions of *in alio vel qua aliud.* The act of understanding is to the possible intellect, the act of loving is to the will, as act to potency, as perfection to its perfectible; the procession is *processio operationis* and cannot be analogous to any real procession in God. But the inner word is to our intelligence in act as is act to act, perfection to proportionate perfection; in us the procession is *processio operati*; in us *dicere* is *producere verbum*, even though it is natural and not an instance of Aristotelian efficient causality. Inasmuch as *dicere* does not involve the imperfection of *processio operationis* it offers an analogy to the divine procession.[64]

Thirdly, is the divine *dicere* a *producere verbum*? Is there truly in God a *processio operati*? Evidently there is an enormous difference between the procession of an inner word in us and the procession of the Word in God. In us there are two acts, first, an act of understanding, secondly, a really distinct act of defining or judging. In God there is but one act. But not only did Aquinas advert to this rather obvious fact but also he assigned the reason for the difference: "id quod procedit ad intra processu intelligibili, non oportet esse diversum; imo, quanto perfectius procedit, tanto magis est unum cum eo a quo procedit."[65] One is apt to object that as the principle and term of a procession approach identity, the procession itself approaches nothingness. But this is simply to disregard what Aquinas most emphatically

---

[63] Godfrey of Fontaines exhibits their logical conclusion. Cf. *Quodl.* VI, q. 7; VIII, q. 2; XIII, q. 3 (*Les Philosophes belges*, Louvain, III [1914], 148-72; IV [1924], 18-33; V [1932], 190-213).

[64] *De Ver.*, q. 4, a. 2 ad 7m.

[65] *Sum. Theol.*, I, q. 27, a. 1 ad 2m.

asserts. The analogy to the divine processions is found only in rational creatures. Not any procession *ad intra* but only intelligible procession is given the property of "quanto perfectius procedit, tanto magis est unum cum eo a quo procedit."[66] In the *Contra Gentiles* Aquinas considered in turn minerals, plants, animals, men, angels, and God to show that in perfect intellectual reflection principle and term are identical without an elimination of the reflection and so without an elimination of the procession.[67] In the *Summa* he is insistent on his point: "secundum emanationem intelligibilem,"[68] "processu intelligibili,"[69] "per modum intelligibilem,"[70] "per modum intelligibilis actionis,"[71] "verbum intelligibiliter procedens,"[72] "secundum actionem intelligibilem."[73]

Obviously Aquinas thought he was making a point. What is it? There are two aspects to the procession of an inner word in us. There is the productive aspect; intelligence in act is proportionate to producing the inner word. There is also the intelligible aspect: inner words do not proceed with mere natural spontaneity as any effect does from any cause; they proceed with reflective rationality; they proceed not merely from a sufficient cause but from sufficient grounds known to be sufficient and because they are known to be sufficient. I can imagine a circle and I can define a circle. In both cases there is efficient causality. But in the second case there is something more. I define the circle because I grasp in imagined data that, if the radii are equal, then the plane curve must be uniformly round. The inner word of defining not only is *caused by* but also is *because of* the act of understanding. In the former aspect the procession is *processio operati*. In the latter aspect the procession is *processio intelligibilis*. Similarly, in us the act of judgment is caused by a reflective act of understanding, and so it is *processio operati*. But that is not all. The

---

[66] *Ibid.*

[67] *C. Gent.*, IV, 11 §§1-7. Observe the initial thesis: secundum diversitatem naturarum diversus emanationis modus invenitur in rebus: et quanto aliqua natura est altior, tanto id quod ex ea emanat, magis ei est intimum.

[68] *Sum. Theol.*, I, q. 27, a. 1 c.

[69] *Ibid.*, ad 2m.

[70] *Ibid.*, ad 3m; a. 2 ob. 2 a.

[71] *Ibid.*, a. 2 c.

[72] *Ibid.*, ad 3m.

[73] *Ibid.*, a. 3 c.

procession of judgment cannot be equated with procession from electromotive force or chemical action or biological process or even sensitive act. Judgment is judgment only if it proceeds from intellectual grasp of sufficient evidence as sufficient. Its procession also is *processio intelligibilis*.

What, then, does Aquinas mean when he writes: "id quod procedit ad intra processu intelligibili, non oportet esse diversum; imo, quanto perfectius procedit, tanto magis est unum cum eo a quo procedit."[74] He does not mean that there can be production, properly speaking, when principle and product are absolutely identical. He does mean that there can be *processio intelligibilis* without absolutive diversity, indeed that the more perfect the *processio intelligibilis* is, the greater the approach to identity. In us inner word proceeds from act of understanding by a *processio intelligibilis* that also is a *processio operati*, for our inner word and act of understanding are two absolute entities really distinct. In God inner word proceeds from act of understanding as uttering by a *processio intelligibilis* that is not a *processio operati*, at least inasmuch as divine understanding and divine Word are not two absolute entities really distinct.

It may be doubted that a pure *processio intelligibilis* is a real procession. If A is because of B without being caused by B, the dependence of A on B seems to be merely mental. It is true that a *processio intelligibilis* cannot be real except in a mind. On the other hand, in a mind it necessarily is real; just as the mind itself and its operation are real, so the intelligibile procession within the mind and the consequent relations of origin are all real. "Mental" is opposed to "real" only inasmuch as one prescinds from the reality of mind.

Indeed, the divine procession of the Word is not only real but also a natural generation.[75] In us that does not hold. Our intellects are not our substance; our acts of understanding are not our existence; and so our definitions and affirmations are not the essence and existence of our children. Our inner words are just thoughts, just *esse intentionale* of what we define and affirm,

[74] *Ibid.*, a. 1 ad 2m.
[75] *Ibid.*, a. 2 c.

just *intentio intellecta* and not *res intellecta*.[76] But in God intellect is substance and act of understanding is act of existence; it follows that the Word that proceeds in Him is of the same nature and substance as its principle,[77] that His thought of Himself is Himself, that His *intentio intellecta* of Himself is also the *res intellecta*.[78] As there is an analogy of *ens* and *esse*, so also there is an analogy of the intelligibly proceeding *est*. In us *est* is just a thought, a judgment. But in God not only is *ipsum esse* the ocean of all perfection,[79] comprehensively grasped by *ipsum intelligere*,[80] in complete identity,[81] but also perfectly expressed in a single Word. That Word is thought, definition, judgment and yet of the same nature as God whose substance is intellect. Hence it is not mere thought as opposed to thing, not mere definition as opposed to defined, not mere judgment as opposed to judged. No less than what it perfectly expresses, it too is the ocean of all perfection. Still, though infinite *esse* and infinite *est* are identical absolutely, none the less truly there is an intelligible procession. The divine Word is because of the divine understanding as uttering, yet "eo magis unum, quo perfectius procedit."

Amor Procedens

As complete understanding not only grasps essence and in essence all properties but also affirms existence and value, so also from understanding's self-expression in judgment of value there is an intelligible procession of love in the will. Evidently so, for without an intelligible procession of love in the will from the word of intellect, it would be impossible to define the will as rational appetite. Natural appetite is blind; sensitive appetite is spontaneous; but rational appetite can be moved only by the good that reason pronounces to be good. Because of the necessity of

---

[76] *C. Gent.*, IV, 11 §6.

[77] *Sum. Theol.*, I, q. 27, a. 2 ad 2m; q. 34, a. 2 ad 1m; *C. Gent.*, IV, 11 §§11, 17.

[78] *C. Gent.*, IV, 11 §7.

[79] *Sum. Theol.*, I, q. 13, a. 11 c.

[80] *Ibid.*, q. 14, a. 3 c.

[81] *Ibid.*, aa. 2, 4.

intelligible procession from intellect to will, sin is not act in the
will but failure to act; it is failure to will to do the good that is
commanded, or it is failure to will to inhibit tendencies that are
judged to be wrong. Because of the same necessity of intelligible
procession from intellect to will, the sinner is driven by a fine
disquiet either to seek true peace of soul in repentance or else
to obtain a simulated peace in the rationalization that corrupts
reason by making the false appear true that wrong may appear
right. Finally, however much it may be disputed whether there
is any *procssio operati* from the word of our intellects to the act
in our wills, it cannot be denied that there is a *processio intelligibilis* from the word of intellect to the act of rational appetite.[82]

Let us now see how Aquinas accounted for the procession of
the Holy Spirit. In the *Contra Gentiles* IV, 19, he inquired: "Quomodo intelligenda sunt quae de Spiritu sancto dicuntur?" In
the first paragraph he stated his intention. In paragraphs two,
three, and four, he examined the nature of love. In the remaining
paragraphs, five to twelve, he applied his analysis to the doctrine
of the Holy Spirit. The three steps in his examination of love
are as follows: first, he argued that in everyone who understands
there must also be a will; secondly, he showed that the basic act,
to which all other acts of will are to be reduced, is love; thirdly,
he pointed out the difference between the presence of the beloved in the intellect and his presence in the will of the lover;
in the intellect he is present "per similitudinem speciei"; in the
will he is present dynamically, as the term of a movement in the
movement's proportionate principle.

But what is this dynamic presence? How is the term of a
movement in the movement's motive principle? Obviously, by
final causality: the end determines the agent. Hence, "sicut
autem influere causae efficientis est agere, ita influere causae
finalis est appeti et desiderari."[83] From the term of movement
there results by final causality an *appeti* of the term; but the
appeti of the term is not in the term but in the motive principle.

[82] On the controversy, see O. Lottin, *Psychologie et morale aux XIIe et
XIIIe siècles*, Louvain, 1942, I, 226-389; also Cajetan, *In Im.*, q. 27, a. 3
§IX ff; ed. Leon., IV, 312.
[83] *De Ver.*, q. 22, a. 2 c.

Similarly, by final causality there results from the beloved the *amari* of the beloved; and this *amari* of the beloved is not in the beloved but in the lover. Next, the *appeti* of the term in the motive principle is one and the same act as the *appetere* of the motive principle for the term; similarly, the *amari* of the beloved in the lover is one and the same act as the *amare* of the lover for the beloved. Hence "est autem amatum in amante secundum quod amatur";[84] "id quod amatur est in amante secundum quod actu amatur";[85] "amor dicitur transformare amantem in amatum, inquantum per amorem movetur amans ad ipsam rem amatam."[86] Finally, if the presence of the beloved in the lover is exactly the same entity as the act of love in the lover, why does Aquinas bother about it? Obviously because he wishes to determine the nature of love and so to show that, while the procession of the Word is a generation, still the procession of Love is not. The object of intellect is in intellect "per similitudinem speciei," but the object of will or love is in the will not by reproduction but as a goal is in tendency to the goal.[87]

Paragraphs five to twelve of *Contra Gentiles* IV, 19, apply the foregoing analysis. First, it is shown that since God understands, He must have a will; further, this will cannot be distinct really from either the divine substance or the divine intellect. Secondly, the will of God cannot be mere potency or mere habit; it must be in act; and since the basic act of will is love, it must be actually loving. Thirdly, the proper object of divine love is the divine goodness which is identical with God; but love is dynamic presence; therefore the love of God for God involves the dynamic presence of God in God. Moreover, since divine loving, divine willing, divine being are identical, it follows that the dynamic presence of God in God is not mere dynamic presence but God. Just as God's thought of God is not mere thought but God, so God's love of God is not mere accidental act but God. Fourthly, the origin of divine love is treated. There cannot be the dynamic presence

---

[84] *C. Gent.*, IV, 19 §7.

[85] *Comp. Theol.*, c. 49.

[86] *De Malo*, q. 6, a. 1 ad 13m. Cf. H. D. Simonin, "Autour de la solution thomiste du problème de l'amour," *Archives d'hist. doct. et. litt. du M.-A.*, VI (1931), 174-276.

[87] *C. Gent.*, IV, 19 §§4, 9.

of the beloved in the lover's will, unless there first is intellectual conception. Further, it is not the concept but the conceived that is loved; hence, divine love necessarily is related both to the Word and to God from whom the Word proceeds. The remaining four paragraphs explain why the procession of love is not a generation, why the Holy Spirit is named Spirit, and why he is named Holy.

As was anticipated, once one grasps the *processio intelligibilis* of inner word from uttering act of understanding, there is not the slightest difficulty in grasping the simple, clear, straightforward account Aquinas offered of proceeding love. Difficulty arises in interpreting Aquinas on this issue from purely subjective sources. A conceptualist is not interested enough in human intellect, to know what *processio intelligibilis* means; and so he is led to take advantage of the complexity of Thomist thought and terminology to invent pseudo-metaphysical theories about *operatio* and *operatum*.[88] After applying these theories to the procession of the inner word, he tries to apply them to the procession of love; and in this he is greatly encouraged by the post-Thomas Augustinian reaction which transformed Augustine's self-movement of soul into self-moving potencies and, above all, denied any influence from the intellect on the will in an alleged defence of the will's liberty.[89]

What Aquinas held is quite clear. In us there is a procession of love from the will, but that is *processio operationis* and irrelevant

[88] On the complexity see pages 101-137 above.

[89] O. Lottin, *loc. cit.*, note 82 *supra*. B. Perez, *La actividad cognoscitiva en los escolasticos del primer periodo postomista*, Madrid, 1948. Peter John Olivi, *In II Sent.*, q. 58 c., Quaracchi, 1924, pp. 412-14; ob. 13a, ad 13m, pp. 400-403, 437-61; ob. 14a, ad 14m, pp. 403-8, 461-515. Gonzalvus Hispanus, *Quaestiones disputatae*, q. 3, Quaracchi, 1935, pp. 27-49. It seems quite plain that the doctrine of vital act was an Augustinian argument against the Aristotelian *pati*. Godfrey of Fontaines, Thomas of Sutton, Nicolas Trivet were resolute Aristotelians. Hervé de Nédellec yielded to Augustinian pressure to the extent of wishing for a *sensus agens*, *op. cit.*, p. 69 (note 18 *supra*). Recall that Aquinas did not evolve a general notion of efficient causality but distinguished analogously the types of emanation on different levels of being see chapter III, pages 132 ff, above); this, I think, is relevant to understanding the Thomist contrast between *movere per modum causae efficientis* and *movere per modum finis* (C. Gent., I, 72 §7; Sum. Theol., I, q. 82, a. 4 c.). See also Simonin, *op. cit.*, pp. 234 ff. (note 86 *supra*).

to trinitarian theory.[90] In us there is a procession of one act of love from another, but that also is irrelevant to trinitarian theory.[91] In us there is a procession of love from the inner word and, as Aquinas very frequently repeated, that is the procession that is relevant to trinitarian theory.[92] In this position Aquinas was following St. Anselm.[93] He was followed by Godfrey of Fontaines,[94] and John of Naples.[95] The extent to which the notion was current merits special investigation but an indication of its currency may be had from a text published by Fr. Balić. In his *Opus Oxoniense* Scotus conceived the procession of the Holy Spirit as procession of love from the will.[96] In the text Fr. Balić has published, Scotus got around to applying his doctrine of partial, concurrent, coordinate causes to the will. The act of will is caused partially by the will and partially by the object presented by the intellect; in confirmation the intention of Augustine is adduced that *amor procedit a mente* and this is followed up by the contention that if the object is only *sine quo non* to the act of love, then the Word is only *sine quo non* to the procession of the Holy Spirit.[97]

[90] *De Ver.*, q. 4, a. 2 ad 7m.

[91] *Sum. Theol.*, I, q. 27, a. 5 ad 3m.

[92] See page 100 above, note 20.

[93] *Monologion*, c. 50 (ed. Schmitt, Edinburgh, 1946, p. 65): Palam certe est rationem habenti, eum non idcirco sui memorem esse aut se intelligere quia se amat, sed ideo se amare quia sui meminit et se intelligit; nec eum se posse amare, si sui non sit memor aut se non intelligat. Nulla enim res amatur sine eius memoria et intelligentia, et multa tenentur memoria et intelliguntur, quae non amantur. Patet igitur amorem summi spiritus (i.e., Deus) ex eo procedere, quia sui memor est et se intelligit. Quod si in memoria summi spiritus intelligitur Pater, in intelligentia Filius: manifestum est quia a Patre pariter et Filio summi spiritus amor procedit.

[94] *Quode. VII*, q. 4; cf. *Les Philosophes belges*, III, 293.

[95] *Quaest. disp. XIII, XXX.* Texts given by M. Schmaus, *Der Liber Propugnatorius des Thomas Anglicus und die Lehrunterschiede zwischen Thomas von Aquin und Duns Scotus*, Teil II: *Die trinitarischen Lehrdifferenzen* (*BGPTM* XXIX, Münster i. W., 1930), p. 132*, lines 11 ff.; p. 138* lines 1 ff.; p. 132, note 51 *ad fin.*

[96] *In I Sent.* (*Op. Oxon*), d. 10, ed. Fernandez, p. 679, ed. Balić, p. 341).

[97] C. Balić, "Une question inédite de J. Duns Scot sur la volonté," *Rech. théol., anc. méd.*, III (1931), 191-208; see lines 418-26.

Via Doctrinae

In his monumental work on medieval trinitarian thought,[98] Dr. Michael Schmaus followed the current division and devoted first over three hundred pages to "die Trinität *in fieri*," and then almost two hundred to "die Trinität *in esse*."[99] But though Aquinas in his earlier works began from God the Father to treat next the generation of the Son and then the procession of the Holy Spirit, his *Summa Theologica* eliminated even the semblance of a logical fiction of a becoming in God. The *Summa* treated first God as one, [100] to turn to God as triune "secundum viam doctrinae."[101] In this presentation the starting-point is not God the Father but God; the first question is not whether there is a procession from God the Father but whether there is a procession in God. After establishing two processions in God, the existence of real relations in God is treated. Only after both processions and relations have been treated, is the question of persons raised.[102] The significance of this procedure is that it places Thomist trinitarian theory in a class by itself.

First of all, it eliminates what Dr. Schmaus considers the *crux trinitatis*.[103] Either the Father is Father by a relation or for some other reason; but neither alternative is possible. If the Father is Father by a relation, then that relation supposes a procession, so that the Father has to generate before being constituted as Father. On the other hand, if the Father is Father not by a relation, then he must be Father either by something absolute or by a negation. Neither will do.

The Thomist solution to this problem cannot be appreciated unless one grasps the *Summa's* structure, which implies a twofold ordering of our trinitarian concepts. There is the order of our concepts *in fieri*, and then processions precede relations and relations precede persons. There is the order of our concepts *in facto esse* and then there are the persons as persons,[104] the persons

---

[98] See *supra*, note 95.
[99] *Ibid.*, pp. 46-378, 379-573.
[100] *Sum. Theol.*, I, qq. 2-26.
[101] *Ibid.*, q. 27, Intro.
[102] *Ibid.*, qq. 27-29.
[103] *Op. cit.*, p. 652.
[104] *Sum. Theol.*, I, qq. 30-32.

considered individually,[105] the persons compared to the divine essence,[106] to the relations,[107] to the notional acts.[108] Now these two orders are inverse. The processions and the notional acts are the same realities. But the processions are in God prior, in the first order of our concepts, to the constitution of the persons. On the other hand, the notional acts are acts of the persons and consequent to the persons conceived as constituted. Once one recognizes this twofold systematization of our concepts, it becomes apparent that Aquinas' solution to the *crux trinitatis* is really satisfying. He maintained a distinction between the property of the Father as relation and the same property as constitutive of the Father. As relation, the property is subsequent to generation; as constitutive, the same property is prior to generation.[109] But how can the same property be both prior and subsequent? The question is not about the property itself but about the systematic order of our concepts;[110] and when there are two systematic and inverse orders, necessarily what is prior in one order will be subsequent in the other.

Secondly, the procedure of the *Summa* reveals very clearly the exact point of application and the measure of significance of the psychological *imago Dei* in trinitarian thought. It reveals the exact point of application. We desire to know *quid sit Deus*, but in this life the only understanding we can attain is through analogy. Philosophy proceeds from pure perfections by the ways of affirmation, negation, and eminence. Faith adds further data. Theology employs the Augustinian psychological analogy, just as philosophy employed the naturally known pure perfections. By natural reason we know that God is absolute being, absolute understanding, absolute truth, absolute love. But natural reason cannot establish that there are in God *processiones intelligibiles*,

---

[105] *Ibid.*, qq. 33-38.

[106] *Ibid.*, q. 39.

[107] *Ibid.*, q. 40.

[108] *Ibid.*, q. 41.

[109] *Ibid.*, q. 40, a. 4 c. Materially the same distinction occurs in *De Pot.*, q. 8, a. 3 ad 7m; q. 10, a. 3; but there it lacks an ultimate basis.

[110] The question is: Videtur quod actus notionales praeintelligantur proprietatibus. In God and *quoad se* there is "ordo secundum originem absque prioritate" (*Sum. Theol.*, I, q. 42, a. 3 c.; cf. ad 2m).

that the divine Word is because of divine undertanding as uttering, that divine Love as proceeding is because of divine goodness and understanding and Word as spirating. Such further analogical knowledge of *quid sit Deus* pertains to the limited but most fruitful understanding that can be attained when reason operates in the light of faith.[111] Thus, the Augustinian psychological analogy makes trinitarian theology a prolongation of natural theology, a deeper insight into what God is.

But the procedure of the *Summa* also reveals the measure of significance to be attached to the *imago Dei*. As we have seen, there is a twofold systematization; first, our concepts are *in fieri*; secondly, their order is reversed and they stand *in facto esse*. Now these two orders stand on different levels of thought. As long as our concepts are in development, the psychological analogy commands the situation. But once our concepts reach their term, the analogy is transcended and we are confronted with the mystery. In other words, the psychological analogy truly gives a deeper insight into what God is. Still, that insight stands upon analogy; it does not penetrate to the very core, the essence of God, in which alone trinitarian doctrine can be contemplated in its full intelligibility; grasping properly *quid sit Deus* is the beatific vision.[112] Just as an experimental physicst may not grasp most of quantum mathematics, but under the direction of a mathematician may very intelligently devise and perform experiments that advance the quantum theory, so also the theologian with no proper grasp of *quid sit Deus* but under the direction of divine revelation really operates in virtue of and towards an understanding that he personally in this life cannot possess.[113]

Hence it is that the psychological analogy enables one to argue that there are two and only two processions in God, that the first is "per modum intelligibilis actionis" and a natural generation; that the second is "per modum amoris" and not a generation; that there are four real relations in God and three of them really

---

[111] *DB* 1796.

[112] *Sum. Theol.*, I, q. 12, a. 1 c.; I-II, q. 3, a. 8 c.

[113] *Ibid.*, I, q. 1, aa. 2, 7. M. Grabmann, *Die theologische Erkenntnis- und Einleitungslehre des heiligen Thomas von Aquin*, Freiburg in der Schweiz, 1948. Y. J. Congar, "Théologie," *DTC* XV, 378-92. M. D. Chenu, *La Théologie comme science au XIIIe siècle*, 3ième ed., Paris, 1957.

distinct;[114] that the names *verbum* and *imago* are proper to the Son, while the names *amor* and *donum* are proper to the Holy Spirit.[115] But do not think that Aquinas allows the psychological analogy to take the place of the divine essence as the one sufficient principle of explanation. The psychological analogy is just the side-door through which we enter for an imperfect look.

Thus, though the generation of the Son is "per modum intelligibilis actionis," though a proper name of the Son is the Word, still Aquinas did not conclude that the principle by which the Father generates is the divine intellect or the divine understanding. In us the inner word proceeds from understanding, and our understanding is really distinct from our substance, our being, our thought, our willing. But in God substance, being, understanding, thought, willing are absolutely one and the same reality. Accordingly, Aquinas not merely in his *Commentary on the Sentences*,[116] but also in his *Summa* makes the divine essence the principle of divine generation. "Sicut Deus potest generare Filium, ita et vult. Sed voluntas generandi significat essentiam. Ergo et potentia generandi."[117] "Illud ergo est potentia generativa in aliquo generante, in quo generatum similatur generanti. Filius autem Dei similatur Patri gignenti in natura divina. Unde natura divina in Patre est potentia generandi in ipso."[118] "... Id quo Pater generat est natura divina."[119] The one divine essence is common to Father and to Son. As the Father's, the essence is the potency by which the Father generates; as the Son's, the

---

[114] *Sum. Theol.*, I, qq. 27, 28.

[115] *Ibid.*, q. 34, a. 2; q. 35, a. 2; q. 37, a. 1; q. 38, a. 2. The difference between essential love and notional love is quite plainly the difference between love considered in its essence (the dynamic presence of the beloved) and love referred to its origin, its principle. The former relates lover to beloved; the latter proceeds. The same distinction might be put by comparing love to *finis operationis* and *finis intentionis* (*De Pot.*, q. 3, a. 16 c.). God's love of God as *finis operationis* is identical with God, and so essential. God's love of God as *finis intentionis* is God as proceeding from God as Judge and Word, and so notional.

[116] *In I Sent.*, d. 7, q. 2, a. 1 sol., and ad 4m; *ibid.*, q. 1, aa. 1-3; *ibid.*, d. 6, q. 1, a. 3 sol.

[117] *Sum. Theol.*, I, q. 41, a. 5 Sed contra.

[118] *Ibid.* c.

[119] *Ibid.*

essence is the potency by which the Son is generated.[120] The *potentia spirandi* is conceived in parallel fashion. Father and Son are one principle because they are one God.[121] They are "duo spirantes" but "unus spirator."[122] As the *potentia generandi* means the divine essence but connotes a personal property,[123] so also does the *virtus spirativa*.[124] The procession of love is not voluntary but natural, even though it is "per modum voluntatis."[125] The same argument in the same passages establishes the existence of both *potentia generandi* and *potentia spirandi*.[126] If one disregard the title of the next article, the contribution of a rubricist, and attends to Aquinas' own question, then its issue is: "Videtur quod potentia generandi vel spirandi significet relationem et non essentiam."[127] It seems to follow that the divine essence is the principle by which the Father generates the Son and by which Father and Son spirate the Holy Spirit; that *potentia generandi* and *potentia spirandi*, while *in recto* they mean the same divine essence, still *in obliquo* connote different personal properties.[128] This is all very far from the type of trinitarian theory in which the Word is generated by the divine intellect and proceeding Love is spirated by the divine will.[129]

---

[120] *Ibid.*, a. 6, ad 1m.

[121] *Ibid.*, q. 36, a. 4 c.

[122] *Ibid.*, ad 7m.

[123] *Ibid.*, q. 41, a. 5 c.

[124] *Ibid.*, q. 36, a. 4 ad 1m.

[125] *Ibid.*, q. 41, a. 2 ad 3m.

[126] *Ibid.*, a. 4 c.

[127] *Ibid.*, a. 5.

[128] Cf. q. 36, a. 4 ad 1m; q. 41, a. 5. As the Son understands essentially "non ut producens verbum sed ut Verbum procedens" (q. 34, a. 2 ad 4m), so the Holy Spirit loves essentially "ut Amor procedens, non ut a quo procedit amor" (q. 37, a. 1 ad 4m). Hence as the divine essence is the Son's potency *ut generetur* (q. 41, a. 6 ad 1m), so also the divine essence is the Holy Spirit's potency *ut spiretur*.

[129] Dr. Schmaus made the supposition that the criterion of Augustinian psychological theory lay in taking the divine intellect as the principle of divine generation, the divine will as the principle of divine spiration. In consequence he records his mounting surprise at the views of post-Thomas Dominicans (cf. *Der Liber Propugnatorius, etc.*, pp. 125-34). Note especially the following from James of Metz: "Sic ergo principium, quo procedit Filius a Patre in divinis, non est intellectus, sed natura et similiter principium quo procedit

Finally, as the reader may have gathered already, the *via doctrinae* of the *Summa* is a masterpiece of theology as science and the apex of trinitarian speculation. But I would not be misunderstood. Coherently enough on their position, conceptualists conceive science simply in terms of certitude. For them the scientific ideal is the certitude one has of the particular and contingent fact of one's own existence. For them the substance of theology is what they are certain about, while the separable accidents are what they consider probable. They cannot be expected to think much of Thomist trinitarian theory which, on its own showing, is no more than an hypothesis which does not attempt to exclude the possibility of alternatives.[130] Still, without in any way deprecating certitude or even solidity, one may point out that the cult of certitude, the search for rigorous demonstration unaccompanied by a still greater effort to understand, has been tried and has been found wanting. It is the secret of fourteenth-century scepticism. Moreover, the same result follows from the same cause at any time; for one can be certain only because one understands, or else because one believes someone else who certainly understands. It is only inasmuch as different concepts proceed from one act of understanding that different concepts are seen to be joined by a necessary nexus. Remove the effort to understand and understanding will decrease; as understanding decreases, fewer concepts are seen to be joined by a necessary nexus; and as this seeing decreases, certitudes decrease. To stop the process, either one must restore the effort to understand or one must appeal not to intellect but to some higher or lower power.

Moreover, the conceptualist ideal of science is not the only ideal. For Aristotle perfect science is certain; but all science is knowledge through causes, and knowledge through causes is understanding and so of the universal and necessary. Because the conceptualist accepts only one element of the Aristotelian ideal,

---

Spiritus sanctus ab utroque est natura non voluntas et hoc dixit (nach Clm. 14 383 steht hier frater) Thomas Parisius in scholis publice, quod non intelligebat Filium procedere a Patre per actum intellectus sicut audivit magister Albertus (Clm. 14 383: tambertus) ab eo" (*ibid.*, pp. 127 f. in note 48). Without insisting on James' accuracy, one cannot well refuse all significance to his testimony.

[130] *Sum. Theol.*, I, q. 32, a. 1 ad 2m.

while modern science realizes the other element, a quite unnecessary abyss has been dug by conceptualists between the Scholasticism they claim to represent and, on the other hand, the contemporary ideal of science. Further, the conceptualist ideal of science has no exclusive claim on the ideal of theology as science. St. Augustine's *crede ut intelligas* no more means "believe to be certain" than it means "believe to have an intellection"; it means "believe that you may understand." When the Vatican Council affirms that reason illumined by faith and inquiring *pie, sedulo, sobrie,* can attain some limited but most fruitful *intelligentia* of the mysteries of faith, *intelligentia* means not certitude, for by faith one already is certain, nor demonstration, for the mysteries cannot be demonstrated, nor intellection, for a mystery is not a universal, but rather obviously understanding.

Nor was understanding as the ideal of scientific theology unknown to Aquinas whose principles, method, and doctrine the Church bids us follows. To ask *quid sit* is to ask: Why? To know *quid sit* is to know the cause—above all, the formal cause in the only manner that causes are known, by understanding. Hence to ask *quid sit Deus* expresses a natural desire; but to know *quid sit Deus* defines a supernatural end. For knowing *quid sit Deus* is understanding God. That understanding cannot result from any finite species but only inasmuch as God himself slips into and mysteriously actuates a finite intellect. But potency that no creature can actuate is obediental and its act, by definition, is supernatural. Short of this supernatural vision of God, we can know *quid sit Deus* only by analogy. But such analogical knowing moves on two levels. By the natural light of reason we argue from pure perfections to the pure act. In the subalternated science of theology we operate in virtue of *ipsum intelligere*, under the direction of divine revelation, without grasping the divine essence, yet truly understanding the relations of properties flowing from the essence, both from the connection between the mysteries and from the analogy of nature. Thus, the ideal of theology as science is the subalternated and so limited, analogical and so imperfect understanding of *quid sit Deus* which, though incomparable with the vision of God, far surpasses what can be grasped by the unaided light of natural reason.

By the measure of the intellectualist concept of theology, the *via doctrinae* of the *Summa* is a masterpiece. It knows just what the human mind can attain and it attains it. It does not attempt to discover a synthetic principle whence all else follows. It knows that that principle is the divine essence and that, in this life, we cannot properly know it. On the other hand, it does not renounce all thought of synthesis to settle down to teaching catechism; for it knows that there is such a thing as imperfect understanding. Systematically it proceeds to that limited goal. It begins where natural theology leaves off. It employs the Augustinian psychological analogy as the natural theologian employs his pure perfections. It develops the key concepts of procession, relation, person. Then it shifts to a higher level, consciously confronts mystery as mystery, and so transposes relations to properties and processions to notional acts. The accurate grasp of the end guarantees the perfection of the method. The perfection of the method automatically assigns the *imago Dei* its proper function and limited significance and no less provides the solution to the *crux trinitatis*. Imperfectly we grasp why God is Father, Word, and Spirit inasmuch as we conceive God, not simply as identity of being, understanding, thought, and love, but as that identity and yet with thought, because of understanding, and love, because of both, where "because" means not the logical relation between propositions but the real *processio intelligibilis* of an intellectual substance. What is truly profound is also very simple.

Yet into the simplicity of the *via doctrinae* in the *Summa* was poured the sum of previous trinitarian and philosophic achievement. Dogmatic development was from the apostolic symbol which briefly acknowledged God, the Father Almighty, Jesus Christ, His only Son, our Lord, and the Holy Ghost. Nicaea affirmed the Son to be truly God, consubstantial with the Father. Constantinople affirmed the divinity of the Holy Ghost. Speculative thought, on the other hand, was clearly present as *via inventionis* in St. Athanasius' deduction that immaterial generation must terminate in a consubstantial being; in the doctrine that distinction between the persons rests on relations as worked out by the Cappadocians,[131] and by St. Augustine;[132] in the elaboration of the

[131] R. Arnou, *De Deo Trino*, Pars I, Rome, 1933, pp. 130-40.
[132] I. Chevalier, *Saint Augustin et les pères grecs*, Étude des relations trinitaires, Fribourg, Suisse, 1939.

notions of person and nature summarized for the East by St. John
Damascene,[133] and for the West in the influential, if not altogether
fortunate, work of Boethius;[134] and, finally, in the threefold problem of person, nature, and relation that came to a head in Gilbert
de la Porré.[135]

But more was needed to make Aquinas' *via doctrinae* possible.
Augustine had to transfer the name, God, from a proper name of
the Father to a common name of the three persons and he had
to explore the possibilities of the psychological analogy. The
systematic distinction between natural and supernatural and so
between philosophy and theology had to be developed.[136] Philosophy had to be cultivated to work out our natural knowledge
of God and to place a scientific psychology at the disposal of
theology's *imago Dei*. Theology had to discover its potentialities
and its limitations as subalternated science. The last two of these
requirements had to be met mainly by Aquinas himself. *In Boetium de Trinitate*, not so strangely perhaps, says nothing of the
Trinity; it studies the nature of knowledge, science, faith, philosophy, theology. The *De Veritate* was still engaged in the translator's task of assigning Aristotelian equivalents to Augustine's
memoria, intelligentia, amor.[137] Still, it offered assured promise
of Aquinas' own triad of *principium verbi, verbum*, and *amor*,[138]
since at least implicitly it formulated the essentials of Thomist
analysis of inner word as definition or judgment expressing un-

[133] J. Bilz, *Die Trinitätslehre des hl. Johannes von Damaskus*, Paderborn,
1909.

[134] V. Schnurr, *Die Trinitätslehre des Boethius im Lichte der "skythischen
Kontroversen,"* Paderborn, 1935.

[135] A. Hayen, "Le Concile de Reims et l'erreur théologique de Gilbert de
la Porrée," *Arch. d'hist. doct. litt. du M.-A.*, X (1935-1936), 29-102.

[136] On the development, see *Theological Studies*, II (1941), 301-306. It
was the lack of systematic notions on nature and the supernatural that gave
St. Anselm and Richard of St. Victor their apparently rationalist mode of
thought and speech. See J. Bayart, "The Concept of Mystery according to
St. Anselm of Canterbury," *Rech. théol. anc. méd.*, IX (1937), 125-66; A.-M.
Ethier, *Le "De Trinitate" de Richard de Saint-Victor*, Ottawa and Paris,
1939; G. Fritz, "Richard de Saint-Victor," *DTC* XIII, 2691-93.

[137] *De Ver.*, q. 10, aa. 3, 7.

[138] *Sum. Theol.*, I, q. 93, aa. 6-8. For Augustinian *memoria* Aquinas substituted *intellectus in actu intelligens et dicens*. For Augustinian *intelligentia*
or *notitia* Aquinas substituted a *verbum* that was definition or judgment.

derstanding.[139] It remains that the *Contra Gentiles* worked out the significance of rational reflection as in the limit involving coincidence of principle and term;[140] and that the *De Potentia*, despite its Richardian elements,[141] not only provided the polished categorization of the factors in intellectual process,[142] but also, by treating the relations before treating the persons,[143] contained some dim anticipation of the master stroke of the *Summa*. Still it is only the *Summa* with its modest appendage, the *Compendium theologiae*, beginning not from the Father but from God, that abandons the Neapolist self-diffusion of the good as explanatory principle; that not merely employs Augustinian analogy to advance from the concept of God as *ipsum intelligere* to the concept of God as the absolute thinking of absolute thought; but also does so in full accord with a concept of theology in which the Aristotelian notion of science is expanded to make room for the Augustinian *Crede ut intelligas*.

Epilogue

From different quarters and in different manners I have been asked to explain my purpose and my method.[144] My purpose has been the Leonine purpose, *vetera novis augere et perficere*, though with this modality that I believed the basic task still to be the determination of what the *vetera* really were. More specifically, my purpose has been to understand what Aquinas meant by the intelligible procession of an inner word. Naturally enough, my method had to be both consonant with my purpose and coherent with my conclusions. Now to understand what Aquinas meant and to understand as Aquinas understood, are one and the same thing; for acts of meaning are inner words, and inner words pro-

---

[139] *De Ver.*, q. 3, a. 2 c.; q. 4, a. 2.

[140] *C. Gent.*, IV, 11 §§1-7.

[141] On the development of Thomist trinitarian theory, see P. Vanier, S. J., *La théologie trinitaire chez S. Thomas d'Aquin* (Paris, 1953).

[142] *De Pot.*, q. 8, a. 1 c.; q. 9, a. 5 c.

[143] *Ibid.*, q. 8 (on relations); q. 9 (on persons); but q. 10 (on processions) and q. 2 (on *potentia generandi*).

[144] M. O'Connell, *Modern Schoolman*, XXIV (1947), 224-34; L. Roy, *Sciences ecclésiastiques*, I (1948), 225-28; F. V., *Bull. théol. anc. méd.*, V (1948), 335 §980.

ceed intelligibly from acts of understanding. Further, the acts of understanding in turn result from empirical data illuminated by agent intellect; and the relevant data for the meaning of Aquinas are the written words of Aquinas. Inasmuch as one may suppose that one already possesses a habitual understanding similar to that of Aquinas, no method or effort is needed to understand as Aquinas understood; one has simply to read, and the proper acts of understanding and meaning will follow. But one may not be ready to make that assumption on one's own behalf. Then one has to learn. Only by the slow, repetitious, circular labor of going over and over the data, by catching here a little insight and there another, by following through false leads and profiting from many mistakes, by continuous adjustments and cumulative changes of one's initial suppositions and perspectives and concepts, can one hope to attain such a development of one's own understanding as to hope to understand what Aquinas understood and meant. Such is the method I have employed and it has been on the chance that others also might wish to employ it that these articles have been written.

The significance of this method is that it unites the ideals of the old-style manual written *ad mentem Divi Thomae* and, on the other hand, the ideal of contemporary historical study. To understand the text, to understand the meaning of the text, to understand the meaning of Aquinas, and to understand as Aquinas understood, are but a series of different specifications of the same act. However, one cannot unite apparently opposed ideals without eliminating their really opposed defects. Method is a means to an end; it sets forth two sets of rules—rules that facilitate collaboration and continuity of effort, and rules that guide the effort itself. The latter aim at understanding, but, since we cannot understand at will, they amount to rules for using chance to defeat mere chance. Still if method is essential for the development of understanding, it is no less true that method is a mere superstition when the aim of understanding is excluded. Such exclusion is the historian's temptation to positivism. On the other hand, the temptation of the manual writer is to yield to the conceptualist illusion; to think that to interpret Aquinas he has merely to quote and then argue; to forget that there does exist an initial and enormous problem of developing one's understanding; to overlook the fact that, if he is content with the understanding he has and the concepts it utters, then all he can do is express his own incomprehension in the words but without the meaning uttered by the understanding of Aquinas.

A method tinged with positivism would not undertake, a method affected by conceptualist illusion could not conceive, the task of developing one's own understanding so as to understand Aquinas' comprehension of understanding and of its intelligibly proceeding inner word. Since that statement of my objective is so impressive as to be misleading, I had best add at once how little I have attempted to do. Aquinas held that only rational creatures offer an analogy to the trinitarian processions. Clearly, then, the analogy lay in their rationality. At once it followed that a purely metaphysical scheme, such as the subtleties concerning *operatio* and *operatum*, could not be relevant to trinitarian theory; for any such scheme can be applied no less to imagination than conception, no less to sensitive desire than to rational love. Again, it followed at once that no conceptualist theory of human intellect could meet the case; for conceptualism consists precisely in the affirmation that concepts proceed not from intellectual knowledge and so intelligibly but, on the contrary, with the same natural spontaneity as images from imagination. I had, then, before me the negative task of detaching from Thomist interpretation the endless tendrils of an ivy mantle woven by over-subtle metaphysicians and conceptualist gnoseologists. This I undertook in positive fashion by writing a series of lexicographical notes on Thomist usage; their purpose was to preclude the misapprehensions on which misinterpretation thrives. By doing my negative work in positive fashion, I simultaneously furthered my own positive end, namely, to show that Aquinas adverted to the act of understanding and made it central in his rational psychology.

This positive task had been anticipated. In his famous *L'Intellectualisme de Saint Thomas*, Pierre Rousselot maintained what was very obvious, however much overlooked, that in the writings of Aquinas it was not the rarely treated concept but the perpetually recurring intellect that was central and basic. If Rousselot was content with a metaphysical intellectualism, others were not. Péghaire's *Intellectus et ratio* showed that understanding was both the principle and the term of all discursive thought, and,

on the other hand, Hoenen's articles in *Gregorianum* brought to
light both the necessity of some intellectual apprehension of nexus
in phantasm and, as well, the recognition of this fact by Aristotle
and by Aquinas.

All that was needed was to put together what had lain apart,
and it could not but come together easily. Aquinas' master, St.
Albert the Great, had no illusions about the basic nature of intellect. In that respect he divided men into three classes—those
who had no need of teachers, those helped by teachers, and those
who could not be helped. For such helplessness two causes were
assigned—natural defect and bad habit. Among such bad habits
was counted a prolonged study of laws without any inquiry into
causes or reasons, so that a man became quite incapable of philosophy.[145] Plainly, Albert's view of intellect included understanding. Now Aquinas would not miss that point. In fact, when
he was out to crush Averroism, he appealed to his stock argument:
"Hic homo intelligit." He might have appealed to conceptual
knowledge of universals; but it was so much more effective to
appeal to the act of understanding: "Si enim hoc negetur, tunc
dicens hanc opinionem non intelligit aliquid, et ideo non est audiendus."[146]

It was a peremptory argument. It still is; for if men will doubt
or deny that they have universal concepts, who will lay it down
as evident that he understands nothing? Nor was Aquinas content
to appeal to the intimate fact that we do understand; he made
that fact the key to knowledge of the human soul: "Dicendum
quod anima humana intelligit seipsam per suum intelligere, quod
est actus proprius eius, perfecte demonstrans virtutem eius et
naturam."[147] But if understanding is the proper act of the human
soul, much more so is it the proper act of the angels who "nec
habent aliam operationem vitae nisi intelligere."[148] Finally, it
takes no great acumen to see that the very Platonist formula,
ipsum intelligere, has no more a Platonist meaning than *ipsum
esse*. As Aquinas did not conceive God as the subsistent Idea

---

[145] S. Alberti, *De intellectu et intelligibili*, Lib. I, tr. III, c. III, ed. Jammy,
Lyons, 1651, V, 252.

[146] *In III de An.*, lect. 7 §690. See pages 75 ff above.

[147] *Sum. Theol.*, I, q. 88, a. 2 ad 3m.

[148] *C. Gent.*, II, 97 §3.

of being, so he did not conceive divine knowledge as the knowl-
edge-beyond-knowledge attributed by Plotinus to the One and
by the pseudo-Dionysius to God. It is not merely that Dionysian
language was at hand and he did not use it, while Aristotelian
arguments were unfamiliar, yet he used them. It is that all he
has to say about knowledge is based on the Aristotelian principle
of identity; that he rejected the Platonist assumption that knowledge is by confrontation; that it is only that assumption which
forces Platonists into the profundity beyond profundity of positing
knowledge beyond knowledge to reach a meaning beyond meaning
that certainly is mystifying and, at least for Aristotelians, likewise
meaningless. We can conceive pure perfection without limitation;
but once limits are denied, we have reached our limit and cannot
go beyond the unlimited. Least of all could Aquinas have lost
himself in the Platonist fog and at the same time steadily progres-
sed from the *Sentences* towards the clear and calm, the economic and
functional, the balanced and exact series of questions and articles
of the *via doctrinae* in the *Summa*, in which the intellectualism of
Aristotle, made over into the intellectualism of St. Thomas, shines
as unmistakably as the sun on the noonday summer hills of Italy.

It seems to me that intellectualism, if once it gains a foothold,
never will be dislodged from the interpretation of Thomist trinitarian theory. If that is correct, I have reached my objective.
Also, of course, if it is correct, many other things follow. To clarify
the purpose of these articles, I hasten to add that I have not
been concerned with them. From the viewpoint of history there
are many questions beyond the bald fact that Aquinas adverted
to understanding and made it central in his psychology. But these
questions are further questions. They presuppose the bald fact
and ask about its measure and degree, its emergence and development, its reinforcement and weakening from combination and
conflict with other influences in Thomist sources and the medieval
milieu. From the writings of Aquinas one can extend inquiry
to other writers, prior, contemporary, subsequent, eventually to
invite some historian of the stature of M. Gilson to describe the
historical experiment of understanding understanding and thinking
thought. My aim has not been to treat such further questions
but to raise the issue of such treatment by settling a preliminary
fact and indicating elementary landmarks.

Perhaps, however, I may express my conviction that many of
the points studied in these articles are very relevant to the history
of the Aristotelian-Augustinian conflict. But, over and above
the historical, there is also a series of theoretical further questions.
It was, I think, very important for me not to touch them, not
merely because their expansion in all directions takes place with
the immediacy of logical implication, but still more because the
theoretical exposition of Thomist thought has already had its
definitive edition from the hands of St. Thomas himself. To put
the same point in a slightly different manner, one may distinguish
two developments of understanding. There is the development
that aims at grasping what Pope Leo's *vetera* really were; there
is the development that aims at effecting his *vetera novis augere
et perficere*. To fail to distinguish between these two aims even
materially, as in the inclusion of both within the covers of the
same book, results not in economy but in confusion. The immediacy of logical implication has no respect for differences of
place and time and no power of discrimination between different
stages of development of an essentially identical philosophic or
theological tradition. One can aim at understanding Aquinas;
one can aim at a transposition of his position to meet the issues
of our own day; but to aim at both simultaneously results inevitably, I believe, in substituting for the real Aquinas some abstract ideal of theoretical coherence that might, indeed, be named
the Platonic idea of Aquinas, were it not for the fact that a Platonic idea is one, while such ideals of logical coherence happen
to be disquietingly numerous. Plainly, there was only one real
Aquinas; plainly, there can be many Thomistic developments.
And though they are many, still there never will be any difficulty
in distinguishing the genuine from the counterfeit. "Ex ope-
ribus eorum cognoscetis eos." A completely genuine development
of the thought of St. Thomas will command in all the universities
of the modern world the same admiration and respect that St.
Thomas himself commanded in the medieval University of Paris.
If the labors of Catholic scholars during the past eighty-five years
have been great and their fruits already palpable, it remains that
so sanguine an expectation has not yet been brought to birth.
For that reason my purpose has been limited to determining on a
restricted but, I believe, significant point what the *vetera* really were.

INDEX OF CONCEPTS AND NAMES

As form and operation: 116-117, 122-123, 140
As form and esse: 165-166
A. as process towards essence (actus imperfecti): 138
A. in agent vs. a. in product: 120-121
A., reflection on to reach singular: 169-170, 171-172
A., what exists in a. as ground of efficient causality: 106-107
Immanent a. is quality for Scotus: 138
    I. a. as pati: 138

ACTIO

A., duplex: 98-99, 110-111 (n. 81), 117-118, 119-124, 126
A., duplex (eff. & oper.) ad dicere et intelligere: 139-140
A. as example of eff. causality: 111
A. and factio: 110-111, 119-120, 121-122
A. synonymous with operatio: 110-111
A. contrasted with operatio: 110
A. in passo: 108 (n. 65), 111 (n. 81), 121-122
A. as actus: 111
A. as predicament: 111 (n. 81), 122-124
A. manens in agente: 132-133, 137, 138
A. in agente: 111 (n. 81)
A. and actus in med. translation: 120-121
A. as threefold (spec., active, productive): 120 (n. 131)
A. as involving movement, as not involving movement : 122-123
A. as of supposit: 77

ACTION(S)

A. vs. term: 126
A., transeunt-immanent: 111, 117-118, 119-124
Transeunt action, as example of efficient causality: 111
               as perfection of patient: 111
               as predicament: 122-123, 141 (n. 4)
A., violent vs. natural: 136
A. and passion as identical: 107-108, 147-148, 178

ACTUS

A. ex actu: 98, 142, 198-199
Actus essendi: 43-44, 86
Actus perfecti: 101-107, 138, 147-148, 165-166
    As a pati: 106-111
    And time: 105-106
    In intellect: 126
Actus imperfecti: 104-105 (cf. 101-107), 138, 147-148
    As a pati: 106-107
A. in Avicenna: 114-115
A. as actuality of virtue : 111
A. secundus, duplex: 120-121
Bruta aguntur et non agunt : 120-121

AEGIDIUS ROMANUS: 189 (n. 18)

Ultimate c. defy definition: 42-43
Nexus of c. in Scotus: 28 (n. 125)
Natural c.: 37-38
Combinations of simple concepts to express coalition of insights: 52-53, 57-58
C. the primo et per se intellectum: 57-58, 154, 158
C. vs. insight (Arist): 32, 139-140, 164-165, 180-181
    Distinction of their objects: 139-140
C. as true or false: 58-60
C. refer to things: 2-4, 151-155
C. of ens: 43-45, 140
C. instruments of knowledge: 154-155, 163-164
C. vs. pre-conceptual: 24-25, 43-44
Separate c. and their synthesis as intelligibilities: 49-56
Distinction of c. eternal: 51-52
Not the concept but the conceived is loved: 203-204
Twofold order of trinitarian c. 206-209
C. linked by intellect in so far as from one act of understanding : 211-212
CONCEPTUALIST(s): 142, 144-147, 151-152, 155-156, 168, 180-181, 186-189
C. on procession of word and love: 203-204
C. ideal of science is certitude: 210-211
C. conceive intellect only in terms of what it does: 186
C. affirms intuition of concrete reality: 186
C. interpretation of Arist. and Aquinas : 186-189
CONCEPTUALIZATION: 14-15, 24-25, 37-45
C. not automatic: 37-38
C. rational in Aquinas: 28 (n. 125), 37 (n. 172), 37-38
C. a matter of metaph. mechanics in Scotus: 28 (n. 125)
C. joins intelligible form to common matter : 57-58
All c. ruled by principle of non-contradiction: 57-58
CONGAR, Y. M. J.: 208 (n. 113)
CONSCIOUSNESS
C. of infinity of intellect: 86-87
C. vs. scientific grasp: 77-79
Sense-c.: 74-75, 147-148
Empirical c. of singular act: 170-171
C. and self-knowledge of soul: 76
Three types of c. concomitant, reflective, rational : 190 (n. 28)
Rational c.: 1, 34, 141, 190 (n. 28)
    R. c. and presence of soul to self: 92-94
CONSUBSTANTIALITY of three Persons (Athanasius): 213-214
CONTINGENT
C. as object of ratiocinativum: 35
C. the object of two virtues of intellect: 119-120

ETERNAL
 E. operation and temporal effects: 115-116
 E. reasons: 90-91, 184
 E. truth: 63-64, 73, 83-84
ETHIER, A. M.: 214 (n. 136)
EUCLID(EAN): 26-28, 36 (n. 166), 41 (n. 194), 41-42, 56-57
EVIDENCE: 61, 65-66, 140, 142, 185, 186, 199-200
EXCLUDED middle, principle of: 33, 71, 87
EXEMPLARS
 Divine ideas as e.: 7
 E. are in example as species intelligibilis in phantasm: 163
EXISTENCE
 Our knowledge of e. of God: 8
 Natural, intentional e.: 150
 Species of e.: 66-67 (n. 82)
 Contingent e. not intelligible in self but in relation to other: 192-193
 Its actuation of matter and form like act of positing synthesis in j.: 49
EXPERIENCE
 E. of agent intellect: 78-79
 E. of possible intellect: 78-79
 E. and concept of being: 43-44
 E. of insight: 25, 31-32, 54-55, 161
 E. our basis for affirming actual being: 43-44, 88-89
 E. vs. sense or memory: 30-31
 Possible e. does not limit metaphysics: see MET
 Mystical e.: 92-93
FACTIO (and cognates): 111, 119-122
FAITH. *See also* BELIEF
 F. and supernatural wisdom: 90-92
 F., philosophy, and theology on God: 207-208
 F. and auditus: 56-57
FALSITY: 2-4
 F. may be had in sense knowledge: 58-59
 F. as non-correspondence of mental and real in composito-divisio: 50
 F. not in terms, but in their conjunction: 49
 F. and linguistic synthesis: 48
 F. and meaning: 2-3, 48, 155
 F. in intellect, not in things: 2-6, 58-59
 F. and logical positivism: 3
 F. as dissimilarity: 58-60
 F. in second operation of intellect, not first: 11, 49, 57-58, 58-60, 175-176
FATHER in Trinity: 206-215
FERNANDEZ: 197 (n. 56), 205 (n. 96)

Its proportion to universe grasped in reflective act of understanding: 192-194

Its influence does not destroy liberty and will: 203-204

Its influence on will in Scotus: 204-205

INTELLECT, AGENT: 11 (n. 48), 25 (n. 122)

Experience of: 78-79

A. i. and intellectual light: 78-80, 185

A. i. in Scotus 25 (n. 122)

Wonder and reflection two functions of a. i.: 47

A. i. the cause of understanding: 47

A. i. as private and individual: 82-84

A. i. as efficient potency vs. possible as natural: 139

A. i. as mover of i.: 127, 139

A. i. as immanent or transcendent: 78-79

Instruments of a. i.: 140

A. i. as related to judgment: 84

A. i. as illuminating: *see* DATA

A. i. converts on phantasm: 160-161

A. i. in Plato: 171-172

A. i. in Aristotle (illuminates, makes intelligible in act, produces
the immaterial, the universal, abstracts) 171-173

A. i. as efficient cause of abstraction: 178

INTELLECT, POSSIBLE

P. i. assents: 61

P. i. not analogous to sense: 76, 148-149

P. i. as passive potency: 131-132

Nature of p. i. understood from object and act: 76, 78-79, 128-130

P. i. and habits, acts: 81-82, 139-140, 185

P. i. as measuring by own principles: 60

P. i. as private, individual: 78-79, 172-173; *see* AVERROES

P. i. as objective, subjective: 20, 81 (n. 163)

P. i. informed by species: 125

P. i. as potency offers no resistance to knowing: 149-150

P. i. as both passive and active: 139-140

P. i. as natural potency agent i. as efficient: 139-140

P. i. does not produce its own act of understanding: 127-128

P. i. is immaterial: 148-149

Has both passive and constructive operations: 167

INTELLECTUAL. *See* INTELLIGIBLE

INTELLECTUALIST, vs. conceptualist: 142, 151-152, 155-156, 184-189,
210-213

INTELLIGENTIA

I. intelligentiae, medieval translation for noêsis noêseos: 188-
189

I. indivisibilium: 156-157, 177

I. in Vatican Council not certitude nor demons nor intellection
but understanding: 211-212

242 VERBUM

INTENTIONAL EXISTENCE: 150-152
INTROSPECTION
    I. in present work: 10-12, 47, 56-57, 93-95
    I. and conceiving trinitarian analogy: 10, 12
    I. and presence of God: 92-93
    I. and content of understanding: 24
    I. and Aquinas: 43, 75-77
INTUITION
    I. as term of discourse: 54-56
    I. and thought: 11 (n. 48)
    I. as insight: 179
    I. as sensible for Kant: 25
    I. of material singulars by Augustinians: 184
    of concrete reality by conceptualists: 186
IRRELEVANT, intellectually: 39-42, 82-83, 140, 146-147
JAEGER, W.: 188 (n. 14)
JAMES of Metz: 210-211 (n. 129)
JOHN Damascene: 120-121, 213-214
JOHN of Naples: 204-205
JOHN of St. Thomas: 100 (n. 16), 141 (n. 4)
JUDGMENT: 58-66
    J. as return to sources in sense and light: 64-66
    J. of met.: 64-65
    J. of natural scientist: 64-65
    J. mathematical: 64-65
    J. as inner word: 1, 4, 5, 6, 47-48, 65-66, 82-83, 140
    J. as knowledge of what is: 7-8
    J. as knowledge of real: 66-67, 82-83, 140, 194
    Knowledge of j. that God is: 8
    Reflective understanding and j.: 11, 47-48, 65-66, 140, 194
    J. in Kant: 25 (n. 122)
    J. as rational: 34
    J. as proceeding from intelligere: 65
    J. regards esse: 43, 86, 194
    Sufficient ground of j.: 47
    Instrumental or material cause of j.: 47
    Synthetic element in j.: 48-59, 65-66
    J. as positing of synthesis: 49, 58-59
    J. as more than synthesis: 49, 50
    J. vs. question, vs. hypothesis: 49, 65-65
    Objective reference of j.: 49
    J. includes knowledge of truth: 50
    Its object not the several terms, but the one proposition: 52-53
    First principles of j.: 57-58
    J. a compositio: 57-58
    J. refers to ens completum: 57-58
    Rational and responsible j. requires intellect in act: 185-186

O. of intellect — proper o. is simply intelligible: 192-193
    proper: 158-159, 161-164, 192-193
    proportionate: 158-159
    first: 158-160, 192-193
    in this life: 158-159
    known only in conversion to phantasm: 158-159
    a form in matter, but not as in matter: 158-159,
    164-165
    indirect o. is singular: 159-160
    proximate o. is the species intellecta: 163-164
    agent o. is the material act of phantasm: 171-
    175
    o. in act is produced by agent intellect: 171-
    175
    present in i. per similitudinem speciei: 201-203
O. as product of act: 128-129, 139-140
O. as efficient cause of act: 128-133, 139-140
O. reveals act, potency, soul: 75, 128-130
Thomist theory of o.: 128-133, 142
O. efficient cause not only of species but of act: 130-131
Pure mathematical o. of Plato: 26-27
    Vs. sensible o. and forms: 26-27
Intellectual light not an o. but a medium: 79-80, 91-92
Material and formal o. of understanding: 80-81
Agent o. of intellect: 139-140, 142, 164-165
O., subject, and critical problem: 88
O. as end of operation: 129-130
O. always a term for some Thomists: 129-131
Immanent o. of intellect: 140
Universal and necessary o.: 152-153
Imagined o.: 178-179
O. of will as partial cause in Scotus: 204-205
O. of love present in will as a goal in tendency to goal: 202-203
O. of divine love and presence in God: 202-204
O. of thought universal and particular: 192-193
O. of intellect and o. of phantasm intrinsically related: 179
O. of apprehensive and formative abstraction essentially same,
    modally different: 180
O. of understanding - compared with external things: 192-193
                    compared with divine essence: 194
O. of sense—a form existing in matter: 158-159
O. of angelic intellect a pure form: 158-159, 168-169
O. necessary for cognitional act: 191-192
OBJECTIVE
    O. reference: 3-4, 20, 49, 68-69, 151-153
    O. and subjective in various systems of thought: 177 (n. 199)
    O. thought vs. subjective thinking: 155

173-174

P. prepared by cogitativa: 173-174

Illumination not of act but of content of act: 172-173

Its illumination: 171-175

How its act can be agent object of intellect: 171-175

Its actual intelligibility when illuminated: 163-164

P. intelligible only in potency: 163-164

Not the p. but what p. represents known by intellect: 163-164

P. actu intellectum is one with possible intellect: 174 (n. 191)

PHILO: 194

PHILOSOPHY

First p. concerned with ultimate reality: 69-71
    is wisdom: 66 (n. 81), 68-69, 71

P. and grammar in Aristotle: 48

P. and presence of God to soul: 91-93

P. distinguished systematically from theology: 213-214

P. cultivated for natural knowledge of God: 213-214

Critical point of p.: 177 (n. 199)

PLACE and time

Irrelevant in scientific explanation: 39-40, 152-154, 177

And individuation by materia signata: 152-154, 177

PLAN and purpose of these articles: 1, 10-11, 12, 45-46, 47, 93-95, 97,
    180-181, 189-191, 214-220

PLATO(NIST): 3, 12, 16-17, 26-27, 29, 32, 40 (n. 187), 82-83, 101, 143,
    146, 153, 158, 171, 179 (n. 199), 183-184, 186-187, 194-195,
    218-220

Christian P.: 194

P. and object of speech: 3

P. and insight, formal cause: 17

Defining as characteristic of P.: 20

P. and knowledge of other (contact): 72-73

P. conceives knowledge primarily as confrontation: 72-73, 183-
    184, 186, 195

P. does not need agent intellect: 171-172

PLOTINUS: 184, 186

POIESIS (and cognates): 107, 113, 119, 132 (n. 209)

POSITIVISTS: 3, 7, 217

POSSIBILITY as object of insight: 42-44

P. and intelligibility: 43-44, 56-57

P. of being: 43-44, 56-57

POTENCY

P. and act: 42-43, 105, 111, 120, 137
    Identity of act, difference of p.: 72

P. and movement: 102-103, 104, 116

P. as principium actionis: 99, 110, 137
                    operationis: 110

P. as principium agendi in aliud: 99, 137

Q. as object of knowledge by understanding: 179
Quidditas vs. res: 180, 192-193
QUID REI vs. quid nominis: 42-43
QUOD QUID ERAT ESSE: 15-25
QUOD QUID EST: 8, 15-25, 34, 35-36, 46, 47, 57, 63, 72, 76, 86, 162-163,
   176; *see* QUIDDITAS REI MATERIALIS, QUIDDITY
RABEAU, G.: 66-67 (n. 82)
RATIO: 7, 34
   R. as meaning of a name: 151-152
   R. as object of thought: 154
   R. is abstract: 154
   R. rei and form: 144-145, 152-154
RATIONALITY
   R. of inner word: 34, 37-39, 140, 146-147, 199-200, 217
   R. of discourse: 34
   R. of human mind and image of Trinity: 1, 34, 45, 141, 217
RAYMOND, P.: 100 (n. 19)
REAL, REALITY
   Knowing r. as r.: 66
   Differences in r. known after r. itself: 88
   Disputes about real distinctions: 177
   R. empirically experienced for Bergson: 103 (n. 33)
   R. is being, the true, for Aristotle: 103 (n. 33)
   Various views on r.: 7, 143-145, 146-147
   R. and appearance: 71, 84
   R. in metaphysics of Aristotle: 68-69
   R. and words: 3, 152-154
   Knowing and r.: 66-67
      Modes of: 3
      Correspondence of: 3, 4-5, 20, 24-25, 69-70, 143-145, 148-149,
      151-153
   R. not the object of external experience: 88
   R. and wisdom: 66-68
   R. not just another essence: 88
   R. divides into essence and existence: 5
   R. is universe: 87
   What is real?: 7
   False concepts of r.: 88, 177 (n. 199)
   Platonist r.: 20, 143-144
   R. and truth: 140
   R. and form: 24-25 (see 15-25 passim)
   R. and thought: 67-68, 143-145
   R. and experience: 45
   R. and truth parallel: 69-70
   R. of movement incomplete, indeterminate: 102-104
   R. and less than essence, more than essence: 105-106

Is synthetic apprehension of motives: 65-66, 186, 192-193

Content of: 85

As analogy for procession of Word: 74

As effecting expression of quod quid est: 72

As effecting transition from knowledge as perfection to k. of other: 72-73

Terminates sweep through all relevant evidence: 186, 192-193

RELATION(S)

R. of origin: 99

Real and notional r., and divine ideas: 6 (n. 24)

Trinitarian r.: 88-89, 206-209

R. the object of insight, not of sense: 29

R. and processions, persons, notional acts in God (order): 206-208, 214-215

R., persons and nature in God: 213-214

R. vs. properties in God: 212-213

Four real r. in God, three really distinct: 208-209

R. between intellect and understanding in God: 99

R. vs. essence in God: 209-211

Three persons distinguished by r.: 210-211

Three types of ground for r. in metaphysics: 112

R. founded on actions: 99

R. of knowledge to known, real nonreciprocal: 174 (n. 190)

RESOLUTIO in principia: 61-66, 140

RICHARD of St. Victor: 214 (n. 136), 214-215

ROLAND-GOSSELIN: 21, 86

RONDET, H.: 53 (n. 26)

ROSS: 21, 102 (n. 25), 154 (n. 73)

ROUSSELOT, Pierre: 217-218

ROY, L.: 215 (n. 144)

SABELLIUS: 197-198

SCEPTICISM and certitude: 210-211

SCHMAUS, M.: 191 (n. 31), 205 (n. 95), 206, 210 (n. 129)

SCHMITT: 205 (n. 93)

SCHNURR, V.: 214 (n. 134)

SCHOLASTICS

Later S. gave divine ideas an esse objectivum: 195.

S. and man as efficient cause of own operations: 134

S. and formal cause: 14-15

S. and epistemology: 72

S. separation from science by conceptualism: 211-212

SCIENCE

Aristotelian notion of s. expanded by Crede ut intelligas: 214-215

Modern s. accepts one element of Arist. ideal, conceptualist another: 211-212

S. in ideal of conceptualists: 210-212

S. in theology: 210-215

S. not occasion or dispositive but representing: 29
S. and knowledge of universal: 32 (and n. 149)
S. the materia causae of knowledge: 80-81
S. as form of organ: 18-19
    Destroyed by violence: 19, 147
"S." of reality: 7, 20, 143-144
S. and intellectual light: 56-57, 64-65, 80-81
S. -knowledge as true or false: 59, 74
Ligature of s. in sleep: 63
S. and judgment: 63, 64 165-166
S. not knowledge of truth: 74
S. as aware: 74-75
S. and moral conduct: 120-121
S. power increased by conjunction with intellect: 173-174
Outer s. are passive: 165-166
S. the first act of material organ: 158
Object of s. a form existing in matter: 158
S. differs radically from intellect in structure: 148-149
S. integration of data in animal: 7, 20
SENSIBIL-E, -IA
S. per se et propria: 102-107
S. communia vs. propria: 41 (n. 192)
S. in actu is sensum in actu: 147-149, 184, 188-189; *see* IDENTITY
SENSIBLE
S. accidents in natural science: 36
Flux of s.: 152-153
S. residue and abstraction: 40-41
S. qualities and mathematical abstraction: 40-42, 64-65
S. apprehended by sense, represented by imagination, illumina-
    ted by agent intellect, understood by intellect: 168
SEPARATION(S)
S. and distinctions belong to 2nd operation of intellect: 156-157
Third degree of abstraction is really a s.: 177
SIGER of Brabant: 189 (n. 18)
SIGNS: 1-2, 152-153
SILVESTER Ferrariensis: 4 (n. 15)
SIMILITUDE, species as: 124, 147-148, 165-169, 167 (n. 150), cf. 202-
    203
SIMON, Yves: 149 (n. 46)
SIMONIN: 135 (n. 225), 202 (n. 86), 204 (n. 89)
SIN: not act in will but failure to act: 201
SINGULAR
Abstract notion of s. vs. knowledge of this s.: 170-172
Knowledge of s. by separated soul: 159-161
Indirect object of intellect: 158-160, 169-170, 178, 192
Sense and apprehension of s.: 4, 158-160
Immaterial s.: 170-171

Fluidity of terminology: 121-122

Gives quite universal definition of action and passion: 122-124

Uses Avicennist active potency in metaphysics of intellect: 125-126 and Aristotelian: 127-129

His theory of object is Aristotelian: 128-129

His difficulty with Ar.'s concept of efficient cause: 132-133

Works of 2nd Paris period: 135

Handicapped by Ar.'s and Avic.'s influence: 138

His metaph. applied confusedly to his psych. by some writers: 139-140

His analysis centres on intelligence not on its products: 142

Intellectualist vs. conceptualist interpretations of: 142, 151-152

Modifies Ar.'s theorem of knowing by identity: 147-148

Conceives perfection as totality: 150-151

Two schools of interp. of apprehensive and formative abstraction: 151-152

Settles recurrent antinomy in Ar.'s thought: 154

Derives proper object of intellect from Ar.: 158-159

His older commentators misled by *De Natura Verbi Int.*: 161-162

Duality of his object of intellect due to Ar.: 162-165

Does not restrict species to forms in cognitive potencies: 164 (n. 126)

Errors in editions of his works (some noted): 166 (n. 144), 209 Authenticity of *Quodl.*: 167 (n. 150)

Perhaps did not advert to a difficulty re reflection on singular: 170-171 (n. 174)

Economic survival in T. of less accurate forms of speech: 174 (n. 191)

Adds 3rd term to Ar.'s matter and form: 177 (n. 199)

Inductive proof of one's interp. of: 180-181

Restricts imago Dei to rational creatures (not so Thomists): 183

His development of Ar. on intellect: 188

The influence of Augustine on his theory of intellect: 188-189

Grasped real distinction of essence and existence: 188-189

His rejection of Plato, Plotinus, Pseudo-Dion. for Ar.: 218-219

His intellectualism (made over from Ar.'s): 217-219

Definitive edition of his thought came from himself: 220

Manuals ad mentem divi T. and modern historical study: 216

Effort required to understand him: 215-217, 219

Data for his meaning are his written words: 215-216

Riccardian elements in the *De Pot.*: 214-215

His thought on verbum not mature in Sentences period: 190-191

Regularly writes as theologian not philosopher: 196-197

More restrained than Scotus on divine processions as production: 196-198

His notion of efficient cause more general than Ar.'s: 198-199 (cf. 116-117)

INDEX OF LOCI

In Boet. de Trin.	i, 190
	iv, Text: pp. 155, 164
	v, Text: p. 214
In Lib. Physic.	iii, Text: p. 123
In Lib. de Anima	ii, Text: pp. 77, 84
	iv, Text: pp. 147, 176
De Natura Verbi Int.	(opus spur.)
	iv, Text: pp. 161-162

LOCI THOMISTICI

Roman and arabic numerals refer to chapter and footnotes in this book where the stated reference to Aquinas is employed.

Contra Gentes

(*Paragraph nn.* [##], *when given, were reached by counting paragraphs in the Leonine manual edition.*)

LOCI ARISTOTELICI

Roman and arabic numerals refer to chapter and footnotes making reference to stated Aristotelian text. Alternative references to pages rather than footnotes are denoted by "Text: p. ..."

Nihil obstat: Joseph HOFFMAN, C.S.C., Censor deputatus.
Imprimatur: ✝ Leo A. PURSLEY, D.D., Bishop of Fort Wayne-South Bend, February 28, 1967.